D1565139

The Numerical Universe of the *Gawain-Pearl* Poet

Florida A&M University, Tallahassee
Florida Atlantic University, Boca Raton
Florida Gulf Coast University, Ft. Myers
Florida International University, Miami
Florida State University, Tallahassee
University of Central Florida, Orlando
University of Florida, Gainesville
University of North Florida, Jacksonville
University of South Florida, Tampa
University of West Florida, Pensacola

Also by Edward I. Condren, from the University Press of Florida

Chaucer and the Energy of Creation: The Design and Organization of the Canterbury Tales (1999)

The Numerical Universe of the *Gawain-Pearl* Poet

Beyond *Phi*

EDWARD I. CONDREN

University Press of Florida

Gainesville · Tallahassee · Tampa · Boca Raton
Pensacola · Orlando · Miami · Jacksonville · Ft. Myers

Copyright 2002 by Edward I. Condren
Printed in the United States of America on acid-free, totally chlorine-free paper
All rights reserved

07 06 05 04 03 02   6 5 4 3 2 1

Library of Congress Cataloging-in-Publication Data
Condren, Edward I.
The numerical universe of the Gawain-Pearl poet: beyond phi / Edward I. Condren.
p. cm.
Includes bibliographical references (p.) and index.
ISBN 0-8130-2554-0 (acid-free paper)
1. English poetry—Middle English, 1100-1500—History and criticism. 2. British
Library. Manuscript. Cotton Nero A. x. 3. Mathematics and literature—History—To 1500.
4. Patience (Middle English poem) 5. Manuscripts, English (Middle) 6. Purity (Middle
English poem) 7. Gawain and the Grene Knight. 8. Pearl (Middle English poem)
9. Mathematics in literature. 10. Numbers in literature. 11. Alliteration. I. Title.
PR1972.G353 C67 2002
821'.109—dc21   2002024392

University Press of Florida is the scholarly publishing agency for the State University
System of Florida, comprising Florida A&M University, Florida Atlantic University, Florida
Gulf Coast University, Florida International University, Florida State University, University
of Central Florida, University of Florida, University of North Florida, University of South
Florida, and University of West Florida.

University Press of Florida
15 Northwest 15th Street
Gainesville, FL 32611-2079
http://www.upf.com

For
Sloane and Peter
Sean
Ellen and Charlie
Hilary and Erin

Contents

Acknowledgments ix

1. Introduction 1

2. Cotton Nero A.x: A Numerical Construct 14

3. *Pearl* 49

4. *Purity (Clannesse)* 74

5. *Patience* 99

6. *Sir Gawain and the Green Knight* 117

Afterword 147

Appendix 1. Geometric and Algebraic Construction
of the Divine Proportion 149

Appendix 2. Construction of Three *Phi*-related Rectangles
within a Dodecahedron 153

Appendix 3. The Poet's Successive Expansion
of His Fundamental Design 157

Glossary of Mathematical Terms for the Nonmathematician 159

Notes 165

Works Cited 187

Index 199

Acknowledgments

Seventeen years have elapsed since those exciting moments when I first held Cotton Nero A.x, Art. 3 in my hands in the British Museum. The intervening years have been punctuated, often at widely spaced intervals, with countless equally exciting discoveries. Through it all I have been sustained by friendships and collaborations too numerous to mention by name and by debts of gratitude it pleases me to mention here. I would first like to thank the Center for Medieval and Renaissance Studies at UCLA for allowing me to reprint sections of my work in this volume: parts of this book appeared in *Viator* 30 (1999) and in the forthcoming book *From Hacket to Haydn* (University of California Press), in the essays "Numerical Proportion as Aesthetic Strategy in the *Pearl* Manuscript" and "From Virgil to Richard Meier: The Music of Poetry and Architecture," respectively.

I am especially grateful for what I have learned from former students: Gary Sanders who took my first seminar on this material in 1985; Matthew Miller whose ethereal reaches perfectly suited the poet's vision; William Bowmer who introduced me to the intellectual pleasures of the Divine Proportion; Aya Peard who brilliantly saw a geometric connection between the five wounds of Christ and the five decorated initials in *Sir Gawain and the Green Knight;* Pavel Ekmekchyan who thinks geometrically; and Philippe Benoit from my most recent seminar. Several colleagues have contributed enormously: Robert Stevick whose revolutionary study of Old English poetry and generous comment on early drafts confirmed my path; Lionel March whose knowledge of medieval mathematics and Renaissance architecture was indispensable; and Yonar Sabar who generously helped me with Hebrew. Several research assistants kept seventeen years from growing into a lifetime: Sandra Cepevicius, William Li, and, with consummate editorial skill as well, Kerri Smith. All the graphic designs were created by Lynne Olson, who amazed me with her high-tech ingenuity. To Amy Gorelick and Gillian Hillis, my editors at the University Press of Florida, I owe much. Not only did they believe in the importance of this book from the very beginning, they also were professional, personable, and, above all, patient throughout.

Finally, in the dedication of this book I hope in yet another way to honor the poet who inspired it. Cotton Nero A.x concerns geometric and spiritual expansion. To the children with whom my wife Gail and I have been particularly blest, and to their spouses who have increased these blessings, I am eternally grateful for making life larger than I could ever have dreamed.

1

Introduction

The poet of Cotton Nero A.x, Art. 3,[1] an imaginative craftsman of the highest order, walks uneasily in the corridors of literary criticism. In contrast to the oft-referenced Londoner named Geoffrey Chaucer and the less-often-mentioned chantry clerk from Malvern named William Langland, the gifted author whom we variously call the *Pearl*-poet or the *Gawain*-poet departed the medieval world leaving nothing personal behind but echoes of a late-fourteenth-century, northwest midlands dialect.[2] A subtle but powerful inhibition prevents us from according this nameless poet as much of an existence as we readily grant his two contemporaries who, but for the scattered records that include their names, would be as anonymous as the northwest midlander. Though a prey to speculation, this anonymity yields a huge benefit. Without a recorded educational background to point to, precise dates and a native shire to explain social motivation, titillating court records to wonder about, or a family history to account for wealth, or its absence, we are forced to confront the very lines of the anonymous text with no more than our own critical skills.[3]

The unique manuscript in which this unknown poet's lines reside presents an unsettling puzzle. The problem centers not only on its informal appearance and unknown history—it has nothing of the presentation quality of Chaucer's Ellesmere Manuscript[4] and the earliest independent reference to it is in the 1614 inventory of a Yorkshire book collector—but also on the apparently uneven quality and disparate subjects of the four poems themselves. Two of these poems, *Pearl* and *Sir Gawain and the Green Knight*, may be finer than anything that survives from Middle English literature, excepting perhaps the *Troilus and Criseyde*. The other two, *Purity* (also known by the alternate title *Cleanness*) and *Patience*, appear to be mere biblical paraphrases, despite their vivid language and narrative appeal. Then, too, it has always been difficult to understand why these four poems are collected in a single manuscript: *Pearl*, an allegorical dream-vision of a man's encounter with a recently deceased girl, probably his daughter, who died before she was two years old; *Purity*, a rambling account of several loosely connected episodes from Scripture, mainly the Old Testament; *Patience*, a retelling of the Old Testament's story of Jonas; and *Sir Gawain and the Green Knight*, an Arthurian romance.

Among the several attempts to explain these alleged inconsistencies of quality and genre, the claim that the poems may be the work of several hands was finally laid to rest, in the opinion of most, by Larry D. Benson (1965) who, while demonstrating that *St. Erkenwald* could not have been written by the *Pearl*-poet, coincidentally presented a persuasive case that the four poems in Cotton Nero A.x all were written by the same author.[5] And so, here the matter has stood for a generation (for 600 years, one might even say): a unique manuscript, composed in a northwest midlands dialect around 1385, containing four Middle English poems, all probably composed by one poet. The evidence at the heart of the present study strengthens this conclusion by demonstrating that all the lines of poetry in the manuscript as well as all its decorated initials express the intentions of one author, intricately planned and almost perfectly realized.

This book alleges nothing to upset current critical opinion. It contradicts none of the excellent studies that have appeared over several decades; indeed it draws upon many of them.[6] Nor does it offer for this quintessentially medieval collection a reading incompatible with the beliefs and traditions of its day. Nevertheless, the chapters that follow propose a thesis that reaches beyond anything that has yet been suggested for this subject: Cotton Nero A.x is not an anthology of four unrelated poems. It is a single, tightly constructed artifact with four movements, each of them connected to the others by precise links that represent and attempt to resolve the central problem facing humanity. It reconciles the measured, corporeal, earthly world of every human being's daily concerns and the limitless, incorporeal, divine world to which all humanity is summoned. The manuscript's immediate surface does, of course, disclose four separate articulations—we could call them metaphors—of humanity's struggle for and against God, while incidentally revealing the futility of the struggle against him:

Lorde, mad hit arn þat agayn Þe stryuen,
Oþer proferen Þe oȝt agayn Þy paye.
(*Pearl* 1199–1200)

Yet none of these poems is entirely self-sufficient, since each receives from the others a dimension enabling it to fit snugly into the wider prospect of the whole manuscript. *Pearl,* for example, concentrates almost exclusively on the afterlife, for which death marks a commencement, while *Sir Gawain* confines itself to life on earth, for which death is a termination. Neither poem, however, remains entirely isolated from the concerns of the other. The Dreamer in *Pearl* imagines the New Jerusalem while mourning his physical loss on a very real spot of earth; Gawain presses on to his earthly destiny while often thinking of Christ and the Virgin. The two poems complement each other.[7]

Though these and other cross-fertilizations are assuredly true, the arguments presented here focus elsewhere by addressing the manuscript's most brilliant source of enrichment, a dimension that has been almost entirely overlooked because it does not inhere in the purely verbal elements of the text. It is the poet's use of mathematics to bridge the worlds of flesh and spirit. The hypothesis proposed here argues that the structural organization underlying each of these poems and determining the shape of the entire manuscript is a numerical design, like the geometric designs on the carpet pages of insular bookart, disclosing a coherent, unified, verbal replica of the universe, a universe the fourteenth century understood to extend from the infinitely small to the infinitely large.[8] The manuscript is a means by which readers can infer mathematically the boundless reality of the Maker of this universe and the eternal destination for which its human inhabitants are created.

By "numerical design" I do not mean "numerology." The two differ from each other as astronomy differs from astrology in the modern world. While numerology assumes that numbers have inherent symbolic meanings related to the divine supervision of the universe, a numerical analysis focuses almost entirely on formal units of text—lines, stanzas, sections, fitts, books, and the like—to discover whether the sizes and shapes of these parts, and their interrelationships, do not perhaps communicate the same meaning that the verbal texture of the manuscript conveys.[9]

Modern literary scholars may be unfamiliar with the compositional plan by which a poet—that is, one who is said to deal with words, ideas, interior life, all things unavailing to measure—would incorporate mathematics into his verbal constructs, or expect an audience to appreciate such a strategy.[10] Yet medieval stonemasons, as Charles S. Singleton pointed out more than a generation ago, often placed intricate carvings on the very roofs of cathedrals, where no one but workmen would ever see them, to make it clear, perhaps especially to themselves, that they were offering their skilled craftsmanship to please, not the eyes of men, but the eyes of God. Whatever the complexity of their designs, God would know (Singleton 1980, 88–89).[11] The record is overwhelming that many an ancient and medieval poet employed numerical construction. A critic who would study such a poet has an obligation, then, to pursue him in whatever direction his poetry leads. If the late Middle Ages believed what Philip Sidney had no difficulty accepting in the Renaissance, that "the poet . . . doth grow in effect . . . another nature,"[12] such that "an artifact is designed as a microcosm of the universe," the student of this artifact must seek the ways in which the artist sees this universe in his work, or shapes his work as a reflection of this universe.[13] If the *Pearl*-poet thought to create the four poems in Cotton Nero A.x as a verbal replica of the mathematics of the universe, we have no choice but to study how, and how well, this plan is executed.

The *Pearl*-poet is neither the first nor the last to bring to literature the notion that mathematical principles afford access to essences. From Plato's *Timaeus,* 53b, it was understood that "the Ordering God" (ὁ τεχνιτής θεός) relied on number to give shape to fire, water, earth, and air and to impose regularity and proportion on the universe (Plato 1961).[14] For our purposes it scarcely matters that Plato believed the transcendental world of Forms existed separately from the Demiurge, whereas Augustine held that they were Divine Ideas existing in the mind of God (Guzzardo 1987, 3). More important by far is the agreement in Plato and Augustine that the world of Forms for the one, and Divine Ideas for the other, were intelligible only through number.[15]

Mathematics enjoyed preeminence for a millennium in the academic curriculum. Martianus Capella passed on the traditions of the seven liberal arts, allegorized as handmaidens at a wedding whose gifts are the disciplines they represent (Stahl 1971, 41–53).[16] And Boethius's immensely influential *De musica* (White 1981) explained that musical harmony arose from the theory of number, whose proportions existed before matter was formed (Augustine 1964, 2.16.164). Indeed, through the entire Middle Ages the disciplines of the quadrivium—arithmetic, music, geometry, and astronomy—rested firmly on Euclidean-Pythagorean principles establishing the mathematical foundation of everything in the universe. From time to time the emphasis given to one or another of these four disciplines would vary. For example, music, which may have given the original impetus to the unification of the higher learning when its harmonies were shown to be obviously related to mathematical proportion, for a time "drifted away from its sisters of the quadrivium," as less rigorous episcopal schools took over from monastic teaching (Beaujouan 1982, 466). But with the advent of the *ars nova* "music once more became [in the fourteenth century] a specialization of masters of arts interested in mathematics" (ibid. 467). Similarly the arrival from Spain of Greek-Arabic science in the twelfth century (Southern 1982; d'Alverny 1982; Beaujouan 1982) undoubtedly altered many of the specifics the Middle Ages had of Plato's mathematics. But the quadrivium remained in essence as Martianus Capella and Boethius described it several centuries earlier.

If the nature and extent of medieval Platonism is not monolithic in its particulars (cf. Southern 1979), neither can it be identified with a single center of learning. Alcuin's treatises on the trivium, written at Achen and Tours at the end of the eighth century, prepared for the number-based quadrivium that Adelard's translations of Euclid made possible.[17] Finally, the Chartrian Platonism that these texts helped synthesize had its fullest expression at Paris in the early twelfth century, leading to an explosion of new learning that the intellectual world has not seen again.[18] Morality, beauty, indeed all human and divine manifestations, which the modern world may consider unrelated concepts, came to be understood as a single idea unified by number. As the music of an opera does not merely accompany a drama, but is as much its very essence as the action unfolding on stage, so mathematics was understood as the divine language of all things. The wonder, then, is not that medieval poets actually thought of using numerical composition to form their works, but that they ever thought literature could be composed without it. The absence from various *artes poeticae* of specific reference to number as a method of construction does not imply that the method did not exist, for there is abundant evidence that poets actually composed this way. It rather suggests that number may not have been considered a property of literary composition, but of the subjects literature addresses, and must therefore be included in any representation of these subjects.

The *Zahlenkomposition* that Ernst Curtius, among others, called to our attention (1953, 502–9) set critics to uncovering the numerical composition of much literature that had long been admired for other reasons.[19] As a result Ovid is now acknowledged as favoring a kind of symmetrical composition known as concentric or ring structure (Otis 1970). The numerical patterns in Dante's *Vita Nuova* and *Commedia* have now been the objects of extended literary criticism for decades (Singleton 1980; Guzzardo 1987). Within English literature, critical awareness of numerical construction seems first to have been noticed as recently as 1960, when A. Kent Hieatt pointed out the influence of the calendar on the structure of Spenser's *Epithalamion*. Since then Old English literature has been carefully examined for numerical construction: by Thomas Elwood Hart (1980) who shows that *Beowulf* is strongly controlled by number, in one instance marking off with hypermetric lines the beginning and ending of a highly significant section that displays parallelism, chiasmus, repetition, and symmetry in precisely measured patterns; and by Robert Stevick (1982, 1994) who demonstrates that several Anglo Saxon poems have been constructed according to prominent mathematical proportions, including the proportion that guided the construction of Cotton Nero A.x, as the chapters below contend.

In Middle English literature the *Pearl*-poet's contemporary, Geoffrey Chaucer, occasionally relies on numerical construction. Two examples may suffice. First, the *Parliament of Fowls* encodes in its three divisions, according to the persuasive arguments of Victoria Rothschild, the twelve months of a year, the fifty-two weeks of a year, and the twenty-nine days of February in the leap year of 1384. Its first mention of St. Valentine's Day occurs in the forty-fifth stanza, to mark February 14th, the forty-fifth day of the year. And the poem as a whole measures 100 stanzas, equaling the one hundred days in 1384 from January 1 to Easter on April 9 (Rothschild 1984, 172).[20] And second, the *Tale of Sir Thopas*, an intentionally wretched piece told by the pilgrim Chaucer himself, slogs through three successively halved fitts, the first containing eighteen stanzas, the second nine, and the third four and a half, before Harry Bailey finally interrupts him, "Namoore of this!" (Burrow 1971). English Renaissance drama seems to have had a special fondness for thirty-three line soliloquies, perhaps to encode a reference to the Trinity and to Christ's thirty-three years on earth. In Shakespeare see Hamlet's famous soliloquy, 3.1.57–89, Cymbeline's speech on the "bloody cloth," 5.1.1–33, and Pericles' on "dull eyed melancholy," 1.2.1–33. In Marlowe's *Edward II* see the thirty-three line soliloquy at 2.5.1–33.[21] In the modern era, though in Spanish rather than English, Jorge Luis Borges organizes "The Total Library," "Doctrine of Cycles," and "The Aleph," to name only three works among several, around the philosophical discussion of mathematics current at the end of the nineteenth century and the beginning of the twentieth. There is a difference, however, between these recent works and Cotton Nero A.x. Whereas Borges begins with believable stories involving ostensibly plausible characters, he often must distort these characters and their situations into irrational relationships to show a connection with his unifying subject, the paradoxes of mathematical thought.[22] The *Pearl*-poet, on the other hand, keeps his mathematics at an unobtrusive distance—neither permitting it to eclipse his immediate subjects nor discussing it esoterically, but clearly employing it in the divisions and sections of his text in order to emphasize the significance of the already highly captivating human stories on the surface.

We might further acquaint ourselves with this tradition of numerical construction by considering two pieces of Latin literature, both well known to the English Middle Ages and to us, where a construction similar to what will be discussed in the following chapters is used in the same way. Long revered as a monument of theoretical criticism, and the probable source of Sidney's loose paraphrase of "Ut pictura poesis" as a "speaking picture," Horace's *Ars poetica* divides its lines unevenly between two subjects, on the one hand the agents responsible for the creation of literature, that is poets and critics, and on the other the products of their creation, poetry and drama. Horace's poem has always been the subject of dispute, especially its title, tone, and genre. Lately the poem as a whole has also become a matter of some uncertainty, having been persuasively interpreted as a parody spoken by a persona of the poet, another "Doctor Ineptus" whose slavish admiration for the style of a former age unfits him for the kind of poetry the authentic Horace creates (Frischer 1991). Conflict over interpretation aside, there has never been disagreement over the dividing line between its two subjects. The first 294 lines concern the craft of poetry as it shapes the two forms of literature then current in Rome, verse and drama. The remaining 182 lines, from 295 to the end of the poem at line 476, focus on the poet and especially his interaction with the critic. As George Duckworth (1962) demonstrated forty years ago, the relative sizes of these two sections are not arbitrary, but conform to the unique proportion, known popularly as the Golden Section and called *phi* (φ) by modern mathematicians. *Phi* satisfies two equations, $a + b = c$, and $a : b = b : c$. That is, $182 + 294 = 476$ and $182 \div 294 \approx 294 \div 476$. To express this second equation in layman's language, 294 is the mean between two extremes, the smaller extreme being 182, the larger being 476. Both resulting ratios—the smaller extreme divided by the mean, and the mean divided by the whole—are practically identical: 0.61904 in the first instance and 0.61764 in the second. Although the mathematics and geometry of the Golden Section will be discussed at greater length in chapter 2, suffice it to say here that this mathematical arrangement underscores perfectly the point Horace makes in the poem as a whole. The craft of poetry is the means by which the lesser extreme, poets and critics, achieve the greater extreme, literature.

A decade or two before Horace created the *Ars poetica*, Virgil wrote a stunning, four-part treatise on farming, called the *Georgics*, which the editor of the Loeb edition has called "perhaps the most carefully finished production of Roman literature" (Virgil 1994, x). It is worth looking at *Georgics I* because here Virgil follows a plan remarkably similar to the strategy governing Cotton Nero A.x. Following a table of contents of 4.5 lines listing the subjects of all four books of the *Georgics*, a section we may dismiss as not actually belonging to the subject at hand, this first book collects the complicated, detailed wisdom on how and when to till fields. It has five sections whose different sizes suggest two rhythms (Le Grelle 1949), one of which fairly leaps out at us from sections 2 and 4 (see figure 1.1). Section 2, having 161 lines, describes the best techniques for preparing soil, while the 204.5 lines in Section 4 discuss the days when such work especially pleases the gods. Virgil is revisiting the subjects of Hesiod's *Works and Days*, producing two sections whose total number of lines equals the precise number of days in a year, or is within a quarter of a day of the precise number. These parts of the book establish a linear rhythm in which the progress of the poem parallels the progress of a year. Departing from this sequential design, a second rhythm embraces the year with sections whose sizes produce the same proportion we saw in the *Ars poetica*, the unique proportion that happens to be the ancient world's most fascinating symbol of the relationship among all things in the universe. But first, let us be clear about the topics discussed in this second pattern. The first section is an invocation to the gods who watch over the fields and send rain, not overlooking Caesar Augustus who may one day become, according to Virgil, the reigning lord of all these deities. The middle section takes note of the changing zodiac as the year progresses. And the final section laments the political strife that keeps farmers and fields from their rightful work, while affirming that these misfortunes, too, are foretold by the heavens.

Virgil, Georgics, Book I - *514 total lines*

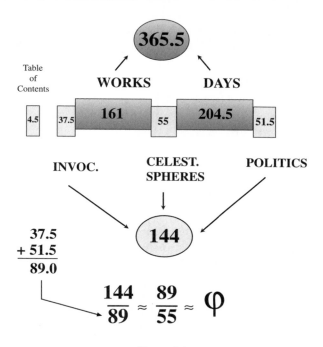

Figure 1.1

At the same time that Virgil's language describes the parallels between the heavens, the earth, and human action, the book's numerical rhythms demonstrate this unity with the Euclidean, Pythagorean proportion that the Greeks called ὁ ἄτομος (the indivisible), a mathematical formula they believed was present in every part of the universe. Parts 1, 3, and 5 of Virgil's five-part poem total 144 lines, the square of twelve and therefore the foundation of the duodecimal system. It thus constitutes one of the ways the ancient world represented the three-dimensional universe. If the first and the fifth of these parts, 37.5 and 51.5, are viewed as a single term having a magnitude of 89, the three resulting terms reveal the same unique proportion we saw above in Horace's *Ars poetica*. Not only do these terms satisfy the additive equation, a + b = c (55 + 89 = 144), but they are also in a continuous proportion, 55 is to 89, as 89 is to 144, where 89 is the mean between two extremes, 55 and 144. As the equation at the bottom of figure 1.1 shows, the larger extreme, 144, divided by the mean, 89, yields approximately the same result as this mean divided by the smaller extreme, 55. The former ratio is 1.61797, the latter 1.61818. These figures are almost precisely the irrational number—that is, "incommensurable," or not amenable to whole-number ratios—that modern mathematicians call *phi* and express to its first five decimals as 1.61803.[23] By arranging his lines in such a way, to show both the measurement of a year and the mathematical proportion shared by all things in the universe, Virgil demonstrates the unity of four orders—not separate orders, but four different expressions of a single order, the earth, mankind, the heavens, and God. We should also take particular notice, for we shall see it again, that the mean in this case, 89, has been split into the two book-ended sections that embrace the body of Virgil's poem: $89 = 37.5 + 51.5$.

The influence of number on the process of creating poetry derives from a long tradition in the history of analytic reasoning, extending from at least the time of Solomon, through the Greeks, and down to the present.[24] The classic biblical reference appears in the Book of Wisdom 11:21, spoken by an unnamed sage understood to be Solomon: "Sed omnia in mensura, et numero, et pondere disposuisti" [But you have ordered all things in measure, and number, and weight].[25] Though it is unclear how *mensura* and *numero* are distinguished from each other as a priori concepts, another scriptural passage, this time from Ecclesiastes, proves helpful by approaching the created universe from an a posteriori perspective:

> Lustravi universa animo meo, ut scirem et considerarem et quaererem sapientiam et rationem: et ut cognoscerem impietatem stulti, et errorem imprudentium. (Eccles. 7:26)
>
> [I have surveyed all things with my mind, to know, and consider, and seek out wisdom and reason, and to know the wickedness of the fool, and the error of the imprudent. (Douay trans.)]

Again the scriptural context, initially at any rate, does not explain how *sapientia* and *ratio* are distinguished from each other. In fact, the Douay translators seem to throw up their hands by selecting "reason" for Latin *ratio*, a translation that may mislead, since modern English "reason" means something very close to *sapientia*, "wisdom," whereas Latin *ratio* has a much wider range of meanings. The translators' choice could well be evidence that they themselves did not know how *sapientia* and *ratio* differ from each other and thus settled for essentially a transliteration. Yet if *ratio* does mean "reason" in the modern English sense, it is unclear why Scripture would say the same thing twice. This is not an example of the echoic half-verse that appears again and again in the Psalms, but a single word whose meaning in the present context Jerome and the Middle Ages must have understood as different from *sapientia*.[26] For the present, a satisfactory understanding of the passage must wait until two other philological matters are cleared up.

The original meaning of *lustro, -are,* was to "purify." But because the usual means of purifying included a thorough encircling examination, the meaning that subsequently attached to the verb gave equal emphasis to abstract purity and to the physical process of encircling and examining that produces it. If in the present passage *lustravi* carries both the abstract and the physical meanings its history implies, then the combination of *sapientiam* and *rationem* produced by such an examination may also have been intended to convey the dichotomy of, respectively, abstract and concrete. The passage as a whole would then mean that a thorough examination of the universe produces (1) an abstract understanding of the disposition of all things, called *sapientia,* and (2) a physical, measurable understanding of how these things are related to each other, called *ratio.* Since the verb *lustro* has an equally important spiritual dimension, the richly suggestive choice of words in Ecclesiastes implies that this intellectual task, at once abstract and physical, produces an understanding that is hardly different from theological perception.

Several of the definitions for *ratio* in Lewis and Short suggest, however, that the word conveys a meaning that is not static, but includes a concept of variables in comparison:

- a business matter; relation, reference, respect to a thing;
- course, procedure, method;
- that faculty of the mind which forms the basis of computation and calculation;
- the reasonable cause of a thing, a ground, motive, reason;
- reasonableness, reason, propriety, law, rule, order, conformity; e.g., Cicero: intervallis imparibus, sed tamen pro rata parte ratione distinctis (divided proportionally by rule [*Republic,* 6, 18, 18]).[27]

This combination of variety among items and constancy of comparison implies something like the "dynamic symmetry" described by Matila Ghyka (1977, ix), drawing upon the Roman architect Vitruvius.[28]

The corresponding passage in the Septuagint also uses a phrase to suggest a dynamic mathematical process: "ζητῆσαι σοφίαν καὶ ψῆφον"(*Septuaginta* 1952, 7:26). *ψῆφος,* literally a pebble, emphasizes the process of calculating (cf. L. *calculus,* pebble). The idea of a constant relationship in a variable environment is precisely captured by the modern English word "ratio," which happens to be the definition listed in Souter's *Glossary of Later Latin:* "the expressed quotient of two quantities," where "quotient" is understood as the result of one quantity divided by another.[29] It is possible, therefore, that *numero* and *mensura,* referring to this same universe in the Book of Wisdom, although from the perspective of the Creator rather than from that of an investigator, implies the same combination of abstract quantity and concrete matter that, when taken together, afford a basis for understanding the relationships among all things. It may be useful to think of Ecclesiastes's more accessible passage as a gloss for Wisdom 11:21, "Sed omnia in mensura, et numero, et pondere disposuisti," where *mensura* means "proportion" and *numero* means "magnitude." The combination of these terms describes the providential design of creation, while *pondere* gives this design corporeal existence.

The possibility that Latin *ratio* includes a mathematical meaning becomes a near certainty in an interesting passage in Augustine's *De libero arbitrio voluntatis* (2.8.80–95), which explains the importance of number in acquiring wisdom. It is clear, initially, that Augustine means more than mere "number" when he uses the word *ratio.* For if he only meant "number," his phrase "ratio et veritas numeri" (2.8.80) would then mean "the number and truth of number," a meaningless sense that Benjamin and Hackstaff avoid by translating the phrase "the order and the truth of number" (Augustine 1964, 54). Yet here, too, Augustine must have in mind something more dynamic than the static concept implied by "order," for in a long Socratic answer to Evodius he adopts the reasoning process of a mathematician, as he amplifies the word *ratio* with a kind of equation. To paraphrase 2.8.90–91: pick any number—4, say—then the fourth number after this number, not counting the number itself, will be double the original number, "by a fixed and unchangeable law." The essence of the passage is not the simple arithmetic, nor the numbers themselves, but the equation that never changes, despite the variable quantities that may appear in the equation. In Augustine *ratio* means the behavior, the system, the scheme, the interrelation of quantities, synonymous with "fixed and unchangeable law," a concept we would understand in modern English as "ratio" or "proportion."

The passage we have been discussing from Ecclesiastes 7:26, as clarified by Augustine's arguments in *De libero arbitrio,* is not proposed as a substitute for the enigmatic Wisdom 11:21. Rather, the two passages together convey a meaning close to Plato's argument at the end of *Epinomis:* "But to crown it all, we must go on to the generation of things divine, the fairest and most heavenly spectacle God has vouchsafed to the eye of man. . . . [I]f, as I say, a man pursues his studies aright [i.e., astronomy, pure numbers, mensuration (γεωμετρία), solid geometry, and harmony] with his mind's eye fixed on their single end . . . he will receive the revelation of a single bond of natural interconnection between all these problems" (991, b, e).

With this provisional understanding, let us proceed to the fixed and unchangeable laws governing the design of Cotton Nero A.x, a perfect example of the natural interconnection Plato describes.

Cotton Nero A.x

A Numerical Construct

As no artist would describe his techniques in detail when he could offer a canvas to show what these skills have wrought, so we begin here with Cotton Nero's grand culminating design and only then will turn to its complicated palette, to the mathematical mix that produces this design. Figure 2.1 lays the manuscript out proportionally, as if it were a line segmented to represent its four poems and their line totals.

The poet of Cotton Nero A.x chose these line totals, I contend, because they demonstrate the most highly revered geometric/mathematical proportion known to the Middle Ages, the Divine Proportion discussed in the previous chapter under the names Golden Section and *phi*. Recalling that discussion, figure 2.2 illustrates the geometric properties of this proportion, shown as a line segmented at the only point, an irrational point at that, at which a magnitude can be cut into two unequal parts such that the three resulting quantities—the smaller segment (CB), the larger segment

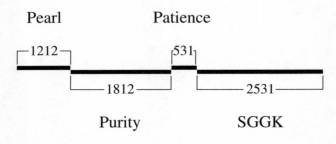

Figure 2.1

From greater to smaller   AB : AC = AC : CB

Or reciprocally, smaller to greater   CB : AC = AC : AB

Figure 2.2

(AC), and the whole line (AB)—create a continuous ratio that leads toward infinity, either the infinitely large or the infinitely small. If we substitute Cotton Nero's line totals for each of these two unequal parts, an extremely interesting thematic relationship emerges. On line AB of figure 2.2:

(1) let the smaller segment CB equal the combined lengths of *Purity* and *Patience;*
(2) let the larger segment AC equal the combined lengths of *Pearl* and *Gawain;*[1]
(3) then line AB equals the length of the entire manuscript.

The ratio of the whole manuscript to the pair of poems at the extremes, as well as the ratio of the two poems at the extremes to the pair in the middle of the manuscript, almost exactly reflect the Divine Proportion (see figure 2.3). Depending on whether one writes the equation by beginning with the

$$6086 : 3743 \approx 3743 : 2343 \approx \varphi \ (\text{i.e., } 1.61803)$$

$$1.62596 \quad \approx \quad 1.59752 \quad \approx \varphi \ (\text{i.e., } 1.61803)$$

Figure 2.3

largest magnitude and proceeding to the smallest, as shown by the equation in figure 2.3 (i.e., whole MS divided by [*Pearl* + *Sir Gawain*] ≈ [*Pearl* + *Sir Gawain*] divided by [*Purity* + *Patience*]), or writes the reciprocal equation, which is not shown in the mathematics of figure 2.3, by beginning with the smallest magnitude and proceeding to the largest ([*Purity* + *Patience*] divided by [*Pearl* + *Sir Gawain*] ≈ [*Pearl* + *Sir Gawain*] divided by the whole MS), both arrangements produce a value extremely close to the Divine Proportion or its reciprocal, namely the modern decimal 1.61803 for *phi*, or 0.61803 for the reciprocal of *phi*. If, when the poet first planned this extraordinary relationship, he disregarded the repeated 12s and 31s in the units and tens columns of the four poems' totals, for reasons which will be suggested below, the ratios of these line totals would be even closer to *phi*: 1.62162 and 1.60869 for the ratios shown in figure 2.3 and 0.62162 and 0.61666 for the reciprocals.

To appreciate the enormity of the poet's mathematical feat, we should recall that medieval mathematicians were forced to use fractions, because the innovation of using Indian decimals (now used universally) was not in widespread use in western Europe until the sixteenth century (Boyer and Merzbach 1989, 303). It is astonishing that this medieval poet, lacking modern calculators and forced to express irrational quantities in complicated fractions, was able to compose his four poems in sizes that reflect the Divine Proportion and to produce thereby a subtle thematic point. The two Hebraic Old Testament poems in the middle of the manuscript, *Purity* and *Patience*, expand visually to include the poems that feature the Christian world of the New Testament, *Pearl* and *Sir Gawain and the Green Knight*. The continuous ratio implied by the Divine Proportion (see below, 31–33, 37) suggests that this Christian context, in turn, expands imaginatively to embrace the entire manuscript and point toward the eternity that lies beyond. The concept of expansion extends to the aesthetic context as well. The two poems at the center of the manuscript, widely understood to be poetically inferior, yield to *Pearl* and *Sir Gawain*, said to be among the finest poems in the English language. With appetite thus whetted, let us for the present put aside this finished product while we consider a few details that point to this final form.

Number Systems

Curiosity over the lack of a standard order among the poems in the various editions and discussions of the *Pearl*-manuscript guides one, paradoxically, to the first indication of the aesthetic strategy that the following chapters suggest. Apart from the nearly universal assumption that the manuscript is an anthology of four, mostly unrelated poems, editors and critics have implied further that the order of its poems has no critical significance. For example, the order in which Sister Margaret Williams (1970) discusses and translates the poems—*Patience, Purity, Sir Gawain,* and *Pearl*—differs from the manuscript's order. A. C. Spearing's elegant study, appearing in the same year, treats the poems in a different order: *Purity, Patience, Pearl,* and *Sir Gawain.* And Charles Moorman's edition of 1977, while scrupulously producing no punctuation marks because the manuscript has none, nevertheless departs from the manuscript's order to choose yet a third arrangement: *Patience, Purity, Pearl,* and *Gawain.* Not until the Cawley and Anderson edition of 1976 and the Andrew and Waldron edition of 1979— which has now become the standard—was there a printed order that followed the manuscript: *Pearl, Purity, Patience,* and *Sir Gawain and the Green Knight.* Yet even the introduction to the Andrew and Waldron edition discusses the poems in Moorman's order, while the text itself omits the manuscript's important arrangement of large and small decorated initials, only noting their existence and placement in a one-page note to the text (Andrew and Waldron 1979, 52).

Trying to decide whether the order of the poems in the manuscript matters leads directly to the discovery of several unusual facts that cannot be coincidental. The first and fourth poems in the manuscript, *Pearl* and *Sir Gawain,* have 101 stanzas each, as has often been remarked. Though *Pearl* adheres to a pattern of twenty sections, five stanzas to each section, it reaches 101 stanzas by including a sixth stanza in its fifteenth section. *Sir Gawain*'s form is not as regular as *Pearl*'s, but despite this irregularity it totals 101 stanzas by assigning 21, 24, 34, and 22 stanzas, respectively, to its four major divisions, or fitts. The quantitative form of these two poems seems to have been as important to this poet as it was to Dante, whose work the *Pearl*-poet may not have known, although his contemporary Chaucer knew it well. Dante gave the three canticles of his *Commedia* 34, 33, and 33 cantos, respectively, for a total of 100 cantos. Criticism has yet to understand why the *Pearl*-poet chose to open and close his manuscript with 101 stanzas, subtly different from the even 100 cantos Dante chose for his *Commedia.* Perhaps he wished to avoid perfection, "for fear of excessive vanity offending God" (Nelson 1973, 33). Or perhaps he was following a tradition pointed out by Karl Menninger (1969, 155–62), in a fascinating book about numbers, that the tribes of northern Europe had a habit, especially in speaking of limits set by law, of allowing an "excess." Many verbal traditions can be attributed to this habit, like "a year and a day," "a thousand and one nights," "a baker's dozen" for 13, *acht tag* for a week, *quinze jours* for two weeks, and perhaps, too, the fondness for 12 as a basic unit of measure.[2]

A richer, more likely explanation undoubtedly accounts for the poet's plan to assign 101 stanzas to both *Pearl* and *Sir Gawain*. The number 101 is the 25th prime number.[3] While every number occupies a position in the integer series, some numbers also belong to other series: odd numbers, even numbers, square numbers, cube numbers, perfect numbers, and so forth. Each series, then, signifies a property attributable to every number in that series. Every number in the prime series, by sharing the divine property of indivisibility, was accorded higher status than the numbers in other series. Quantities in the prime series were understood in the Middle Ages to be inherently more self-contained, integral, "finished," than the quantities signified by numbers in other series. Let us postpone a discussion of prime numbers in Cotton Nero A.x until we become aware of a few simpler numerical curiosities that nonmathematicians might be expected to notice.

Table 2.1 shows that the total number of lines for each of the manuscript's four poems exceeds a multiple of hundreds of lines by a very small amount, 12 extra lines each for *Pearl* and *Purity*, 31 extra lines each for *Patience* and *Sir Gawain and the Green Knight*. Alert modern readers familiar with *Sir Gawain*'s appearance in the manuscript may object that the 101 "bob" lines in the poem, that is, the two-syllable line preceding each "wheel," as in lines 15, 32, 55, 80, and so forth, are all written in open spaces to the right of the main text, usually a couple of lines above the beginning of the wheel, and therefore do not occupy manuscript lines at all. I reply that the artful pattern shown in table 2.1 is sufficient proof that the poet thought of these bobs as lines unto themselves, regardless of whether the scribe (even if the scribe were the poet himself) was instructed to conserve space and therefore save 101 lines of expensive vellum. Similarly those familiar with published versions of *Sir Gawain* may object that the poem has only 2530 lines, rather than 2531 as indicated here. But this is to overlook the Old French caveat "Hony soyt q. mal penc," which immediately follows the line "He bryng vus to His blysse   Amen" (2530). If this proverb is considered part of *Sir Gawain*, as it is certainly part of the manuscript, then the total number of lines in the poem is 2531, precisely

Table 2.1

Pearl	Purity	Patience	Sir Gawain
1200	1800	500	2500
+ 12	+ 12	+ 31	+ 31
1212	1812	531	2531

completing the manuscript's highly artful, and hardly coincidental, pattern.

The well-known Old French adage (if we may digress for a moment) has long been a vexing presence in the manuscript, its thematic relation to the four poems still unclear. It is, of course, a proverb used as the motto of the Order of the Garter, founded by Edward III in 1348. Whether the poem existed before the founding of the order, or the reverse, is impossible to determine in the absence of historical evidence. Nor does the Old French expression itself help with questions of provenance, since it is very probably older than either the Order of the Garter or Cotton Nero A.x.[4] If *Sir Gawain*'s composition was roughly contemporaneous with the founding of the order, the poem would have to have been composed at least forty years before Cotton Nero A.x was copied out—a possibility, but highly unlikely in view of the complete absence of other surviving manuscripts. Further, the poet's obvious piety would undoubtedly clash with the political overtones that colored the founding of the order, suggesting that the poem and the Order of the Garter are unrelated to each other in all but the coincidental appearance of this single epigraph. Gollancz's assertion, that the motto is "in a somewhat later hand" (1971, 8), may have influenced Andrew and Waldron to claim that the "Garter motto appears to have been added to the poem in order to associate it with that order" (1979, 300). To the extent that this remark implies their further acceptance of a later hand, I cannot agree. In addition to the line's necessity to achieve the numerical symmetry noted above, its visual appearance also argues that it is contemporaneous with the rest of the manuscript.

Plate 1 reproduces folio 124 verso where the motto appears, after one blank line, in a large display script approximately the same size as the word "**a**men" at the end of line 2530. But the shape of the characters in the

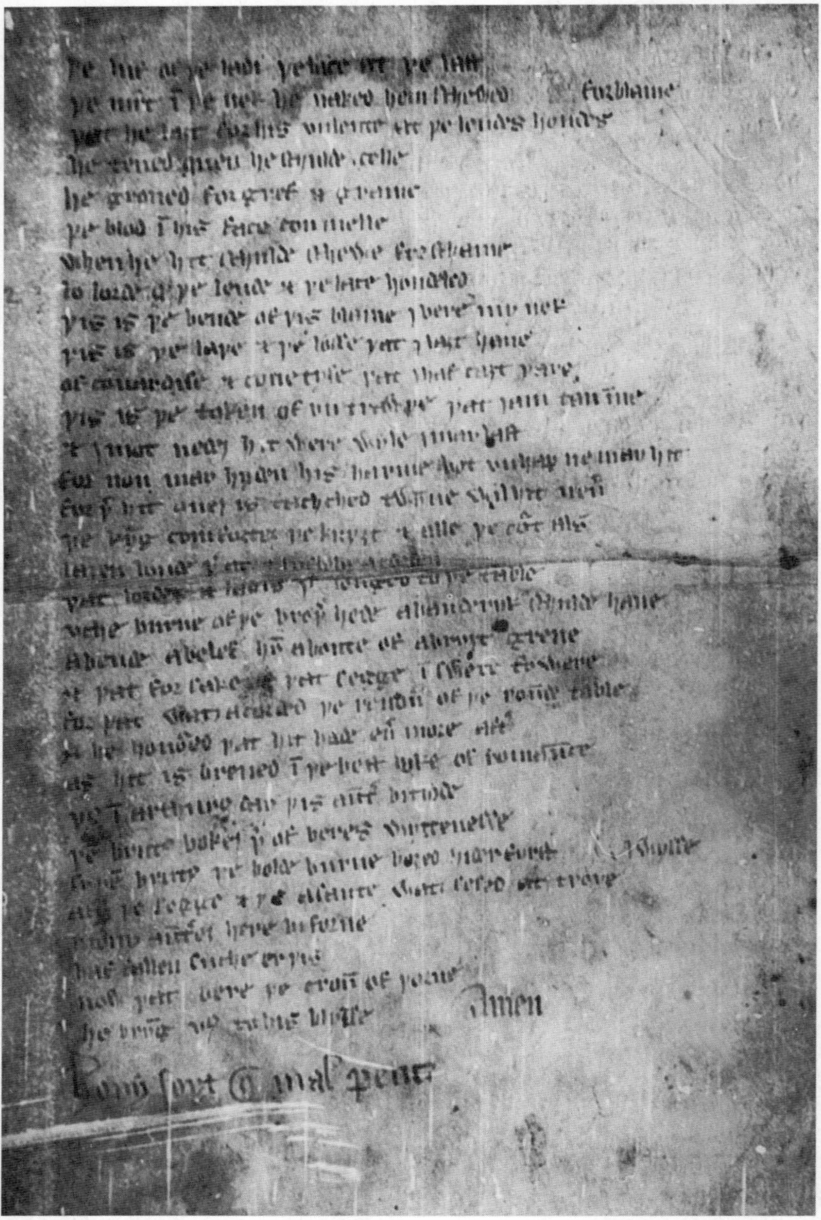

Plate 1. MS Brit. Lib. Cotton Nero A.x. Folio 124 verso. Reproduced by permission of the British Library.

motto, the slant of the *ductus,* and the careful alignment with the left margin, all suggest that it was written by the same hand that wrote the rest of the manuscript, and written at the same time. If anything was added later, it was the word "**a**men," which is separated from "blysse" by a space large enough to accommodate eight uncial characters and has a narrow, almost Gothic appearance very different from the bookhand elsewhere in the manuscript. Moreover, its letters descend slightly, whereas beginning at about the middle of the page the lines start slanting upward, a tendency that continues for the remainder of the page, including, though to a lesser extent, the final Old French *devise.*

Another curiosity that would leap out at anyone who had received a fourteenth-century education in the quadrivium is the number 531, the line total of *Patience* as well as the last three digits in the line total of *Sir Gawain.* This number, a reversal of the first three odd numbers (1, 3, and 5),[5] is the sum of the first four "perfect" numbers: 1, 6, 28, and 496 (Boethius 1: chap. 20; Heath 1921, 74–75), magnitudes which were thought important enough to be represented by the four parts of the nave in the Great Church of Cluny III (Peck 1980, 58, summarizing Conant 1963, 33).[6] Even more intriguing to a fourteenth-century reader, the manuscript's division into two perfectly balanced halves, with a basic 3000 lines in each half, suggests that the small excesses in the poems—12 extra lines each in the first two poems, 31 each in the second twosome—were intended to signal a way in which the two halves of the manuscript are differentiated.

Let us pay particular attention to these excesses, for they encode an extremely important tension within the manuscript, rising to a motif associated with the progress of theological history. These numbers would have been indicated by the left hand, the units and tens hand, in the finger counting system described by Bede (Blair 1976, 166–69; Menninger 1969, 201–8) and might, therefore, be considered a kind of signature or key, analogous to a key in music. These left-hand numbers show that the first two poems are written in the "key of twelve," as it were, a signature confirmed by their basic duodecimal sizes of 1200 and 1800, which would have been indicated by Bede's right-hand numbers, the hundreds and thousands. The 31–line excess for *Patience* and *Sir Gawain* presents a somewhat different signature. In the integer series the number 31 has little significance, unlike the number 12 which indicates the duodecimal system. But 31 also happens to be the 10th prime number, since the prime series began with the number 3 in the Middle Ages (see chap. 2, n. 3). That *Pa-*

tience and *Sir Gawain* have basic decimal sizes of 500 and 2500 lines, respectively, strongly implies that the 31–line excess in these two poems represents, not itself, but the 10th prime number. That is, the third and fourth poems in the manuscript are written in "the key of ten." The overall result is a combination of two interesting patterns. First, tension between the duodecimal and decimal systems, similar to the dynamic chosen by Dante. The consistent terza rima and 33 cantos each in *Purgatorio* and *Paradiso* honor the Trinity, while the 34 cantos in *Inferno* represent the duodecimal system by displaying the factors of 12 (3 x 4). But the *Commedia*'s 100 total cantos measure the entire poem by the decimal system. Cotton Nero employs the same technique. The two poems in its first half are measured by the duodecimal system, as their twelfth-integer signatures indicate, while the second half of the manuscript announces its poems with the 10th prime number in the signatures and organizes them within the decimal system.[7] And the second pattern is the progress toward mathematical unity as the manuscript proceeds from the first poem to the fourth: *Pearl*'s 1212 lines and *Purity*'s 1812 can each be factored ten ways. *Patience* has only four factors.[8] And the prime number of lines in *Sir Gawain*, 2531, represents a perfect unity, divisible only by itself and 1.

The prime series, which the 101 stanzas in both *Pearl* and *Sir Gawain* and the 31–line excesses in *Patience* and *Sir Gawain* would have brought to the attention of a medieval mind, is unlikely to occur to a modern reader, because the modern world uses only four series of numbers, the integer series (1, 2, 3, 4, 5 . . . to count totals), the odd series (1, 3, 5, 7, 9 . . . for numbering the sequence, for example, of addresses on one side of a street), the even series (2, 4, 6, 8, 10 . . . for the addresses on the opposite side), and the series of dozens, a remnant of the duodecimal series, reserved for bulk purchases of small items. Tennis scores, 15, 30, 40 (an abbreviation of 45), and an implied 60 for game, follows a system of quartering the sexagesimal series, modeled after either the four 15-minute segments of a clock's full 60-minute cycle or the four 15-*sous* divisions of the basic French monetary unit in the fourteenth century, worth 60 *sous* (Whitman 1968, 66–82). This series, as well as the fascinating history of tennis scoring, is now entirely lost, even to most tennis enthusiasts. Still another series, the "twenty series," perhaps influencing the twenty stanzas in all but one of *Pearl*'s sections, now survives only in vestiges like French *quatre-vingt* and English "score," which originally meant to scratch a mark into some surface to signify twenty (Menninger 1969, 49–50). On the other hand, the medieval world, according to Martianus Capella, understood and used constantly in its mathematics an extensive array of numerical series: feminine, masculine, triangular, cube, square, perfect, and a variety of others, including the Fibonacci series, devised by Leonardo of Pisa in the early thirteenth century (see below), and the series of prime numbers (Stahl 1971, 158–62).

It is possible that the *Pearl*-poet intended to give two of the poems in his manuscript a prime number of stanzas because every prime number implies that something has been brought to completion, to unity, to a fruition that may only exist *in potentia* elsewhere. The repetition of a complicated rhyme scheme in *Pearl* and the repeated form of the bob and wheel in *Sir Gawain* make the 101 stanzas of these poems unavoidably obvious. But nothing in the formal presentation of *Purity*, including the small ticks in the left margin every fourth line,[9] gives any reason to think it is other than a continuous narrative of 1812 lines with occasional decorated initials at irregular intervals. Yet this poem too may have as complex a design as *Pearl* or *Sir Gawain*, although such a design remains hidden from view. If this is true, *Purity* may differ from these two stanzaic poems only by lacking the obvious editorial signs that readers would need in order not to miss what now only exists *in potentia*. In fact, without rewriting a single word, the poet could easily have displayed *Purity* as a series of twelve-line units, like *Pearl* three to a page. Viewed thus, its 1812 lines reveal an inchoate series of 151 groups. Now 151 is the 35th prime number. Hence, in the first half of the manuscript, these twelve-line groups that have not yet been made explicit in *Purity*, compared to *Pearl's* fully displayed twelve-line stanzas, produce in the prime series the ratio of 35 : 25, or 7 : 5. This was a very important ratio during the Middle Ages, a convenient substitute for $\sqrt{2} : 1$, the ratio of the diagonal to the side of a square measuring 1 on each side.[10] Architects and geometers undoubtedly relied on this ratio to prepare the plan of St. Gall, as did Villard de Honnecourt for the thirteenth-century Cistercian church appearing in his *Sketchbook*. The same proportion seems to have been the basic module for St. Michael's at Hildesheim and one of the modules used in the cathedrals at Chartres and Amiens (Hiscock 1999, 6, 10–12).

The second half of the manuscript yields a different, yet equally interesting potential ratio of primes. Again, *Patience* is not written in rhymed stanzas, but in the same continuous narrative form as *Purity* and with the same ticks in its margins every fourth line. But to consider only individual four-line units leaves the poem with a form consisting of 132 four-line units plus a single three-line unit, an inelegant design that has encouraged some critics to imagine a scribe who carelessly dropped a line.[11] Unlike *Purity* whose 1812 lines can be factored by 12, *Patience*'s 531 lines can only be factored by 3 (177 times, although 177 is not a prime number) and 9 (59 times, the 16th prime number). If the poem is imagined, therefore, as another inchoate arrangement, this time of nine-line units, four to a page, the ratio of its prime number of units to *Sir Gawain*'s prime number of stanzas, *Patience*'s 16th prime to *Sir Gawain*'s 25th prime, or $4^2 : 5^2$, represents the longer leg and the hypotenuse of the Pythagorean 3–4–5 triangle, the cornerstone of all geometry.[12]

These relationships in Cotton Nero A.x have understandably escaped the notice of critics, not only because the poet chose not to call attention to them, but also because number theory has lost its appeal in the modern world. Among literary critics in particular, numeracy is an unintelligible foreign language. Yet there is nothing alarming about the coexistence of different numerical series. The modern world is not inconvenienced by using the duodecimal system for time (12 hours = day or night at the equinox), small lengths (12 inches = 1 foot), and the quantities of small items (dozens), while the decimal system measures everything else. Even while measuring the same thing, multiple systems comfortably exist side by side. References to a year, say, do not make it impossible to refer to the same length of time as either a twelve-month period, or a fifty-two-week period. The fact that individual days and years have been obviously marked by the divine artificer—alternating day and night for the one, summer and winter solstices for the other—does not make it impossible for individuals to conceptualize a week, though no heavenly scribe has drawn specific attention to it. Of course one must be clear about which system is in use at any given time. An Anglo-Saxon coast warden would be anxiously queried when reporting "manige hund vikinga scipa" off the coast. Are these "many hundreds of Viking ships" long hundreds (120 in each group) or short hundreds (100 ea.)?[13]

A serious problem does arise, however, from the inherent imperfection of all whole-number systems, including the two systems just mentioned as well as the Babylonian/Sumerian compromise, the sexagesimal system, which partakes of both the duodecimal system and the decimal system. (In the sexagesimal system of counting, 60 is understood as ten 6-unit groups; in the decimal, six 10-unit groups; and in the duodecimal, five 12-unit groups.) All three systems mislead us into accepting their versatility, especially when measuring the whole of Cotton Nero A.x (less its signature lines, that is). The manuscript's 6000 basic lines may be viewed as 1000

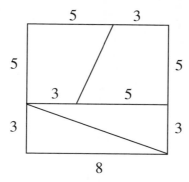

Figure 2.4

units in the sexagesimal system, 600 units in the decimal system, and 500 units in the duodecimal system. Note, however, that Dante, while working within the duodecimal system, must add an extra canto to *Inferno* to produce the perfect hundred cantos he needs to complete the *Commedia* in the decimal system. Every fourth year we must add an extra day to our calendar to correct the inability of the duodecimal system to reconcile the annual orbits of the moon about the earth and the earth about the sun. The integer series, or natural number system, has its faults too, as an old conundrum demonstrates well. Figure 2.4 illustrates a square of dimension 8, cut into sections as shown.[14] Its area is obviously 64 square. But when we rearrange its four sections, as shown in figure 2.5, the area is now 65 square.[15] The sexagesimal system, too, is only partly adequate for measuring *Pearl*, nineteen of whose sections indeed have sixty lines, but they are distributed among five stanzas each, in twenty sections. It is no help at all in measuring *Sir Gawain*. It would be well to keep these imperfections in mind as the following chapters unfold. The numbers and proportions dis-

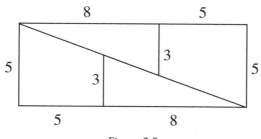

Figure 2.5

cussed here point toward a perfect intention, one that could not, within the realm of poetry/mathematics, be more closely achieved.

The foregoing remarks may seem to fly in the face of a somewhat different Renaissance belief. M.J.B. Allen notes that Plato, according to Marsilio Ficino's interpretation of the *Republic*, thought of the sexagesimal system, and especially its foundation, the perfect number 6, as God's time:

> Plato had intended us to look beyond the realm of Fate that 12 signifies to the higher realm of Providence; and to set another, a hexadic, time, God's time, over and against both the decades, the centuries, and the millennia that we measure by 10 and its multiples, and the dodecadic time of the Sun, the Moon, and the stars, and the calendars we base upon them. He had intended us, that is, to set a perfect, golden time over and against both the iron time, the clock time, of nature's and of man's present imperfection and mutability, and the silver time of the celestial spheres. (Allen 1994, 80)

The number 6 was called "perfect," not because the hexadic or sexagesimal system was thought to be without flaw, but because the divisors of six, namely 1, 2, and 3, are neither deficient nor superabundant but add up to the number itself (see chap. 2, n. 6). Even more curious than the suggestion that God's time is the sexagesimal system, which is in fact no more immune to defect than any other whole number system, is the phrase "golden time." To a seventeenth-century mathematician the term "golden" meant "division into extreme and mean ratio," the technical meaning of Golden Section. There is only one such division. It is incommensurable, that is, impossible to express as a whole-number ratio. But the commensurable hexadic system is entirely amenable to whole-number fractions. While the *Pearl*-poet may have been in general agreement with Plato (at least with Ficino's interpretation of him), he would have taken exception to calling the hexadic system "golden," and naming it "God's measure." To the *Pearl*-poet, God's measure is the miraculous, flawless, incommensurable Divine Section, the name that the seventeenth century's Golden Section would supersede. It holds Cotton Nero A.x together in a continuous ratio that implies a divine path to infinity and eternity. More on this ratio later; now, back to the manuscript.

Ratios and Proportions

Even if one were to remain within the whole number series, the relative lengths of the poems in Cotton Nero A.x produce interesting ratios, evident only if we mentally separate from each poem the extra-line signature indicating its "key," as the poet himself seems to have done. Though *Pearl* and *Purity* in the first half of the manuscript have relative lengths of 2 : 3 (a perfect fifth, musically speaking), and *Patience* and *Sir Gawain* in the second half are in a 1 : 5 ratio, *Pearl*'s relation to the whole manuscript is the same as that of *Patience* to *Sir Gawain:*

$$\text{Pearl : MS} = \text{Pa : Sir Gawain}$$

$$1200 : 6000 = 500 : 2500$$

$$1 : 5 = 1 : 5$$

Similarly, *Sir Gawain*'s relation to the whole manuscript is the same as *Patience*'s to *Pearl:*

$$\text{Sir Gawain : MS} = \text{Pa : Pearl}$$

$$2500 : 6000 = 500 : 1200$$

$$5 : 12 = 5 : 12$$

This importance that *Patience* apparently has for the whole manuscript, as a kind of linchpin holding its four poems together, especially since it comes third in the manuscript, suggests a significant parallel with the fundamental literary unit of Old English poetry, the four-beat line. That three of the poems in the manuscript (*Purity, Patience,* and *Sir Gawain*) employ the "alliterative long line," a descendant of the Old-English four-beat line, makes it likely that this parallel was intended. *Pearl* has at least one feature of the older line, alliteration, though its tetrameters lack the length and the caesura that characterize the other three poems.

The Old English poetic line consists of an a-line and a b-line, each with two accented units and a variable number of unaccented units, as in *Wanderer* 32:

´ ´ ‖	´ ´
Waraδ hine wræclast, ‖	nales wunden gold
a-line ‖	b-line
[An exile's path protects him,	not at all decorative gold]

While a prominent caesura keeps the a-line and b-line separate, the two half-lines are linked by alliteration. The third beat in the line, that is, the first accented unit of the b-line, determines the alliteration shown in both accented units in the a-line. The fourth beat in the line stands apart, since it virtually never alliterates with the rest of the line. It is clear, then, that the third accent in an Old English poetic line is the key unit holding the line together. The alliterating lines in Cotton Nero do not follow precisely the Anglo-Saxon metrical form—a caesura does not occur regularly in every line, nor do important units of meaning always fall naturally on the alliterating syllables, as typically happens in Anglo-Saxon poetry. Nevertheless, vestiges of the older meter are still present.

Adhering to a principle of expansion that we will see again, Cotton Nero A.x seems to have adopted the rules governing a single Anglo-Saxon poetic line as a rubric for determining the arrangement of poems, emphasized here with modern alliterating titles that emulate the alliteration in an Old English line:

Pearl   Purity   ‖   *Patience   Gawain*

The two-poem first half and two-poem second half remain distinct from each other by exceeding a multiple of even-hundreds of lines by different amounts that signal the two different numbering systems they employ. Yet the two halves are also similar. Linked chiasmically, each half consists of one stanzaic poem set in the Middle Ages and one continuous narrative poem set in biblical times. Each half has a basic 3000 lines. Additionally, the mathematical ratios among the four poems suggest that *Patience*, like the first beat of an Old-English b-line, links the two halves of the manuscript.

The expansion we have just seen—from the form governing a single line to the same form embracing six thousand lines—is also implied in the manuscript's geometry. If certain parts of the manuscript are compared to other parts, in various combinations, the resulting ratios duplicate the several expanding ratios of Villard de Honnecourt's famous thirteenth-century diagram of rotating squares, shown in figure 2.6, each of which doubles the area of the one it encloses. For convenience we shall call the innermost square the first square, having a dimension of 1. The next larger square, which doubles the area of the first, we shall call the second, and so forth.

The ratio of the first half of the manuscript to the second is shown in figure 2.7, where *Pearl*'s 1200 lines and *Purity*'s 1800 lines total 3000 to balance the 3000 of the second half comprising *Patience*'s 500 and *Sir*

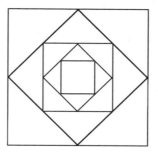

Figure 2.6

Gawain's 2500. This same ratio is represented as one side of Villard's first square to another side of the same square.

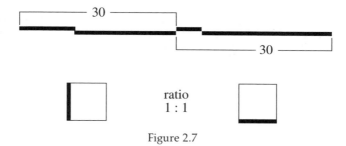

ratio
1 : 1

Figure 2.7

The first three poems compared with the final poem is the same as the ratio of a side of the second square to a side of the first square, as represented by figure 2.8. The resulting ratio, 35 : 25, or 7 : 5, a rational convergent for √2 : 1, discussed above, is shown as the diagonal of a square mea-

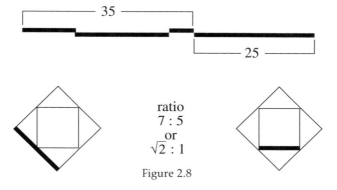

ratio
7 : 5
or
$\sqrt{2} : 1$

Figure 2.8

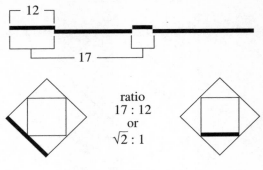

Figure 2.9

suring 1 on each side to a side of the square. A side of the second square is, of course, equal to the diagonal of the first square. Modern mathematicians would write the ratio 7 : 5, as the equation $7 \div 5 = 1.4$, which is very close to the modern notation of $\sqrt{2}$ as 1.41421.

An even more accurate substitute for the same irrational number is demonstrated by (*Pearl* + *Patience*) : *Pearl,* shown in figure 2.9 as, again, a side of the second square to a side of the first square. In modern notation: $17 \div 12 = 1.41666$; and $\sqrt{2} = 1.41421$.

The third ratio in Villard's rotating squares is represented in the *Pearl*-manuscript by the whole of the manuscript in relation to either half, as in figure 2.10.

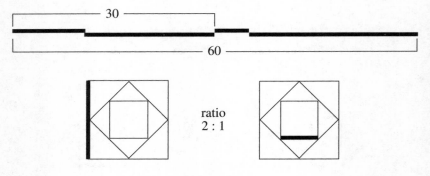

Figure 2.10

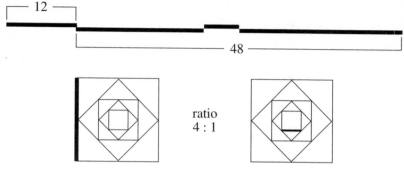

Figure 2.11

Finally, the fourth ratio in this simple comparison of parts of the manuscript, the last three poems in relation to the first, or 4 : 1, echoes Villard's fifth square in relation to the first square, shown in figure 2.11.

While these and other proportions held great appeal for the Middle Ages, especially those that produce pleasing harmonies in music—the fifth, the third, and the fourth intervals—the poet of Cotton Nero A.x determined the size and shape of his manuscript by relying on still another proportion, the mean held preeminent by mathematicians from Euclid through the Renaissance: division into extreme and mean ratio, known variously as the Divine Section, the Golden Section, and *phi*. As has already been suggested in chapter 1 and at the beginning of this chapter, this proportion recommended itself to the poet, not because of its reputation among mathematicians, but because it precisely echoes the major theme of his poetry. An understanding of a few rudiments of this mathematics—only its shallows, mind you, so this lay brother does not have to venture beyond his depth—may provide useful background for the chapters that follow.

Every ratio is a comparison of two numbers or quantities, expressed as *a* : *b*, or 3 to 4, or 3 : 4, or 3/4. A proportion is an equation showing that two ratios are equivalent, as 5/10 = 1/2, or 5 : 10 = 1 : 2. A proportion normally has four terms, *a* is to *b* as *x* is to *y*, unless it refers to a continuous proportion, in which case the middle term is repeated, *a* is to *b* as *b* is to *c*. There are, of course, many kinds of proportion, the most familiar of which are arithmetic, geometric, and harmonic.[16] The former two are normally shown as continuous series. The arithmetic progression shows each term exceeding its predecessor by the same fixed amount, shown in such series as 3, 6, 9, 12 . . . or 5, 10, 15, 20 . . . and so forth. A geometric progression shows each number exceeding its predecessor by a fixed rate, for example 3x in the series 1, 3, 9, 27, 81 . . . or 5x in the series 4, 20, 100, 500, 2500. . . . The more complex harmonic proportion is achieved "when the three terms are such that 'by whatever part of itself the [third] exceeds the second, the second exceeds the [first] by the same part of the [first]'" (Heath 1921, 85, quoting Porphyry). The numbers 3, 4, and 6 are in harmonic proportion, since 6 exceeds 4 by 1/3 of 6 and 4 exceeds 3 by the same 1/3 of 3. Similarly 4, 6, and 12 are in harmonic proportion, 12 exceeding 6 by 1/2 of 12 and 6 exceeding 4 by the same 1/2 of 4.

The proportion that controls Cotton Nero A.x, technically known as division into extreme and mean ratio, combines the arithmetic and harmonic means. It too may be shown as a continuous progression, but is unique among continuous progressions by simultaneously satisfying two equations: (1) the ratio of its first term divided by its middle term equals the ratio of the middle term divided by its third term; and (2) the sum of the first term and the middle term equals the third term. To state the equation algebraically, not only does $a \div b = b \div c$, but also $a + b = c$. As we will see below, this ratio is the same irrational number for every division into extreme and mean ratio. Hence, a demonstration using whole numbers can only be an approximation. The quantities used by Virgil in *Georgics I*, discussed in the previous chapter, precisely satisfy one of the two equations required of this unique proportion, the additive equation, but only approximate the other. That is, 55 + 89 accurately equals 144, but the ratios expressed by 55 : 89 and 89 : 144 only approximate each other and *phi*, albeit very closely: $55/89 \approx 0.61797$; $89/144 \approx 0.61805$; $1/\varphi = 0.61803$.

The more familiar terms signifying division into mean and extreme ratio, Golden Section and φ, are postmedieval creations. The former term was borrowed and adapted from a famous remark by Kepler in the early seventeenth century, where it seems to refer to the Pythagorean theorem: "Geometry has two great treasures: One is the theorem of Pythagoras; the other, the division of a line into extreme and mean ratio. The first we may compare to a measure of gold; the second we may name a precious jewel" (Boyer and Merzbach 1989, 50). The latter name, *phi*, was suggested in the early twentieth century after the first letter in the name Phidias, the Greek sculptor who based his works on this mathematical proportion. In the Middle Ages, this precise ratio was known as "The Divine Proportion," the phrase used by Luca Pacioli as the title of his 1509 dissertation for which Leonardo da Vinci provided the illustration. Kepler himself used this name when he was not waxing poetic.[17] A thirteenth-century editor of Euclid, Campanus of Novara—mathematician, chaplain to Pope Urban VII, and canon of Paris Cathedral—inserted in his edition a remark of his own that captures the significance the Middle Ages attached to this Divine Section:[18]

> Mirabilis itaque est potentia lineae secundum proportionem haben-tem medium duoque extrema devisae. Cui cum plurima philoso-phantium admiratione digna conveniant, hoc principium vel praeci-puum ex superiorum principiorum invariabili procedit natura, ut tam diversa solida tum magnitudine tum basium numero, tum etiam figura irrationali, quadam symphonia rationabiliter conciliet.

> [Wonderful therefore is the power of a line divided according to a ratio having a mean and two extremes: since most things worthy of the philosophers' admiration accord with it, this foundation or pre-eminence proceeds from the invariable nature of higher foundations, that a certain harmony can rationally unite solids that are so diverse, first in magnitude, then in the number of bases, then too in their irrational shape.]

Luca Pacioli accords the Divine Section the fullest manifestation of divinity by noting that it shares with God four principal attributes:[19] (1) Unity. The supreme epithet of God Himself. It is a unique species, the only proportion that has miraculous power. (2) Trinity. As there are three persons in God, there are three terms, never more, never less, in the Divine Section. (3) Secret and Occult. As God cannot be properly defined nor un-derstood through words, the Divine Proportion can never be designated through intelligible numbers, but is called irrational by the mathemati-cians. (4) Unchangeable. The proportion remains the same, whether it in-heres in a large or small quantity.

This wonder in which the Divine Proportion is held remains unabated to the time of Kepler, a century after Pacioli. In a 1608 letter to Tanckius, Kepler speaks of the Divine Proportion with words that combine math-ematics and mysticism:

> A peculiarity of this [Divine] proportion lies in the fact that a similar proportion can be constructed out of the larger part and the whole; what was formerly the larger part now becomes the smaller, what was formerly the whole now becomes the larger part, and the sum of these two now has the ratio of the whole. This goes on indefinitely; the divine proportion always remaining. (Herz-Fischler 1998, 174)

The notion that number is the basis of everything worthy and beautiful in existence prompted the famous cry of Jean Mignot during an argument with his Italian clients over the principles that should govern the construction of Milan cathedral, begun in 1389, "ars sine scientia nihil est."[20] While language was the foundation of the grammar, rhetoric, and logic comprising the trivium, in a kind of preparation for the higher learning,[21] number theory, together with three practical applications of number, became the foundation of the next sequence, the quadrivium. Martianus Capella had laid out the original order of these four disciplines (Stahl 1971, 125–227): arithmetic, an innate feature of human understanding that included more than the elementary counting and calculating its meaning carries today, followed by three practical applications: geometry (quantity at rest), astronomy (quantity in motion), and music (quantity in relation to itself).

Boethius accorded greater importance to music than to geometry or astronomy when compiling the standard arithmetic and music textbooks for the quadrivium (White 1981, 163) and therefore rearranged the order in Martianus by placing music next after arithmetic, thus conferring theoretical status on the concept of harmony, better known as proportion (Peck 1980, 21). Boethius's work was not original, however, since he followed very closely the *Introductio arithmeticae* by Nicomachus of Gerasa (fl. A.D. 100). Yet Nicomachus derived much of his material from Euclid, whose *Elements* (ca. 300 B.C.) was the great summary of earlier Babylonian, Egyptian, and Greek mathematics. Nicomachus wisely collected all ten of Euclid's proportions in one convenient place, whereas Euclid scattered them through several books. It is probably accurate, therefore, to say that the Middle Ages learned of the division into extreme and mean ratio from "the tenth mean of Nicomachus," rather than from Proposition 2, 11 in Euclid's *Elements*. When the schoolmen of Chartres understood mathematics as "the link between God and the world, the intellectual key which unlocked the secrets of the universe" (Masi 1983, 32–33), they had Nicomachus's proportions in mind. Thierry of Chartres would appeal to the equilateral triangle to explain the equality of three persons in the Trinity, "the square of [whose] sides unfolds the ineffable relationship between the Father and the Son" (Masi 33). The *Sketchbook* of Villard de Honnecourt provides numerous examples that geometric and arithmetic proportions extend to a model of the perfect cathedral, as Otto von Simson pointed out a half-century ago and Nigel Hiscock has thoroughly demonstrated very recently. Of particular importance for our interest here, Chartres makes

abundant use of the Divine Proportion and the pentagon that is constructed from it in both its ground plan and its elevations (von Simson
1989, 208–10).

It is often thought, though incorrectly, that division into extreme and
mean ratio was introduced to the Middle Ages by the mathematician
Leonardo of Pisa, better known as Fibonacci (Filius Bonacci), through the
mathematical series that bears his name. Actually, the Fibonacci series has
a distinctly nontheoretical cast. Published in Leonardo's most important
work, the *Liber abaci* (1202), it solves a specific brain twister expressed in
commercial terms:

> How many pairs of rabbits will be produced in a year, beginning with
> a single pair, if in every month each pair bears a new pair which be-
> comes productive from the second month on? (Boyer and Merzbach
> 1989, 256)

As a solution Fibonacci devised a series of numbers in which any two successive numbers, added together, produce the next number: 1, 1, 2, 3, 5, 8,
13, 21, 34, 55, 89, 144, ad infinitum. As the series increases, the ratio of each
number divided by its predecessor approaches the Divine Proportion,
bracketing it with ever closer approximations that are alternately larger
and smaller than *phi*. The numbers in the Fibonacci series turn up in surprising places, for example, in the arrangement of petals in a pine cone,
seeds in a sunflower, and leaves on a tree branch.

However charming this account of the medieval "rediscovery" of
Nicomachus's tenth mean may be, it is very likely a fiction, for "there is no
indication whatsoever that Fibonacci realized that any connection existed
[between the Fibonacci series and division into extreme and mean ratio]"
(Herz-Fischler 1998, 144). Nor is there evidence that division into extreme
and mean ratio had ever been forgotten. Since its discovery in the ancient
world, perhaps giving rise to the discovery of irrational numbers by Hippasus of Metapontum before 410 B.C., division into extreme and mean ratio has been an ever present cornerstone in mathematics. Fibonacci himself, though apparently unaware of the relation between his series and the
Divine Section, nevertheless displays a full knowledge of division into extreme and mean ratio at several places in his mathematical works. Whether
we call it "the Section," after the Greeks ἡ τομή, the "Divine Section," as it
was known throughout the Middle Ages, the "Golden Section," after the
name Kepler apparently gave to its relative, the Pythagorean theorem, or

phi, as modern science now refers to it, there is no doubt it is an irrational number, impossible to measure precisely. Modern mathematicians approximate *phi* as the ratio 1.61803 : 1.

As a kind of miraculous formula, *phi* affords access to complicated geometric forms, in particular the pentangle (known popularly as a regular, five-pointed star), the most prominent symbol in *Sir Gawain*, which would be extremely difficult, if not impossible, to construct without recourse to *phi* (Hiscock 1999, 193). Of crucial significance for the strategy of the manuscript we have been discussing, a pentangle implies a pentagon, as a pentagon implies a pentangle. To connect the points of a pentangle is to enclose a pentagon; to draw the diagonals of a pentagon is to construct a pentangle.[22] Both shapes, pentagon and pentangle, are locked in a continuous progression of references to each other, geometrically toward infinity, poetically in Cotton Nero A.x toward divinity. See appendix 1 for a technical discussion of how the Divine Proportion was calculated by geometric and algebraic methods.

From the perspective of the ancients, division into mean and extreme ratio was a coherent system of relationships that could demonstrate a connection to infinity, the power to replicate itself and expand indefinitely, the very feature Kepler described to Tanckius. It was this feature, one presumes, that would later recommend itself to the *Pearl*-poet as the most appropriate device for his literary purpose. As long as the ancients remained within the fields of algebra and geometry, they were secure in their belief that number was the foundation of all existence. "Euclidean geometry," in the words of the contemporary scientist John D. Barrow (1995, 14–15),

> was held up as a piece of absolute truth about the nature of the world. It was not merely a piece of mathematical reasoning about a possible world; it showed how reality truly was. It underpinned the belief of theologians and philosophers that there was reason to believe in the existence of absolute truth. Moreover, we had discovered it, and understood it. Thus we could have confidence in our ability to appreciate, at least partially, absolute truths about the Universe.

With their "Section," the Neopythagoreans constructed the five-pointed star as the symbol of their sect and the dodecahedron, a regular solid whose twelve faces are regular pentagons, as their symbol of the universe. It was only when they attempted to assign specific magnitudes to the geometric structures in which they had such confidence that difficulties arose. Despite their religious belief in the power of division into extreme and mean ratio, they could not measure the section with any whole number system. And the whole number system was an even more fundamental tenet of belief than the section. Thus was developed the concept of incommensurability—"irrational numbers" in modern parlance—a concept that may have cost the life of Hippasus, who was deemed heretical for being the first to recognize its challenge to their beliefs (Heath 1921, 154; Boyer and Merzbach 1989, 71–72). At length, acceptance of incommensurability became unavoidable, especially when Aristotle supplied the proof of its existence (Heath 91).

Although the *Pearl*-poet was writing almost two millennia after the Greeks worked their way through this problem with irrational numbers, he faced a similar challenge: how to reflect incommensurability in the design of a text subject to precise measurement. Fortunately poetry does not require the same degree of scientific precision that mathematics requires. The *Pearl*-poet is not demonstrating a mathematical proof; he is using "irrational" mathematics as analogy in a literary work dealing mainly with theology and faith. Like everyone who had received a good fourteenth-century education, the *Pearl*-poet would have been thoroughly familiar with the mathematics of his day from the regular course of instruction in the quadrivium.[23] The relationships explained in the excursus of the preceding pages would not have exceeded his learning nor been impossible to grasp as an aesthetic tool: *phi* enables an ordinary square shape, an unimproved lot as it were, to be converted into extraordinary shapes that are inherently more fascinating, more elegant, than the plain shape to which it was applied. And *phi* also provides, as Kepler explains in his letter to Tanckius, quoted above, a tangible means of expressing a path leading to infinity, whether infinitely large or infinitely small. Hence, the geometry of Cotton Nero's linear measurement is a perfect analogue of what the literary content of the manuscript has been progressing toward thematically.

Mathematics and Poetry

The separation between the modern world's "two cultures" has unquestionably widened since C. P. Snow eloquently called it to our attention long ago. As a result, if we have paid little attention thus far to whether medieval mathematics has more than passing significance for Cotton Nero A.x, many a reader has undoubtedly brought two questions increasingly to mind: (1) Is there anything in the literal language of the manuscript, as distinct from the total number of lines and stanzas in its various parts, that justifies so prolonged and detailed a concentration on mathematics? (2) What contribution can mathematics make to poetic structures and themes that are entirely accessible in the very words and sentences of the manuscript? A single response should properly be made to these questions, not only because the matters they raise develop simultaneously in Cotton Nero A.x, but also because they were not as remote from each other in the Middle Ages as C. P. Snow feared they are in the modern world. Nevertheless, they are more easily discussed separately.

The many literal references to number in the manuscript are impossible to ignore. *Pearl* gives pointed attention to the twelves noted in John's description of the New Jerusalem in the Apocalypse: 12 tiers, 12 foundations, 12 gems, 12 steps, 12 furlongs of height, breadth, and length, 12 gates, 12 fruits of life, ripening 12 times each year (*Pearl* 992–1079; cf. Apoc. 21:12–21). John mentions, as well, the twelve groups of twelve thousand virgins each, one group from each of the twelve tribes of Israel, totaling 144,000 (*Pearl* 869–70; cf. Apoc. 7:4, 14:1–5). That this throng is mysteriously transformed, when attending the Lamb, into 100,000 (line 1107), for which there is no authority in John, may be related to the tension between the duodecimal and decimal systems, the former being associated with the Old Law, the latter with Christian salvation.[24] In addition to these literal references to twelve, the manuscript also includes twelve pictures, four preceding *Pearl*, two between *Pearl* and *Purity*, two between *Purity* and *Patience*, one between *Patience* and *Sir Gawain*, and three at the end of the manuscript.[25] So, too, each folio has 36 precisely ruled lines—three twelves—showing two barely noticeable strokes in the left margin where each new stanza begins in *Pearl*. The same ticks appear at every fourth line in *Purity* and *Patience*, and at the beginning of each new stanza in *Sir Gawain*.

The dimensions of Noe's ark are shown very prominently in *Purity* (314–19) where they copy precisely the dimensions in Genesis 6:15, perhaps to recall the mathematical congruity Augustine notes in *The City of God*, 15.26, between the ark, man, and Christ:

> For even [the ark's] very dimensions, in length, breadth, and height, represent the human body in which He came, as it had been foretold. For the length of the human body, from the crown of the head to the sole of the foot, is six times its breadth from side to side, and ten times

its depth or thickness, measuring from back to front. . . . And therefore the ark was made 300 cubits in length, 50 in breadth, and 30 in height. (1950, 516)

A more important reference to number, literarily speaking, occurs in Gawain's first vesting scene, where the poet sees fit, "þof tary hyt me schulde" (*Sir Gawain* 624), to halt the drama of his poem for almost fifty lines (619–65) to dwell on the pentangle on Gawain's shield. The method of constructing this figure and its intricate geometric properties interest the medieval author as much as the five groups of attributes that its points signify. He carefully explains that "vche lyne vmbelappez and loukez in oþer" (628), perhaps meaning that each line passes over one line and then under the next until it touches each of the other four, uniting all five. Yet each of the lines is but a segment of a single line, an "endeles knot" (630). Secured with language in the poem, as it secures itself in geometry, lines associating the pentangle with learning both introduce and conclude the poem's description of the knot. As introduction, the knot is associated in the pre-Christian era with wise King Solomon (625), the same Solomon who said in the Book of Wisdom that all things have been ordered in measure and number and weight (Wisdom 11:21), an enigmatic statement that we suggested in the previous chapter refers to the mathematical design of the universe. To conclude the description, the knot is associated with "learned people" in the English Christian era who call the figure "the noble pentangle" (*Sir Gawain* 664–65; Andrew and Waldron translation in note).

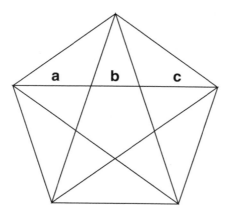

Figure 2.12

The attention that the poet gives to this figure certainly derives from its fame among all educated people in general, as the poem says. Yet this fame originally attached to the pentangle primarily because of the esteem in which its properties were held among mathematicians and geometers from the time of Plato's Academy through the quadrivium and down to the present day (Herz-Fischler 1998, 134 ff.). Each line of a regular pentangle intersects two other lines at precisely their Divine Sections. Conversely, each line is intersected by these other two at the two places that are its own golden cuts—two places because each line shows three stages of the Divine Proportion in expanding magnitudes. In figure 2.12, since a = c, then:

$$b : a = a : (b + c) = (a + b) : (a + b + c) = 1/\varphi$$

It is evident that, in order to construct a regular pentangle, one must first know how to divide a line into extreme and mean ratio. It is also evident from figure 2.12 that a pentangle is intimately related to a pentagon: one pentagon is constructed by connecting the points of a pentangle, another appears at the center of every pentangle. If each of the five legs of the larger pentagon in figure 2.12 is extended in both directions to meet two other extended legs, the resulting figure is another, larger pentangle. In the opposite direction, from greater to smaller, to draw the diagonals of a pentagon is to create a pentangle, within which a new pentagon appears, presenting another opportunity to draw diagonals for yet another, smaller pentangle. And so on in both directions, toward a dimension infinitely large and toward a dimension infinitely small. Finally, as noted above, a regular pentagon is the shape of each of the twelve faces of a regular dodecahedron, the fifth and most perfect Platonic solid, considered by the Neopythagoreans the symbol of the universe. All of these mathematical and geometric relationships matter very deeply to the manuscript under discussion.

A satisfactory answer to the question of whether mathematics can make a contribution to the literal subjects in Cotton Nero A.x is more difficult to shape, for the manuscript's elusive subject may actually lie beyond a human capacity to understand, as argued the new moral theology of the *moderni* whom Peter of Spain inspired (Wallace 1991, 94–95). In general divine literature attempts to make some attribute of God more understandable—his omnipotence, omniscience, love, and so forth. These qualities, however, cannot avoid taking their definition from some interaction, real or imagined, between God and humanity. Hence, divine mercy, for example, acquires in our understanding the limited dimension needed for a specific act of forgiveness. To say "God's mercy is infinite" is to create an unrealistic abstraction, or at best to draw on our limited ability to imagine some horrific offense against God that still would not exceed his capacity to forgive. Again, it is we who would be defining the limit of God's virtue, an ontological impossibility when, by definition, all his attributes are limitless.

Let us not be persuaded that the overall subject of the *Pearl*-manuscript is the felt life it portrays, or the human dilemmas it features. On the contrary, the manuscript continually forces readers to confront the very concept of infinity—not infinite power, or infinite love, but infinity itself. In varying degrees each of the four poems in the manuscript attempts to bring characters and readers to the very edge of infinity—to the point of the Beatific Vision, or at least to some epiphany about the nature of God—and then to back off.[26] Throughout *Pearl* the dreamer-narrator struggles to recover his lost pearl, yet must retreat when he seems closest to regaining it; he labors to understand the arguments offered by the *Pearl*-maiden, but continually sinks back into his usual processes of quantified reasoning; he longs to cross the water to join the procession toward the Lamb, only to awaken abruptly, as if from the cold water he imagines he steps into, for a disappointing return to his original condition. Even his sight of the wounded Lamb "is only momentary, and does not involve any deeper penetration into the divine mysteries: there can be no question of the Dreamer achieving the highest kind of mystical experience" (Spearing 1970, 115). Attempting to describe the Maiden, he misses the center and emphasizes the periphery, the borders of her dress, and the edges of her beauty. Heaven too materializes in vivid metaphors, parables, and splendors, while its essence remains unassayed. Readers remain as excluded from God's presence as is the Dreamer, whom we accompany back to the mound on which he earlier fell asleep.

The second poem in the manuscript, though named *Purity* or *Cleanness* by modern editors, concentrates on the opposite, *fylþe*. Again, we hear the word of God, observe a divinely inspired hand writing three words on Belshazzar's wall, even meet briefly three emissaries who may be angels representing the Trinity ("samen alle þrynne" [*Purity* 645]), yet we never meet God face to face. Similarly in *Patience*, obvious symbols of God continually appear: in the divine instructions ordering Jonas to preach in Ninive; in the raising and calming of a storm; in the three days Jonas spends in the belly of a whale; in the whale's carrying out a divine order; in the mysterious appearance and subsequent withering of a woodbine; in the gentle rebuke Jonas receives at the end of his story; and in many other images. Yet God himself remains beyond our understanding, as the symbols themselves recede from view.

The last poem in the manuscript, *Sir Gawain and the Green Knight*, seems more remote than the others from the contexts normally associated with God. Yet a supernatural presence is dramatically implied in the decapitation of the Green Knight (*Sir Gawain* 417–66), who not only remains indifferent to the severing of his head from his body, but miraculously retrieves it, calmly tucks it under his arm, and returns to his horse. The poem later attributes this power to the "myȝt of Morgne la Faye" (2446), as perhaps do the knights of the Round Table, who greet Gawain's return as if he had done no more than slay a giant or two. Like these knights, Gawain remains uncertain of the lessons he may (or may not) have learned. But a medieval reader attentive to motifs developed elsewhere in the poem and in the manuscript as a whole, seeing Bertilak "resurrected" whole at his second meeting with Gawain, and realizing that Gawain himself has returned relatively unscathed from the Green Chapel, would not be unaware of the providential hand of God, however much he may still fail to understand it.

While it may be true that the literary text of Cotton Nero never actually shows mankind achieving salvation or even approaching an understanding of God, the mathematical underpinning of the manuscript does present a precise, concrete method of approaching a spatial parallel to this understanding. To appreciate how the poet combines number and theme we might first notice that images of circularity pervade the manuscript. Each of its individual poems calls attention to circular movement by repeating in concluding lines details that first appeared at its beginning. Matching the Dreamer's return in *Pearl* to the little spot of earth on which he fell asleep, verbal echoes link the last line of the poem with the first, the singular "perle" of line 1 growing into plural "perlez" of the last line, while the unnamed "prynce" of the first line becomes a particular reference to Christ at the end of the poem:

Perle plesaunte, to prynces paye (1)
Ande precious perlez vnto His pay. (1212)

Purity both opens and closes with one of the beatitudes. "Blessed are the pure in spirit, for they shall see God":

'Þe haþel clene of his hert hapenez ful fayre,
For he schal loke on oure Lorde with a leue chere.'
(27–28)

Ande clannes is His comfort, and coyntyse He louyes,
And þose þat seme arn and swete schyn se His face.
(1809–10)

The final line of *Patience* repeats its first line, with the single addition of the word "noble" modifying "poynt." Though the word *poynt* has many meanings, including "virtue," "truth," "instance," and so forth, it was also the single word identifying the lengthy debate over infinity, for the debate over the divisibility or indivisibility of a point initiated discussions of the continuum (Eldredge 1979). It is also worth noting that the occurrence of the word in *Pearl* line 891 signifies a musical note or chord, a meaning not impossible in *Patience:*

Pacience is a poynt, þaȝ hit displese ofte. (1)
Þat pacience is a noble poynt, þaȝ hit displese ofte. (531)

The last poem, *Sir Gawain,* in addition to commencing at Camelot, following Gawain on his quest, and, like *Pearl,* completing a circle by returning to Camelot, also orchestrates a ring structure of four separate items to bring readers from Troy to Britain at the beginning of the poem, from Britain back to Troy at its end:

Siþen þe sege and þe assaut watz sesed at Troye (1)
Felix Brutus (13)
Ay watz Arthur þe hendest (26)
Rekenly of þe Rounde Table alle þo rich breþer (39)

For þat watz acorded þe renoun of þe Rounde Table (2519)
Þus in Arthurus day þis aunter bitidde (2522)
Syþen Brutus, þe bolde burne, boȝed hider fyrst (2524)
After þe segge and þe asaute watz sesed at Troye. (2525)

The reverse order in which these details are recalled at the end of *Sir Gawain* reflects in isolated particulars the two concentric rings of the entire manuscript, as seen from a distance in figure 2.13. The two poems on

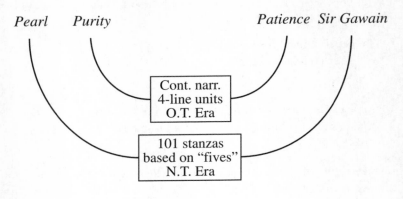

Figure 2.13

the inner ring, *Purity* and *Patience,* are written as continuous narratives, rather than in stanza form, and governed by four-line units, every fourth line ticked off in the margin, nine ticks to a page. In addition, the predominant metrical form in both of these medial poems is a slightly softened, four-beat, alliterative line. But for the caesura that occurs only irregularly, they almost exactly copy the Anglo-Saxon meter that flourished four centuries before Cotton Nero A.x was created. Both of these poems also have similar Old Testament settings.

The two poems at the manuscript's extremities, *Pearl* and *Sir Gawain,* do not present a form starkly different from what we find at its center. Instead, they combine prominent strains of the old meter with features of more recent metrical forms to produce a harmonious synthesis of English literature through the fourteenth century. Rather than continuous narratives, they are both composed in stanza form, 101 stanzas in each, with *Pearl* following a complicated rhyme scheme throughout and *Gawain* concluding each stanza with its rhyming bob-and-wheel. Both poems call attention to the number 5 as a continuing motif, *Pearl* assigning five stanzas to all but one of its twenty sections, and *Sir Gawain* showing five lines in each stanza's concluding bob-and-wheel. *Sir Gawain* also gives great attention to the five groups of fives associated with the five-pointed star on Gawain's shield. The mathematics of the Divine Section (see appendix 1) is derived from the square root of 5. The comment from Kepler to Tanckius, quoted earlier in this chapter, does not stop with the description of the Divine Proportion, but shifts immediately, without explanation, into a paean in praise of the number 5, as if the number 5 would naturally come into the mind of anyone who was thinking of the Divine Section:

> I believe that this geometrical proportion [i.e., the Divine Proportion] served as idea to the Creator when He introduced the creation of likeness out of likeness, which also continues indefinitely. I see the number five in almost all blossoms which lead the way for a fruit, that is, for creation, and which exist, not for their own sake, but for that of the fruit to follow. (Herz-Fischler 1998, 174)

Finally these two poems take place in a setting more closely associated with the New Testament than the Old. To work from the center of the manuscript toward its outer limits, then, is to witness an expansion: from the Old Testament to its historical and religious outgrowth in the New; from an older poetic form to a more recent form that integrates both the old and the new. That the manuscript is also shaped by the Divine Proportion suggests that this expansion will continue until the New Testament era itself—the very age that produced these poems—embraces yet wider contexts bringing eternity and salvation within reach.

It may be of interest to point out here, though we shall see it again in chapter 5, that the general directions of the little-known Hebrew Kabbalah agree perfectly with the central thesis and the methodology of Cotton Nero A.x. The word *Kabbalah* has come to mean "mysterious cult" in the modern era, but the Kabbalists themselves seem to use the word in the same way the Greeks used the word *oracle*, that is, to signify a prediction, a gloss, a cryptic saying. While there have never been more than a few serious students of the Kabbalah, perhaps because of widespread traditions that one must not begin its study before the age of forty, its most active periods were the twelfth and thirteenth centuries in central Europe, followed by a resurgence of interest in sixteenth-century Spain, Italy, and Germany. Although no clear evidence suggests an awareness of the Kabbalah in fourteenth-century England when the *Pearl*-poet was creating his work, or that England had even a single active Hebraist in the Middle Ages, it would be a mistake to conclude from this silence England's complete ignorance of the discipline, for this would imply a wider ignorance of European thought in general, a charge impossible to support.

English theologians were not unaware of the *Postillae* of Nicholas of Lyra (fl. 1314), whose liberal quotations of Hebrew texts in the original language testify to a respect for Hebraic study. Nor could they have overlooked the attempt of Pope Clement V at the Council of Vienne in 1311 to

stimulate interest in creating a chair of Hebrew and other semitic languages at Oxford, Paris, Bologna, and Salamanca (Weiss 1952, 1 ff.). A
mere century after the *Pearl*-poet created Cotton Nero A.x, Pico della
Mirandola in Italy and Johann Reuchlin in Germany—both well known to
John Collet and well respected by him—were arguing strongly that the
study of ancient Hebrew texts was indispensable for a deep understanding
of Christianity. And if Lionel March's suggestion is correct, that Alberti's
volute rosettes in the facade of Santa Maria Novella in Florence encode the
tetragrammaton by using a system of equivalence between letters and
numbers, called *gematria*, an awareness of the Kabbalah must have been
abroad in Florence well before Pico della Mirandola was promoting its importance around 1490 (1998, 194). It seems unlikely that the highly educated author of *Purity* and *Patience*, both of which show a deep familiarity
with Old Testament tradition, would not have known of a significant intellectual current on the Continent that argued for the importance to Christianity of the careful scholarly study of ancient Hebrew texts. I am not
claiming, however, that the Kabbalah was active in England during the
Pearl-poet's lifetime, that he was well versed in it, or that his manuscript is
indebted to it. Though such is not impossible, I only suggest that the fundamental concepts of the Kabbalah, contained in the commentaries on the
Zohar and on the books of Enoch and Abraham by Kimchi, Rashi, Ibn Ezra,
and others (Reuchlin 1983, 91–92), are remarkably similar to the organiza-
tional principles of Cotton Nero A.x.

According to Reuchlin, whose *De arte cabalistica* is the most extensive
discussion of the Kabbalah for gentiles (and the nearest in time to the
Pearl-poet), the Kabbalah has three principal emphases: (1) many of the
books of the Old Testament cryptically foretell the advent of Christ, while
also describing several of the cornerstones of Christianity; (2) much of the
Kabbalah's methodology is equated with Pythagoreanism; and (3) the
techniques of the Kabbalah, called the "practical Kabbalah," especially its
belief in legions of good and bad angels responsible for all celestial and
earthly movement, are useful to penetrate the mysteries of divinity (18–
21, 95, 347 ff.).

The Kabbalists make much of the conversion of the tetragrammaton
into the pentagrammaton. The most prominent example of this conversion
is the expansion of the four letters of one of the names for God, YHVH,
into the five letters of the Hebrew form of the name Jesus, YHSVH.[27] The
intriguing line of reasoning leading to this conclusion, according to
Reuchlin, begins when "the angel Raziel was sent to Adam . . . to console
him [with] the first Kabbalah of all":

The primal sin will be purged in this way: from your seed will be born a just man, a man of peace, a hero whose name will in pity contain these four letters—YHWH—and through his upright trustfulness and peaceable sacrifice will put out his hand, and take from the Tree of Life, and the fruit of that Tree will be salvation to all who hope for it. (73)

The ancients dearly hoped that the name of this savior would contain the letter S in the middle, which stands for "in mercy": YH-in mercy-WH. Although this hint of expansion into the name Jesus appears in book 1 of Reuchlin's *De arte cabalistica* (77), it is not amplified until near the end of book 3, where Marranus (one of the characters in Reuchlin's extended dialogue) explains that the Christians believe they have the best pronunciation of the tetragrammaton "in the name of YHSVH, the true Messiah" (353). By using a form of *gematria* it is possible to show that the S in the middle of the name means both "cross" and "tree" (353–55).

While much of the reasoning accompanying Reuchlin's exegesis sounds elliptic, dependent on an arbitrary linking of numbers and meanings, and in any case requires transposing some characters to make the neocabalist, or "Christian-cabalist" case, it is clear that the expansion of the tetragrammaton into the pentagrammaton, of the four-letter name for God into his five-letter name, in Reuchlin's mind the expansion of YHWH into YHSWH (that is, Jesus), has interesting significance for Cotton Nero A.x. The two poems containing Old Testament episodes, *Purity* and *Patience*, are overwhelmingly composed in four-line syntactic units and divided by decorated initials into sections with line totals divisible by four. Of eighteen sections—thirteen in *Purity*, five in *Patience*—only one, the final section in *Patience*, does not have a line total divisible by four. The two poems set in the New Testament era, *Pearl* and *Sir Gawain*, are governed by a five-based system, *Pearl* in every section but one and in its 101 stanzas signifying the 25th prime number, *Sir Gawain* in its five-line bob-and-wheel, in its basic 2500 lines, and in its 101 stanzas signifying the same 25th prime number. Thus, the *Pearl*-manuscript, like the Kabbalistic expansion of the tetragrammaton into the pentagrammaton, similarly expands its measuring system from a base four to a base five—the number so admired by Kepler—when it widens its perspective from the two medial poems to the two poems at its extremes.

The manuscript's linear advances through time and theology, similar to what the Kabbalah articulates, coupled with the circular forms of the poems themselves, make concrete and accessible the paradox of mortal man living with his immortal soul. The final poem in the manuscript, *Sir Gawain and the Green Knight*, shows us a nearly contemporary society, specifically King Arthur's court and one of its knights, facing corporal challenges that torment humanity in every age. *Pearl* spends most of its time at the very threshold of eternity, before returning us and its dreamer to an empty bereavement. In other words, from a purely human perspective, the manuscript would progress from right to left in the graphics of this study, as Hebrew is read, beginning with the trials and temptations of Gawain and concluding with the Maiden's eternal abode in heaven. It is not entirely fanciful to imagine a parallel with the entrance of a typically flawed Christian into a church at the rear of the nave from which may be viewed in the distant choir symbols of the spiritual enlightenment toward which the faithful are encouraged to progress. By contrast, from the perspective of the Creator—as well as our limited faculties can imagine that perspective—the manuscript moves from left to right, beginning in *Pearl*'s heavenly realm and proceeding to Gawain's earthly setting. The divine perspective, then (to sustain the ecclesial simile), arises in the east, like the sun, passes over the graves of the departed faithful, shines through the stained glass of the apse, takes voice in the choir, and reaches the suppliants in the nave who strive for holiness and eternal repose with their forebears, thus completing a circular path. Both directions pass through the point at which the earthly meets the divine, signified by the two poems at the center of the manuscript that focus exclusively on Scripture, the only object believed to be both heavenly and earthly, having been inspired by God and written by human hands.[28]

Finally, let us note that for any given magnitude the irrational Divine Section, which provides the engine to drive this extraordinary design, can be found in linear measure with utter simplicity, as shown in appendix 1, by using no more than a straight edge and a pair of dividers. The manuscript contains, therefore, another analogue to its central thematic point. Heaven, salvation, even God—concepts impossible to comprehend fully— are accessible with utter simplicity, or as the *Pearl*-maiden might put it, accessible only with childlike innocence. Let us turn, then, to the first of the poems in Cotton Nero A.x, the plush dream vision *Pearl*, a humble, tender elegy on the one hand, and a powerful reconstruction of the universe on the other.

Pearl

Pearl holds immense appeal for even the most casual reader. Its plush texture, its effortless rhythm, and its pathos draw us forth, from mound to stream and beyond. We want to enter the poem, to present an amicus brief to end the maddening debate between the lost Maiden, now found, and the Dreamer who lost her and lacks the ability to understand her new state or the apotheosis it brings. The linguistic subtlety that produces this effect, so different from the muscular language of *Sir Gawain*, has long been appreciated.[1] And the thematic movement of the poem, though perhaps not of the Dreamer, from spiritual torpor to the threshold of salvation encapsulates a universal wish, certainly of everyone in the Christian Middle Ages, if not of all time. Especially dazzling is the poem's rhythmic glory: a four-beat line throughout; twelve-line stanzas of only three rhymes each; the third rhyme sustained for all five stanzas in a section; a recurring echo as the first line of each stanza picks up the final sound(s) of the preceding stanza;[2] and the poem's overall circularity—so like a pearl—as the narrator returns to his original setting and the poem's last line repeats its opening line.

These metrical complexities tend to outshine less obvious marks of beauty that are nonetheless equally remarkable. Indeed, the poem's most compelling theme is initiated with a gentle linguistic crescendo in its opening stanzas. No fewer than seven images of growth and expansion in the initial lines of stanzas 2 through 6 effectively reverse the pearl's fall and apparent disappearance in the first stanza, "I leste hyr in on erbere; / Þurȝ gresse to grounde hit fro me yot" (9–10). Although line 13 refers to the same loss, its verb "sprange" conveys energy and life. Another image of vitality reaches the Dreamer's ear as sweet song, while spices and blossoms "sprede" (25) over this spot of earth and suffuse his thought. One of these plants, "pyonys" (44), may seem to have been added merely for a floral superabundance. In fact, as Barbara Nolan has pointed out, peonies do not bloom during August in England. What they add to the poem is evident in their alternate name, *pentaboron;* their petals number five, a magnitude of major importance in this poem and in the manuscript as a whole (Nolan 1977, 172). The fourth stanza adds voice to this motif of expansion, in the speech "I . . . expoun" (37) on that spot. By this point in the section so many images of flowery renewal, springing spice plants, and expanding size command our attention that the loss of a pearl not only recedes from view, but seems to have been a prerequisite for releasing such vitality. The fifth stanza gently recollects the restriction of a fleshly loss in the hand clasped for cold (50), in the enclosing of the pearl (53), and in the Dreamer's falling (57) to the ground. Yet the implied reach of the hand, the suggested beauty of the pearl in its setting, and the "floury flaʒt" (57) on which the Dreamer falls sustain a vital impulse. All of this prepares for the dramatic opening of the second section, "Fro spot my spyryt þer sprang in space" (61).

Not unlike the separation of body and soul to which a later elegy calls attention by sadly asking dolphins to "waft the hapless youth," while the once living youth, now an "angel," is eagerly asked to "look homeward . . . now,"[3] the Dreamer in *Pearl* leaves his sleeping body on the flowery mound where his cherished possession was lost, while his soul springs free to encounter this possession's spiritual significance. The unfolding poem, however, blurs this dichotomy. In the opening lines the pearl seems to represent the corruptible world, for it is lost in the ground where riches are run to rot (26). The spirit that springs into space must then refer to the Dreamer's soul. But as the poem proceeds, the Dreamer brings to his encounter with the Maiden in Paradise a soul limited in its vision to the sentient self he left behind, while the Maiden, now risen and in union with the Lamb, is identified with the pearl. The point of this paradox may be traced to properties of the continuum, where there is little distinction between flesh and spirit. If every object of creation is connected to every other object, as the mathematics of the quadrivium makes clear, then something of the Dreamer's soul, the part it shares with God, must remain behind, and something of his flesh, the part it shares with matter, must spring into space. This internal discomfort that comes of being both flesh and spirit, unique to humanity let us note, may seem to be a struggle between two aspects of one being, the intellect and the will:

I playned my perle þat þer watz penned,
Wyth fyrce skyllez þat faste faʒt.

Þaȝ kynde of Kryst me comfort kenned,
My wreched wylle in wo ay wraȝte.
(53–56)

But this assumption would misunderstand the unfolding point. Here the
tension is constant, as with the color purple, say, that is always both blue
and red, never struggling between the one and the other, and with the
Roman de la Rose, which owes as much to the Garden of Love as to the
Earthly Paradise (Spearing 1970, 117–23). And Douglas Thorpe, speaking
of *Pearl*, grants that "We can distinguish literal and figurative, body and
spirit, but to separate them is finally impossible, at least for us who dwell
in a physical world."[4] If the Maiden whom the narrator meets in his dream
is an image of his actual daughter, she provides a fine representation of
these two seemingly contradictory motifs, a figure identified with the
Dreamer, yet an expansion above and beyond the Dreamer. That she is an
image in his dream, the product of his own mental vision, yet now residing
in heaven, intensifies the paradox.

As soon as the narrator reaches the otherworld of his dream, the clash
that might have been predicted grows in intensity through the rest of the
poem. Beginning with his first glimpse of the Maiden, he seems more at-
tracted to her outlines, her borders and their adornment, than to the girl
herself:

Al blysnande whyt watz hir beau biys,
Vpon at sydez, and bounden bene
Wyth þe myryeste margarys, at my deuyse,
Þat euer I seȝ ȝet with myn yȝen;
Wyth lappez large, I wot and I wene,
Dubbed with double perle and dyȝte;
Her cortel of self sute schene,
With precios perlez al vmbepyȝte.
. . . .
Pyȝt watz poyned and vche a hemme—
At honde, at sydez, at ouerture—
Wyth whyte perle and non oþer gemme,
And bornyste quyte watz hyr uesture.
(197–204, 217–20)

An unwitting irony occurs in the Dreamer's description of the Maiden's
first gesture toward him, when he says she greeted him "wyth a lote lyȝte"

(238). Since "lyȝte" may be either an adjective, meaning light in weight, used metaphorically of a pleasant greeting, or a noun implying the light that illuminates, the phrase means both "a joyful voice" and "a greeting infused with light [and with the divinity light implies]." Despite this rich opportunity to see in the Maiden's greeting evidence of the divine presence, the Dreamer apparently notices only her airy social demeanor, for he adds to this description of her greeting the physical details that seem to strike him clearest of all, "þat swete in perlez pyȝte" (240). Evidence of this limited capacity extends to the next stanza where an identical opportunity is identically missed. Are you the pearl I lost, he asks, now "in a lyf of lykyng lyȝte, / In paradys erde" (247–48)? His own words here suggest the true significance of the Maiden's sanctified state, the light of Paradise, especially since the literal meaning of "paradys" cannot be unknown to him. Yet instead of understanding a spiritual significance, he completes the thought in a sentient way, forcing us to infer that he intended only a metaphoric meaning for paradise, "In paradys erde, of stryf vnstrayned" (248).

Shortly thereafter, the meeting takes an awkward turn, confirming in a series of triplets that the Maiden and the Dreamer inhabit two entirely different worlds. First, the Dreamer exuberantly mentions three thoughts that give him pleasure, wholly understandable if he is a grieving father: that finding what he thought he had lost brings him joy; that he will now live with her in bright groves; and that he yearns to be with her on the other side of the stream (283–88). She flatly states in stanza 25 that these thoughts are errors, explaining her opinion in three succinct arguments in the next two stanzas. Crushed, he makes a pathetic plea in stanza 28, unfortunately couching it in purely physical terms—calling the girl a treasure whose value is nil if it brings no joy, and calling himself an exile bereft of feeling. The Maiden judges his remarks harshly, "'Thow demez noȝt bot doel-dystresse'" (337), inviting the judgment that she lacks compassion. Never mind the extraordinary permission she manages to secure later for the Dreamer, that he might catch a glimpse of the New Jerusalem (967–68), her attitude to him here seems insensitive, as defiant as Cordelia's to Lear. What she says is not actually offensive; indeed, her explanations of medieval Christian theology are apparently sound, according to those who have studied the matter.[5] But she says it with a surprising lack of sympathy. Instinctively readers want to see her greet her father (if father he is) with the kind of warmth his bereavement yearns for. During their later exchanges regarding the truths of theology, we would welcome a Socratic conversation, where she might inquire why he holds certain views, followed by a gentle explanation of how these views are somewhat wide of the mark. But we get none of this. Instead, from her opening lines she levels at him charges that he is mistaken (257), mad (267), that he is "no kynde jueler" (276), and that he speaks before thinking (292–94).

Rather than see this attitude of the Maiden as a blemish in the poem, we might more profitably think of it as a sharp reminder that absolute truths do exist. These impasses in the poem, when the Maiden and Dreamer have entirely different viewpoints that seem unlikely ever to coincide, operate very much like several passages in the *Consolation of Philosophy,* or any other allegorical confrontation between self and soul. The Dreamer sounds like Boethius—the character, not the author—complaining about his lot in life; the Maiden like Lady Philosophy futilely explaining the difference between transitory and permanent goods as she exhorts Boethius to recognize good and bad fortune for the imposters they both are. The Maiden in *Pearl* possesses a truth very different from the Dreamer's, as absolute, exacting, and infinite as the mathematics holding the manuscript together. Her truth has no room for the Dreamer's brand of relativist thinking. The meeting of the Maiden and the Dreamer, therefore, captures well one of the challenges facing humanity, the obligation to reconcile the human emotions and values that may incline one to think and act in a certain way, with spiritual truth that may prompt the same person to act in an entirely different way. This is not to say that divine law lacks compassion. On the contrary, as *Patience* makes abundantly clear, divine compassion is infinite, offered unhesitatingly again and again to Jonas and to the Ninevites, as it is offered to the workers in the vineyard in the parable cited by the *Pearl*-maiden, and as it will be offered countless times to the Dreamer, despite his inability or unwillingness to grasp the Maiden's explanations. But Christ's gift of infinite mercy should not be confused with the Maiden's role as spokesperson for divine truth.

Now chastened, or at least making the sounds of new knowledge, the grieving narrator seems to accept the Maiden's exhortation to humility and patience. With this little unpleasantness out of the way, he now inquires about her new life. Yet here again the answer he receives is not what he expected: she has been "Corounde . . . quene in blysse to brede / In lenghe of dayez þat euer schal wage" (415–16). The theological point implicit in the word "blysse" and the clear reference to infinity in "euer schal wage" go over his head entirely, as he narrows in on the temporal word "queen," taking it to mean that she has usurped the Virgin's role. His argument rests on another worldly concept inappropriate to heaven: his sense of justice reckoned in temporal terms. God would not "wryþe so wrange away" (488) from a just decision, he claims, but more likely, in view of the Maiden's brief life on earth, settle upon her a rank of countess "Oþer ellez a lady of lasse aray" (491). Although "quene," "countes," "damysel," and "aray" are all words with which he deals daily, their implication of relative rank has no place in heaven and perhaps should not consume much earthly energy, a thought that seems not to occur to him.

To make the ideas of equality and infinity in heaven more accessible to her recalcitrant guest, the Maiden reaches for one of the most troubling parables in the New Testament, the parable of the vineyard (497–576; cf. Matt. 20:1–16). As a result, what had threatened to become only an impasse now reaches open argument. The Dreamer is not alone here in his impulse to resist the parable. In every age, congregations exit churches on the Sunday when this parable is read with troubled thoughts as they contemplate what might happen to them, if they paid their employees, or were paid by their employers, as the workers are compensated in Matthew. Yet the lesson has a simple beauty, despite the apparent caprice of the vineyard owner who insists on his right "'To do wyth myn quatso me lykez?'" (566). Every human being has a solemn responsibility throughout life to attend to a personal contract with the Creator. Let us imagine this contract geometrically (the metaphor is mine here, rather than the poet's), as one of the vertical legs leading up to the apex of an angle. Trouble arises only when one looks horizontally to compare his progress with another's. But that other workman must attend his own contract, must keep his own path straight until he reaches the same apex. The progress of this second worker has nothing to do with the first worker's obligation, which ought always to tend upward. So too, the vineyard workers in *Pearl*, glancing sideward more often than upward, grumble that others are more handsomely rewarded in worldly ways than they are.

Like these vineyard workers, *Pearl*'s Dreamer-narrator alleges unfair treatment. Although the specific lesson of the parable concerns equality in the context of eternity, he can only imagine equality as a temporal concern, emphasizing once again his dependence on a reasoning that would undoubtedly be judged sound by many a mortal:

'In sauter is sayd a verce ouerte
Þat spekez a poynt determynable:
"Þou quytez vchon as hys desserte,
Þou hyȝe Kyng ay pertermynable."
Now he þat stod þe long day stable,

And þou to payment com hym byfore,
Þenne þe lasse in werke to take more able,
And euer þe lenger þe lasse þe more.'
(593–600)

He errs by focusing on the amount of work, a worldly concern, rather than
on the fulfillment of a contract entered into with the lord of the vineyard.
The parable implies that eternal life is earned by successfully discharging
one's obligations to God, not by measuring one's worldly work in comparison to another's. The penny promised for fulfilling this contract does not
symbolize salvation or even grace, but divine approval, a judgment on
which grace will be granted and salvation will ultimately depend. As such
it cannot be doubled for those who worked four hours or tripled for those
who worked the whole day; it is already infinite. Thus all workers receive
the same infinite reward. Still mired in the way the world measures value,
the workers in the vineyard, like the Dreamer in *Pearl*, have no understanding of the scene unfolding before them. The grumbling workers ignore the significance of the penny, in order to compare the length of their
earthly labor against another's; the Dreamer looks at the rank of queen
while missing the concept of eternal bliss.

Notwithstanding this oblique exegesis, the parable of the vineyard provides a homely analogue to the most important structural design of *Pearl*,
expansion in stages from the mundane to the infinite. It takes the *Pearl*-
maiden more than two sections (601–744) to explain the delicate distinction between the innocent who have never lost their childlike nature and
the righteous who recover their innocence through contrition. But these
arguments rely heavily on abstract reasoning, on premises that lie outside
the ken of someone like the Dreamer. It is precisely here that the poem,
suddenly and with apparent illogic, brings us back to the Maiden's physical
being, long after the Dreamer has praised the beauty of her array and the
excellence of the pearl she wears on her breast. A single stanza, perhaps
with greater effect than the Maiden's lengthy explanation, teaches us by
way of allusion, metaphor, and example how to interpret the parable of the
vineyard. It is a curious stanza, as surprising for what it says as for when it
says it. Ironically, it is spoken by the Dreamer.

'O maskelez perle in perlez pure,   745
Þat berez,' quoþ I, 'þe perle of prys,
Quo formed þe þy fayre fygure?
Þat wroȝt þy wede he watz ful wys;

Þy beauté com neuer of nature—
Pymalyon paynted neuer þy vys,   750
Ne Arystotel nawþer by hys lettrure
Of carped þe kynde þese propertéz;
Þy colour passez þe flour-de-lys,
Þyn angel-hauyng so clene cortez.
Breue me, bryȝt, quat kyn offys   755
Berez þe perle so maskellez?'

It is certainly possible that the two surprising allusions in this stanza, Pygmalion and Aristotle, have only proverbial force, emphasizing degree and nothing more. Pygmalion symbolizes the best portrayer, as he does in the poet's Ovidian source; Aristotle is a familiar symbol of the wisest mathematician-philosopher. Their skills are easily attributed to the heaven-portraying, philosophizing Maiden. Nevertheless, the references seem out of place, like names dropped for effect and then forgotten. For after denying that the Maiden's perfection could have been produced by Pygmalion or explained by Aristotle, the poem returns to the Maiden herself and to the heavenly home bestowed on those who love the Lamb.

One crucial word in this stanza offers guidance to the poet's strategy here. Unfortunately, it is a textual crux. Every edition I have seen prints the last word of line 755 as "offys," modern English "office." (In plate 2, line 755 is the second line from the bottom.) This reading ignores what looks like a deliberate, vertical, superscript pen stroke to the right of the second *ascenda*. There is, in addition, a slightly larger separation than expected between the third and fourth letters, suggesting that the scribe wanted a little extra room to accommodate this superscript stroke. In other words, the stroke was intended. When a medieval manuscript has a superscript mark oriented vertically it usually indicates omission of the consonant *r* in combination with some vowel, though not *er* which this manuscript indicates by a superscript mark in the shape of a *c*, as shown over "nev*er*" in line 749, again over "nev*er*" in line 750, and over "nawþer" in line 751. If this superscript stroke in line 755 is not just a blemish in the manuscript (my own visual inspection of the manuscript at the British Library convinces me that it is not a blemish), then it is probably an abbreviation for *ri*, opening the possibility that the second and third letters are a tall *s* and a *t*. If this is all true, the word is probably *o s t r i y s*, the genitive singular or plural of "oyster," producing the following meaning for "quat

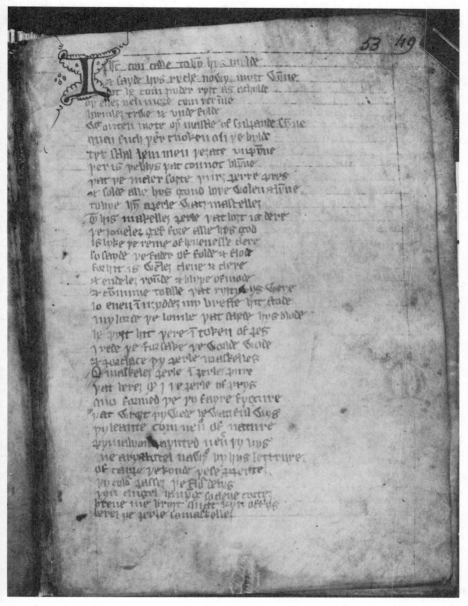

Plate 2. MS Brit. Lib. Cotton Nero A.x. Folio 49 recto. Reproduced by permission of the British Library.

kyn os*triys*": what kind of oyster(s).[6] Such is how Talbot Donaldson reads the line, "What kind of oysters produce a pearl like you?" (1972, 76). This potential reading has obvious significance for the poem's main symbol, a pearl.

Read thus, the stanza takes shape as a complicated cluster of related metaphors. Pygmalion brought raw inanimate matter to a higher state of perfection as a statue of consummate beauty with which he fell in love. He was rewarded when Aphrodite brought the statue to an even loftier perfection as the living Galatea, who returned Pygmalion's love. Aristotle, though "primarily a philosopher and biologist . . . was thoroughly *au courant* with the activities of the mathematicians" (Boyer and Merzbach 1989, 98).[7] By remaining in the penumbra of this stanza's allusions, his influential treatise *On Indivisible Lines*, which discusses the infinite in arithmetic and geometry as well as incommensurables, suits perfectly the secondary importance that mathematics assumes for the entire manuscript—always unstated, off the page, a silent presence supporting the thematic subjects advanced by literal language. The third item of comparison in the stanza creates exactly the same image, though in a different medium. An oyster crafts an ordinary grain of sand into an exquisite pearl.[8]

The most significant line in the stanza may actually be missed, for it sounds at first like mere hyperbole, though a poet of this precision and power does nothing for so meager a reason. It is the Dreamer's comment, "Þy beauté com neuer of nature" (749). Yet the Maiden herself did come from nature. The Dreamer had seen her before (164). Nearer to him than aunt or niece (233), she is the little child whom he knew well. If she was his own child, now deceased and slipped into the earth, she came from *his* nature. All this notwithstanding, he now suggests that her present condition—her fair figure, her beauty, her face, her color, her angelic bearing—are not the properties of the natural girl he once knew. Like Galatea, she has been transformed by a force he does not know.

What makes the observation extremely important is its location at line 749. This is the precise point in this poem of 1212 lines that medieval mathematicians would call its Divine Section (Golden Section or *phi* in modern parlance): 1212 x 0.61803 = 749.05, or line 749. It is one of only two points—depending on whether measurement begins from left to right, or right to left—at which a line can be divided into extreme and mean ratio, the one that produces a continuous proportion, constantly repeated as it approaches infinity.

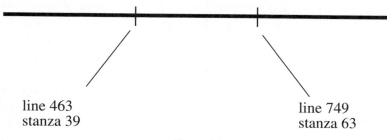

line 463
stanza 39

line 749
stanza 63

Figure 3.1

An oyster, Aristotle, Pygmalion, and the Divine Section are more than proverbial presences casually inserted in a random stanza. They demonstrate the kind of expansion that creates a higher reality. They show that the power of the irrational number *phi* and the power of God are not analogous but continuous. They suggest further that the early fourteenth century's intense philosophical debate on the continuum—primarily a focus on a geometric point, a mark of no dimension, to discover whether it is indivisible or infinitely divisible—implies a wider discussion of infinity and a consideration of magnitudes that are infinitely large as well as infinitely small.[9] It is significant, therefore, that the geometrically reciprocal point at which *Pearl* can be divided into extreme and mean ratio, displaying the smaller extreme at the left as shown in figure 3.1, contains the philosophic reciprocal of the point made in stanza 63. Lines 463 ff. (1212 x [1 - 0.61803] = 462.95) identify a theological principle in which everyone is understood to be a member of the "mystical body of Christ." As the head is never jealous of the arm that wears a bracelet, or the finger that wears a ring, so there is no rivalry among the members of this mystical body. If the argument in stanza 63 appeals to the expansion the Divine Proportion makes possible, here in stanza 39 the same point is made in the opposite direction, from Christ, "þe Mayster of myste," to every individual, allegorized as a single finger or digit. At both points where the Divine Proportion segments *Pearl's* 1212 lines, the poem stresses the harmony among all things, from the Greatest to the least. Of significance for the thesis advanced here, the distinction the poet accords these two stanzas is a declaration of the organizing principle on which Cotton Nero A.x is based.

While acknowledging that every hypothesis awaits the firm footing of demonstration (for which see chapter 4, on *Purity*), let me repeat that the organizing principle of Cotton Nero A.x is the Divine Proportion. Further, the poet has taken the most elevated geometric shape arising from the Divine Proportion as the form of the first poem in his manuscript. That is, the form of *Pearl* is based on the form of the fifth Platonic solid, a dodeca-hedron. Although a regular dodecahedron would probably not occur to a modern reader, no one can fail to notice that the numbers five, twelve, and twenty have prominence in *Pearl:* all but one of its sections have five stan-zas; each stanza has twelve lines; and the entire poem has twenty sections. If exposed to the medieval quadrivium, however, one would recognize im-mediately that these very dimensions describe a regular dodecahedron: five edges to each face; twelve faces; and twenty apexes. I shall explain why a dodecahedron is especially appropriate for the design of *Pearl,* but it will be instructive to pause for a brief discussion of how this first poem in the manuscript expresses the most highly revered of all regular geometric shapes.

Since each face of a dodecahedron is a regular pentagon, it follows that the fundamental building block of a dodecahedron is the same Divine Sec-tion discussed in the previous chapter and used as the controlling propor-tion throughout Cotton Nero A.x. Neither a pentagon nor its intimately related pentangle can be constructed without the Divine Section. That there are twelve of these faces causes some uncertainty over their relation to the many twelves in *Pearl.* In addition to the frequent occurrences of the number twelve noted in the previous chapter, subtler occurrences of the same number appear in the twelve sections constituting the exposition part of the poem (sections 5–16), in the 120-line hymn where the Maiden praises her marriage to the Lamb (781–900), and in her 12-line final speech in the poem (965–76), especially since this speech's twelve lines do not appear in a single 12-line stanza—the speech bridges two stanzas. From one perspective the twelve lines in each of *Pearl's* stanzas suggest the twelve sides of a dodecahedron, but from another view the five stanzas of each section could represent the five edges of a pentagon. One may well ask, then, is a five-edged face of this twelve-sided dodecahedron repre-sented by the five stanzas in a typical group of stanzas, or by one of the twelve poetic lines in a single stanza? And if by five stanzas, is not another dilemma presented? In *Pearl* there are twenty pentagonal sections, but only twelve pentagonal sides in a dodecahedron.

While the twelve lines in each stanza and all of the other twelves in the poem certainly represent the duodecimal system of measurement and the dodecahedron based on that system, a subtle conversion occurs when a group of twelve-line stanzas completes a sixty-line section. As a simple diagonal across two side-by-side squares leads to the miraculous Divine Section (see appendix 1) and in turn affords access to more complex, richer figures, and eventually toward infinity, so lines originally arranged in a duodecimal system eventually produce a section that also participates in the decimal series. That there are twenty sections in *Pearl*, all but one of which reveal graduations from a duodecimal base to a decimal base, enforces the parallel with geometry in which twelve sides produce twenty vertices.[10] That is, each section of *Pearl* and each stanza in a section, viewed as single units, suggest the twelve five-edged faces of a dodecahedron, but all of *Pearl*'s sections together suggest a dodecahedron's twenty vertices.

To appreciate more fully how the twenty sections of *Pearl* represent the twenty vertices of a dodecahedron we must suspend our usual habit of describing a poem's verse form in terms of individual stanzas, in favor of a close look at the texture of all sixty lines in a section. The rhyme scheme of a single stanza in *Pearl* is normally indicated thus:

$$a\,b\,a\,b\,a\,b\,a\,b\,b\,c\,b\,c$$

Such a description overlooks the importance of the third rhyme, which is much greater than its two occurrences here would indicate. This same sound resonates throughout an entire section, appearing as the rhyme word in the tenth and twelfth lines of each stanza and again in the first line of the next stanza, usually in initial or medial position. The technique not only crosses borders between stanzas, but between sections as well. Thus, we might more profitably look at a scheme that marks the occurrence of this sound throughout a whole section, including the three lines before the section and the one line following. Here is a representation of these echoing sounds for the 64–line run from line 358 through line 421, though any other section would illustrate the technique equally well:

CxCCxxxxxxxxDxDDxxxxxxxxDxDDxxxxxxxxDxDDxxxxxxxxDxDDxxxxxxxxDxDD

The three uppercase Cs represent the third rhyme in the preceding sixth section, "fleme" (358) and "deme" (360), and the echoic sound in the first line of the seventh section, "demed" (361). A different echo marks the seventh section, the recurring sound of "-ysse" represented by uppercase D for the cluster at lines 370, 372, and 373, again for the cluster at lines 382, 384, and 385, and so forth. These uppercase letters counterpoint the regular stanza divisions, since they stretch across stanza breaks. Thus, without disturbing the numeric scheme that represents the five edges of a regular pentagon, these recurring sounds suggest spikes in an otherwise flat line (to use images from modern technology). Each of these echoic patterns of spikes across an expanse of 52 lines, from line 370 through line 421 in the example above, represents one vertex of the dodecahedron, twenty in the whole poem. That each cluster contains three repetitions in quick succession may also refer to geometry, since each vertex of a regular dodecahedron is constructed by the intersection of three pentagonal edges. The recurrence of the same sound across stanzas may have still another geometric reference by representing the indivisible point that the ends of two edges share as they form a pentagon's 108° angle at a vertex.

Although it matters little what dimension the poet had in mind for his dodecahedron, since shape and proportion are more important than size, he had to begin with something concrete—to convert virtue into essence, in Boethius's and Pacioli's terms (see below). A dodecahedron needs only one measurement to be completely constructed, namely the length of an edge. If one tests every likely dimension, a 12-unit edge alone leads to the results discussed here and in the following chapters. Each pentagonal face, then, has five edges measuring 12 units each. (Any unit may be used: centimeters, inches, feet, et cetera.) An interesting fact now presents itself. Even though one lacks a means of measuring angles, and in this respect duplicates the condition of a medieval geometer, it is nevertheless relatively easy to approximate a regular pentagon by using five slender, movable objects, all of exactly the same dimension. Anyone can quickly arrange a pentagonal shape on a desk, for example, with five new pencils all from the same box and presumably the same size. If the angles are kept equal, they will inevitably and necessarily measure 108°. But it is impossible to *draw* a perfect pentagon without first knowing the length of the pentagon's diagonal (the straight line joining any two nonadjacent angles). Again, one might try experimenting with a simple compass and a ruler, only to learn that it cannot be done. To discover the length of this diagonal the Divine Proportion is an absolute necessity. If each edge of the dodecahedron is to be 12, one need merely multiply this length by *phi* (12 x 1.61803) to learn the length of a diagonal on one of its faces, 19.416. By drawing a line to this precise measure, the two end points of this line will position two of the nonadjacent angles of the desired pentagon. Completing the figure is then straightforward, though a second use of the diagonal measurement computed earlier provides a useful check for accuracy. Completing the dodecahedron by joining twelve such pentagons is equally straightforward.

Let us now return to the poet's thematic purposes. From ancient times through the Renaissance the fifth Platonic solid was considered a symbol of the universe.[11] When Luca Pacioli said that this Divine Section shares four attributes with God (see chap. 2, 33), he added a fifth as an afterthought, which deserves quoting in full:

> A fifth . . . attribute can be added to the above not undeservedly. This is: just as God has conferred being to the heavenly virtue by another name, called the fifth essence, and through it on to the other four simple bodies, that is the four elements: earth, water, air and fire, and through these [He conferred] being to every other thing in nature, likewise this holy proportion of ours gives the formal being, (according to the ancient Plato in his *Timaeus* [section 16.D.1]) to heaven itself conferring to it the figure of the body called Dodecahedron, or the body with twelve pentagons. (Herz-Fischler 1998, 172)

For those who shared Pacioli's learned background, a dodecahedron was a manifestation of the heavenly essence, God's first expression of the extended world. As the heavenly virtue, an abstraction, became a physical entity signaled by a change of name, "virtue" becoming "essence," so the Divine Proportion, an equally abstract concept, received its first physical expression as the geometric shape that is constructed exclusively from it, the dodecahedron. If a statue was once elevated to a living person, as in the Pygmalion story, then a dodecahedron can be elevated, burnished, smoothed into the shape of a sphere—the shape of the universe at its largest dimension, a pearl at a significantly smaller dimension. The obvious circularity of *Pearl* is especially pertinent. The last line of each stanza is echoed by the first line of the succeeding stanza, with the final line of the poem recalling the opening line, as if the poem's first line were to succeed its last line and the poem were to begin again. All of this creates an overwhelming sense of something round with a seamless surface, like its main subject the pearl. Based upon precise mathematics and drawing upon both the duodecimal and decimal systems to measure straight lines, sharp angles, and flat sides, the poem achieves a perfectly spherical shape.

Mathematical and geometric perfection is more than analogous to ontological/theological perfection; it is part of the same continuum. The acts that enable someone or something to approach these perfections are themselves more than similar or analogous; they are part of the same process. As one approaches mathematical perfection, moral or theological perfection draws nearer. Gerardus Ruffus, as summarized and quoted by Masi, uses a similar argument to explicate Boethius's chapter on secondary and composite numbers (*De institutione arithmetica* 1:15):

> such reasoning can be interpreted as an allegory of how man knows God. Numbers may be imperfect in respect to themselves but perfect in relation to others[,] so the knowledge of man can be imperfect in itself but comprehend something of the perfect. "So our manner of knowing goes from composed things to simple, from the imperfect creatures to perfect beings, from created things to God" (Masi 1983, 90 n).

It is important, therefore, that the penny in the parable of the vineyard be understood as a middle term facilitating this expansion, like the Divine Proportion, a mean between two extremes, a "determynable" (594) coin of exchange on the one hand, a symbol of the key to eternal salvation on the other. The relation between the vineyard owner and his penny is the same as the relation between the divine geometer and *phi*. The initiator in each case—the lord of the vineyard and the Lord of all—reaches for some symbolic device to make understandable the connections among all things. The largesse of the vineyard owner in expanding the workers' lot from the physical labor of a few hours to the eternity of the spirit, as symbolically promised in the wages of a penny, emulates the largesse of the Creator in conferring on all things lesser images of his divinity.

With a dodecahedron now complete, and using formulas well known to the fourteenth century, the poet would now be able to calculate all of the shapes associated with the fifth Platonic solid, widely understood as a symbol of the universe. Let us, then, temporarily put aside specific calculations to discuss a hidden property of a dodecahedron that has particular importance for this study. Within every dodecahedron there can be constructed three identical rectangles whose twelve corners (3 rectangles x 4 corners each) touch the central points of the twelve faces of the dodecahedron, as shown in figure 3.2. Appendix 2 describes the method by which the poet could have calculated the size of these rectangles. The length and width of each of these rectangles are in a *phi* ratio. We have seen that the initial

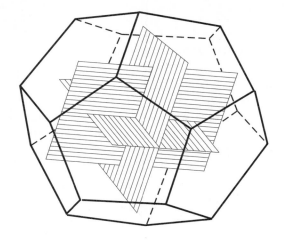

Dodecahedron
with 3 *phi* - related, inscribed retangles

Figure 3.2

poem in Cotton Nero A.x describes not only the surface of the earth, where we find the Dreamer mourning a loss, but also the eternal context, or rather the supratext to which the Dreamer's spot of earth is a hypertext (to use modern metaphors once again). In short, by imaginatively visiting both heaven and earth, *Pearl* depicts the three-dimensional universe as the Middle Ages understood it. It is perfectly suited, therefore, to represent a three-dimensional shape, specifically the dodecahedron.[12] The three remaining poems in the manuscript, by recounting events that happened, or might have happened, on the two-dimensional surface of the earth, are equally well-suited to represent, and be represented by, the three rectangles found within this dodecahedron. The geometry of a dodecahedron with its three inscribed planes is replicated by *Pearl* and its three accompanying poems. We shall save for later chapters the explanation of how the geometric designs of these three remaining poems, like a dodecahedron's inscribed rectangles, encode the Divine Proportion.

The dodecahedron we have been discussing, with edges measuring 12, when fully constructed does not produce a single dimension that refers to anything in the sections or subsections of Cotton Nero A.x, excepting the number 12 itself. If, however, we expand the diagram in the manner described in chapter 2—that is, extend the edges of its pentagonal sides until they meet other extended edges to complete a five-pointed star, and then connect the points of this newly constructed star to complete another pentagon, from which yet another star will be formed from extended sides, and so forth—after the third expansion a shape is produced that has enormous significance for the remainder of the manuscript. Since each expansion requires two applications of *phi* (the first measures the extension of a pentagonal side to form a new pentangle, the second measures each line connecting two adjacent points of this newly formed pentangle, that is, a side of a newly formed pentagon), the original dimension 12 must be multiplied by 1.61803 six times to reach the pentagonal size from which the poet seems to have constructed his manuscript. As we shall see, this is a pentagon with sides measuring 212. Again, we must remember that in the fourteenth century calculations were made without a convenient system of decimals. Instead, a cumbersome method of fractions was used, necessitating a continual process of rounding off and much more approximating than would make modern mathematicians comfortable.[13]

Notwithstanding the poet's need to use approximations, the six applications of *phi* with their assumed rounding are remarkably close to what can be produced with modern calculators:

Table 3.1

12	times φ	=	19.416	rounded off to	19
19	"	=	30.742	"	31
31	"	=	50.158	"	50
50	"	=	80.901	"	81
81	"	=	131.060	"	131
131	"	=	211.961	"	212

The last three of these figures, 81, 131, and 212 are extremely important dimensions for chapter 4. Until then we shall leave the mathematics of the manuscript, while we consider more conventional lines of critical thought.

There has been much discussion of two eccentricities of form in *Pearl*. The first is a sixth stanza in the fifteenth section (stanza 76, lines 901–12), whereas every other section has five stanzas; the second is a decorated initial at line 961, beginning stanza 81, the final stanza of section sixteen, whereas every other decorated initial in the poem marks the beginning of a new section. It is a brave critic indeed who would argue that these are mistakes, especially the addition of stanza 76, which would have to be called an inadvertent addition of colossal proportions, rather than a simple error of omission or a repeated word. That a poet who reveals meticulous craftsmanship everywhere else simply became so deeply engrossed that he kept writing another stanza, which he would not have included had he not had a momentary lapse, is simply impossible to accept. It seems more probable that this "extra" stanza was intended to bring the poem to a total of 101 stanzas, identical to the 101 stanzas in *Sir Gawain and the Green Knight*, enabling the stanza count of both poems to reach the 25th prime

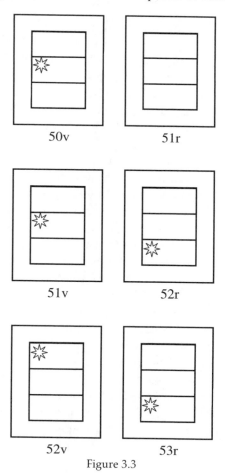

Figure 3.3

number. The poet's reason for placing this extra stanza at the end of section 15, rather than randomly somewhere else, will be clear shortly.

The latter instance—a decorated initial at line 961—is only slightly less difficult for editors and critics to dismiss as merely "misplaced" (Andrew and Waldron 1979, 52). To assume, as many do, that stanza 81 mistakenly received a decorated initial under the influence of the additional stanza in section 15 requires critical gymnastics. In the manuscript's scheme, where each page accommodates 36 lines, that is three 12-line stanzas,[14] a 5-stanza section takes up one stanza less than two complete pages. Thus, each new section begins one stanza earlier on its page than the position occupied by the beginning of the previous section. The illuminator (if he was other than the poet) could understandably have established a pattern of expectation without regard to other indications of metrical form. The poem's first section begins in the top position on folio 39r,[15] the second in bottom position on folio 39v, the third in middle position on folio 40v, and so on. Top, bottom, middle, top, bottom, middle, top. . . . Since the fifteenth section begins with the middle stanza on folio 50v, such an illuminator would expect the sixteenth to begin at the top of 51v, the seventeenth at the bottom of 52r, and so forth. But the fifteenth section has six stanzas, as shown in figure 3.3, which represents the open manuscript as it would appear to a reader, with the verso of one folio on the left, recto of the next folio on the right, and with each page's three stanzas indicated by three rectangles. Therefore the sixteenth section correctly begins—decorated initial in its proper place—with the middle stanza on 51v, the seventeenth with the top stanza on 52v, the eighteenth with the bottom stanza on 53r, and so forth. The pattern is complicated by the surprising appearance of a decorated initial at the bottom stanza on 52r, as if it too were beginning a section. Those who would argue that the illuminator has obviously made a mistake in creating this decorated initial are faced with having to explain why this craftsman, alert enough to avoid drawing an initial letter for the sixth stanza of section 15, lost his attentiveness four stanzas later when he drew the mistaken initial at line 961, then recaptured his wits, noticed his mistake, and set the poem back on track by correctly drawing an initial for the next stanza (973) to begin section 17.

A much simpler explanation—Ockham to the rescue—can account for the initial at 961 than the tortuous speculation about how an error might have been made: *the author intended it.* Is it not also more gracious, if an error must be assigned, to lay this error at critics' feet for failing to find the

poet's design, than at the poet's and/or his collaborator's for failing to remain alert? A claim of authorial intent, however, raises further questions:
Why here? And why at all?

Whereas every other decorated initial marks only a structural separation,
the beginning of a new five-stanza section and a new concatenation, the
decorated initial opening stanza 81 (line 961) is the only visual indicator in
the poem marking a point of thematic significance. This is the one point in
the poem where the Maiden and the Dreamer are most closely in accord.
Not only is this the stanza where the Dreamer asks the Maiden to take him
to her "bygly bylde / And let me se þy blysful bor" (963–64), but it further
underscores their closeness by being the only stanza in the poem that includes words from both the Dreamer and the Maiden. But, again, why does
the poet limit their duet to this single stanza? And does this stanza have
further structural significance to match its thematic importance? To answer these questions calls for a brief explanation of yet another context.

The various forms and degrees of intensity in Man's relation to God
have a wide range of expression. The *Dream of the Rood*, for example,
focuses mainly on the first stirrings of religious *awareness*, while *Piers
Plowman* movingly describes the worldly impediments that must be
purged before further progress can be made. Scripture itself, especially the
teachings of Christ in the New Testament and of the Glossa Ordinaria for
the Old and the New, bring theological *illumination*. Other literature, like
Wanderer and *Seafarer*, explore the *dark night of the soul* that, if survived,
may lead to the most profound kind of religious *union* possible, as the
writings of several mystics attest. Indeed, Richard Rolle, a mid-four-
teenth-century mystic whose writings the *Pearl*-poet may have known,[16]
describes this full range of expression as five steps of religious maturation
(marked by the italicized terms in the previous sentences, which correspond in the following quotation from *Form of Living* to the bracketed
numbers that immediately precede the verbs signaling each step):[17]

A man or woman þat es ordaynd til contemplatife lyfe first God [1]
enspires þam to [2] forsake þis worlde and al þe vanite and þe
covayties and þe vile luste þarof. Sythen he [3] ledes þam by þar ane,
and spekes til [þ]ar hert, and als þe prophete says, 'He gifes þam at
sowke þe swetnes of þe begynnyng of lufe.' And þan he settes þam in

wil to gyf þam haly to prayers and meditacions and teres. Sithen, when þai have [4] sufferd many temptacions, and foule noyes of thoghtes þat er ydel, and of vanitees, þe whilk wil comber þam, þat can noght destroy þam, er passand away, he [5] gars þam geder til þam þair hert, and fest anely in hym; and opens til þe egh of þair sawls þe ʒates of heven, swa þat þe ilk egh lokes intil heven. And þan þe fire of lufe verrali ligges in þair hert and byrnes þarin, and makes clene of al erthly filth. (H. E. Allen 1931, 118–19)

Pearl, perhaps uniquely, tracks very closely all five of these steps by assigning—almost exactly—one-fifth of its length, approximately twenty stanzas, to each of these thematic groups. In the first of these groups (secs. 1 through 4, lines 1–240) the Dreamer slowly becomes aware of his dreaming surroundings, their beauty and their artifice, which finally culminate in the appearance of the Maiden, the most rarefied, beautiful, and elevated presence in a landscape already more curiously beautiful than anything in his prior experience. The second major division extends from the beginning of the conversation between the Dreamer and the Maiden (241) through the end of section 8 (480). These twenty stanzas expose the errors in the Dreamer's initial response to the Maiden's presence. His reliance on his physical faculties, his presumption that his future will be spent with the Maiden, and that he can cross the stream to embrace her, are the very beliefs that paradoxically separate him from her and must be purged before further steps can be taken. If this second division points out what is wrong with the Dreamer, the next division (481–720) provides illumination by pointing out what is right with the rules that govern the spiritual order. But this third division remains in the theoretical realm, where metaphors, symbols, parables, and a mystical return of the righteous back to innocence at best approximate truth. Thus it provides a logical background for the pivotal fourth division (721–960), which continues to illuminate as it details the rewards for those who recover from their dark night: spotless innocents respond to Jesus' call; the Dreamer gives his first evidence of yielding to the wonder and the truth of what he is learning; and the Maiden prays a lengthy prayer describing the harmonious music of heaven that accompanies those who come before the Lamb.

The crowning achievement of this fourth division, however, is the elevation of the Dreamer to a new level of spiritual commitment, occurring during the exchanges between the Maiden and the Dreamer beginning with stanza 76, the extra stanza in section 15. From this point to the conclusion of stanza 80 (line 960) we see a microcosm of the Dreamer's progress through the whole poem. His opening remark, though chastened and respectful, combines an understanding of the difference between the earthly and the spiritual with a lack of this same understanding:

I am bot mokke and mul among,
And þou so ryche a reken rose.
(905–6)

The different appeal these two images present suggests he has learned what separates earth from heaven. But by failing to realize that there is no difference in kind (cf. *kynde*) between rotting earth and a blooming rose, other than a brief span of time, he implies that he still misses the point of the Maiden's earlier reference to a rose:

For þat þou lestez watz bot a rose
Þat flowred and fayled as kynde hyt gef.
(269–70)

Nevertheless, the remaining references to eternity (908) and innocence (909) confirm the Dreamer's progress. As a result, when he inquires in the next stanza whether so spotless a maid does not have for herself and her retinue equally spotless "wonez in castel-walle, / Ne maner þer ȝe may mete and won" (917–18), we credit him with honest solicitation, rather than recall the limited vision he evinced when he first saw her. In turn, and in kind, the Maiden gently explains the difference between the Old and the New Jerusalem. As if twelve sections of arduous teaching and learning could not do what the proximate locale of the New Jerusalem can do, the Maiden fully transforms the Dreamer by explaining the most important distinction between the two cities: in the Old Jerusalem Christ earned for mankind the right to eternal life, but the New Jerusalem *is* eternal life where "glory and blysse schal euer encres" (959). Though his commitment is now complete, the Dreamer has one more sentence to speak. We must recognize, therefore, that before he utters the first word of this four-line sentence he has already progressed to the elevated level of spiritual commitment that makes him yearn for what it asks. The moment is precious, signaling entry into the final phase of mystical union, aptly marked by a uniquely placed decorated initial at line 961.

'Motelez may so meke and mylde,'
Þen sayde I to þat lufly flor,

'Bryng me to þat bygly bylde
And let me se þy blysful bor.'
(961-64)

The fifth and final division of *Pearl*, in general the poem's last four sections, has an indistinct beginning, for the Maiden's twelve-line response
(965-76) to the Dreamer's plea to see "þy blysful bor" bridges sections 16
and 17. It is the Maiden's exit speech, for upon its completion we hear her
no more. Instead, we experience with the Dreamer, not the splendor of the
New Jerusalem, but the splendor of John's description of the New Jerusalem. These last four sections depart from the progress usually found in
mystic writers, where union normally occurs, by taking the Dreamer and
us to the very threshold of heaven, imbuing him and us with an overwhelming desire to enter (1153-60), and then exiling us again (1169-70).
The poem could not do otherwise. As wayfarers still wandering through
time, in contrast to the Maiden now out of time, both the Dreamer and the
mortal reader must wait in continual uncertainty until summoned. Thus it
is that the poem, with its dark-night-of-the-soul *reprisée*, leaves us to our
familiar state of uncertainty, underscored by a subtly ambiguous conclusion.

The Dreamer's first reaction to the sudden loss of his dream, dissolved
by his rash attempt to enter the stream, seems accurate:

To þat Pryncez paye hade I ay bente,
And ȝerned no more þen watz me geuen,
And halden me þer in trwe entent,
As þe perle me prayed þat watz so þryuen,
As helde, drawen to Goddez present,
To mo of His mysterys I hade ben dryuen.
Bot ay wolde man of happe more hente
Þen moȝte by ryȝt vpon hem clyuen;
(1189-96)

Had he been patient, remaining on his side of the stream as the Maiden
instructed him in lines 965-76, he might well have learned more. Yet doubt
is cast on his capacity for patience of this kind, when the echoing phrases,
"I syȝe" and "I knew," of section 17 (cf. 986, 998, 1019, 1021, 1033, 1035)
make it sound as if the Dreamer and John have become one in the frequently repeated formula in the Apocalypse itself, "Et vidi. . . ." His earlier
objection that the Maiden has usurped the role of the Virgin is far from his
thought, even as his own words come close to usurping John's. He still

seems not to recognize that her words to him pertain more to his life on earth, after he returns from this dreaming epiphany, than to the dreaming vision itself. It is hard to say what the Dreamer means by the word "happe" in the gnomic lines 1195–96. Does he have in mind merely the joy of beholding the New Jerusalem visually in his dream, or does he recognize that salvation can never be a matter of man's deserving, only of God's giving?

Further doubt arises from the assurance of the poem's final stanza. The Dreamer has undoubtedly recovered from the threshold of despair at which we found him in the opening lines of the poem. But the opposite of despair is not certainty, only hope. Yet at the end of the poem the Dreamer strikes a clear note of self assurance, as if he were now absolutely certain he is already among the saved:

> To pay þe Prince oþer sete saȝte
> Hit is ful eþe to þe god Krystyin;
> For I haf founden Hym, boþe day and naȝte,
> A God, a Lorde, a frende ful fyin.
>
> (1201–4)

Here the Dreamer sounds more like the Pharisee than the publican in the famous parable recounted by Luke (18:9–14). The poet does not literally remind us of this parable, but it is hardly coincidental that, immediately after he recounts the scene of the Pharisee and the publican, Luke says that Jesus rebuked his disciples for hindering little children from coming to him, "Amen I say to you, whoever does not accept the kingdom of God as a little child will not enter into it" (Luke 18:17).

The Maiden may have wanted to guide the Dreamer gently back to the hill on which he fell asleep, when she instructed him to proceed along his side of the stream "tyl þou to a hil be veued" (976). That the Dreamer makes his bold move into the stream well before reaching this hill suggests he has only partly received the Maiden's instruction. He will return, of course, to the life of "þe god Krystyin" (1202) he has probably always been, perhaps stumbling in his maturity toward a happiness he hardly understands or deserves, as the Maiden herself may have done when she was but two years of age.

4

Purity (Clannesse)

Of all the poems in Cotton Nero A.x, *Cleanness* typically draws the least praise. Closer to narrative than homily, yet more diffuse than focused, it neither presses forward to a central climactic action nor contributes to an evident allegory. Unlike many a medieval narrative, for example, the procession of nine groups of suppliants in Chaucer's *House of Fame,* who exhaust all combinations of fame sought and fame granted, and the seven levels in Dante's *Purgatorio* that correspond to the deadly sins, *Purity,* to use the title a majority of critics prefer, seems to ramble eclectically through three random stories: Noe and the Flood; the stories of Abraham and Lot, culminating in the destruction of Sodoma and Gomorra; and Baltassar's Feast.[1] Some attempt at unity may be detected in the emphases these stories have been given, slightly different from their counterparts in the Old Testament. Though by no means a distortion of Scripture, the versions in *Purity* elevate the motif of cleanness, especially the avoidance of its negative *fylþe,* to a central theme. Nor do the poet's adjustments of biblical sequences seriously violate chronology, as when he provides a context for his main thread by selecting some, but not all, of the other biblical stories that surround his three main points of interest and adds brief paraphrases of the New Testament's wedding feast (51–168; cf. Matt. 22:1–14) and the life of Christ, especially his Incarnation and Nativity (1067–1109). Yet Andrew and Waldron typify the usual view of the poem, as they valiantly laud what they imply is the single, humble virtue of both *Purity* and *Patience:*

> Superficially, the art most in evidence here is the direct persuasive art of the sermon, with its explicit moral exhortation, its affective *exempla* and its warnings of the consequences of sin. The poem's audience . . . is cast in the role of recipient of instruction, a role akin to

that of a congregation hearing a sermon. This relationship between poet and audience, implicit for the most part in *Cleanness,* presented more explicitly in *Patience,* creates a didactic context for the purely aesthetic qualities in both poems and defines the poet's ruling concern as that of pointing out Christian principles and encouraging his audience to follow them. (1979, 17)

Fine, as far as this goes, but hardly the sort of excellence that might lift the poem above the reputation of, say, the *Parson's Tale* or one of the Monk's *exempla* in the *Canterbury Tales*—closer, in fact, to Dorothy Everett's comment that the "poem's scheme," though more ambitious than that of *Patience,* "is not entirely successful" (1955, 70). In contrast to these modest opinions of the poem, Charlotte Morse suggests an organization reflecting Augustine's conception of the ages of history, either a three-age or seven-age conception, with the advent of Christ presented as history's culminating event.[2] Although the former two responses treat the poem somewhat simplistically in suggesting a kind of didacticism without addressing the nature of the lesson, while Morse casts a more interesting light on philosophical conceptions than the poem itself does, one can understand fully the appeal of such readings. Conditioned to appreciate literature as a verbal account of events and ideas, expressed in the traditional way language has always conveyed meaning, most modern readers expect that these events and ideas themselves set the terms on which *Purity*'s reputation must rest. But this assumption, by touching only the surface, overlooks entirely the important structural contribution the poem makes to the entire manuscript.

Purity's arrangement into parts is marked by decorated initials of two different sizes. Three large decorated initials at lines 1, 557, and 1157 presumably indicate that the poem has three main divisions, while ten smaller decorated initials at lines 125, 193, 249, 345, 485, 601, 689, 781, 893, and 1357 mark sections that lie within these divisions.[3] In other words, the first large division, covering lines 1–556, has six sections of 124, 68, 56, 96, 140, and 72 lines. The second large division, from line 557 through line 1156 (a total of 600 lines), numbers five sections of 44, 88, 92, 112, and 264 lines. The final division, extending from line 1157 to the end of the poem (656 total lines), has only two sections of 200 and 456 lines. The three divisions and thirteen sections are shown in figure 4.1, aligned with enough episodes to provide a rough orientation.

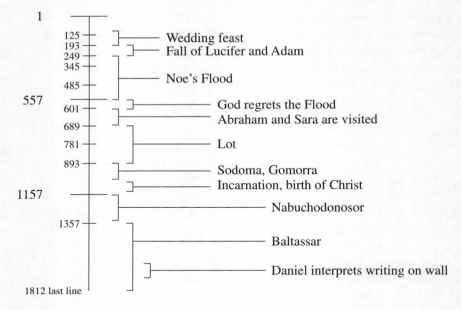

Figure 4.1

Although there does seem to be an approximate correspondence between the poem's three large divisions and its three main episodes, the same cannot be said for its sections. For example, the decorated initial indicating the beginning of section 9 at line 689, is placed eight lines after the opening of God's 31-line speech to Abraham (682–712). And the decorated initial at line 1357, marking the beginning of the final, longest section in the poem, appears twenty-five lines after the narrative transition from Nabuchodonosor to Baltassar, as if the poet had to delay the appearance of the thirteenth initial until two hundred lines filled out the twelfth section, regardless of when a shift in subject matter occurred. The poet apparently had a specific plan for the divisions and sections of his poem independent of the material his text would contain. It would be wrong, therefore, to assume that the text determines where the manuscript's divisions should occur. In fact, the reverse is true: the divisions in the manuscript determine the size, if not the content, of the text, not only for *Purity* itself but for all four poems in Cotton Nero A.x. In the case of three of these poems, *Pearl, Purity,* and *Patience,* the specific number of lines to be assigned to each section was also clearly understood before the poems were written. Explaining why *Purity* compels this conclusion is the task of this chapter. But let us first give some attention to the poem's elusive thematic unity, which seems to proceed from the premise that, in the eyes of the Hebrew nation, there was no greater good than contributing to the strength of the tribe.

Biblical stories and their meanings often fix themselves forever in the unchanging context in which we originally hear them—the more familiar the stories, the more firmly are they fixed. We readily associate the parable of the wedding feast with the subject of proper attire, the allegorical equivalent of an unsullied soul (Matt. 22:1–14; *Purity* 51–160). The poem strongly reinforces this equation: "Thus comparisunez Kryst þe kyndom of heuen / To þis frelych feste þat fele arn to called" (161–62).[4] But a look at the past, at whether or not those attending this feast have prepared themselves for salvation, allegorically speaking a preparation symbolized by wedding garments, is not its only contribution. We should also be aware of the main point of interest at a wedding feast, the young forward-looking couple at the center of the event, if not at the center of the narrative, now beginning a new life together and coincidentally foreshadowing the marriage of Christ and his Church. The same may be said of the familiar story of Noe (Gen. 6–9; *Purity* 293–556). While our thoughts are typically dominated by images of the Flood, a parade of every known species of animal, and thoughts of an angry God's retribution against a people fallen into sin, we are apt to miss the meaning conveyed by the arrangement of the survivors. Every creature is part of a couple. All are disposed two-by-two, as if the implied bridal couple above were now celebrated in fable, a tableau of the world positioned for a new beginning. That Noe and his wife provide a model of an ideal couple, accompanied by their offspring who now have wives of their own, emphasizes the parallel between animals and people. Never mind that for the sake of humor the Corpus Christi Cycle would later emphasize the constant bickering between Noe and his wife, here they are a microcosm of a family apparently living as nature intended, using natural powers conferred by God to "increase and multiply and fill the earth" (Gen. 9:1). The first large division of *Purity*, then, though presenting examples of uncleanness in the unpresentable clothing at the wedding feast and the unacceptable conduct of Noe's countrymen, gives implicit emphasis to the family units that might increase and multiply by their own creative acts.

Purity's central division, too, shows multiple instances of uncleanness.

But the series of episodes it presents shifts the focus from uncleanness, per se, to conditions that thwart a tribe from reaching its full strength: advanced age, fruitless practices, and the unavailability of husbands. Lest we miss the reason for divine wrath at the second condition in this group of three, God

> dyscouered to [Abraham's] corse My counsayl so dere,
> Syþen he is chosen to be chef chyldryn fader,
> Þat so folk schal falle fro to flete alle þe worlde.
> (683–85)

Since the customs at Sodoma and Gomorra will hardly carry out God's "counsayl" to populate the world, the cities are destroyed. Three peripheral episodes provide explanatory footnotes to this central event. The story of Sara precedes the event; the story of Lot occurs at its center; and two antithetical motifs, the stench of the destroyed cities and the birth of Christ, provide a conclusion.

Long past her productive years, Sara is incapable of delivering another son to Abraham. Thus her miraculous fertility at age ninety-one is an unusual gift from God, especially cherished in retrospect, for the son who would be born to her was none other than Isaac, from whose line came the foundation of Israel. Immediately following this prefatory material, the poem, following Scripture, turns its attention to the central episode of Sodoma and Gomorra, in the middle of which Lot curiously offers his daughters to the rabble outside his gates who are eager to debauch the young men visiting his home. It is unseemly to modern ears—and to medieval ears as well, one suspects—that a father would offer his daughters to strangers, especially in the presence of the daughters' intending husbands. But this is to take the lines too literally. The force of the lines, in view of Lot's expressed motive, "Bot I schal kenne yow by kynde a crafte þat is better" (865), seems to convey something like this: "Look at my beautiful daughters. These are the kind of partners you ought to be seeking, not the young men who are my guests."

Genesis has a fitting conclusion to the episodes regarding Sara's pregnancy and Lot's offer of his daughters. It is the subsequent strategy of the daughters themselves (Gen. 19:30–38). Though God instructed Lot to take his entire household safely away from Sodoma, the future husbands of these daughters prefer to remain behind, perishing in the fire and brimstone that rain on the city. Now bereft of men whom they might marry and with whom they could beget a new generation, these two daughters contrive to lie with their father, plying him with wine until he has no knowledge of what he is doing. One of their resulting sons became the father of the Moabites, the other the father of the Ammonites.

Purity says nothing of this strategy concocted by Lot's daughters, perhaps because their actions have ambivalent force, testifying on the one hand to a natural impulse to increase and multiply, but on the other to an incestuous begetting, the symbolic explanation for later strife with the Moabites and Ammonites (Deut. 23:3; Judges 3; 2 Kings 8; 1 Esdras 9:1). Instead, *Purity* concludes this long central division in the poem with two powerful but antithetical images. First, there is a vivid description of the stench and sterility of what had once been Sodoma and Gomorra, a part of Paradise, now appropriately called the Dead Sea (1005–48). There is no authority in Genesis for this highly original detail. Second, a literal birth ensues, picking up a motif introduced as far back as the beginning of the first major division in the poem, the account of the wedding feast, and sustained by the pairing of animals in Noe's ark and by Sara's miraculous childbirth in her old age. Most surprising for a poem featuring primarily Old Testament stories, this literal birth is the New Testament's birth of Christ. The poem's strategy is now clear. Its apparently random collection of biblical stories has become a powerful crescendo embracing everything from the opening of the first large division of the poem to the conclusion of the second. The effect of this ascent is made possible as much by converting intermediate stages into a subtle continuum as by the magnitude of its final stage, the ontological and spiritual miracle of the coming of Christ.

To appreciate this strategy let us recapitulate its separate stages. First, the relatively unremarkable wedding feast with which this crescendo begins (51–160), though bringing together a young man and woman whose main thought is undoubtedly the love they bear for each other, nevertheless keeps this couple offstage, while the anticipated fruit of their union remains unspoken, a silent hope for their future. The second stage, concerning Noe and the Flood, does not lessen the traditional understanding that sinners will be destroyed and the sinless saved, but also advances the image of males and females in pairs and the loving purpose for which nature brings them together. A significant advance occurs at the third stage of this thematic movement, when the vindictive God of the first division softens to an instructive God, permitting humanity to redeem or destroy itself. The gift of a son comes to Sara and Abraham through a natural event—natural conception and natural birth—yet its occurrence in Sara's ninety-first year, foretold to the incredulous Sara by three visitors to her home, when she was "so hyȝe out of age, and also [her] lorde" (656), confirms a divine suspension of natural law. Thus the event has both natural and supernatural dimensions. As this remarkable birth opened the poem's second division, the final stage in its thematic progression provides closure by describing another birth, now weighing heavily on the supernatural side. For the birth here is the birth of Christ. Lines that are usually called the "Incarnation passage" (1052–1148) emphasize a departure from natural laws in both the conception of this infant in a virgin's womb,[5] and in the identity of the infant as God:

> Þat euer is polyced als playn as þe perle seluen.
> For, loke, fro fyrst þat He lyȝt withinne þe lel mayden,
> By how comly a kest He watz clos þere,
> When vnkkyst watz no vergynyté, ne vyolence maked,
> Bot much clener watz hir corse, God kynned þerinne.
> And efte when He borne watz in Beþelen þe ryche.
>
> (1068–73)

Let us note the complex motif that culminates in this final stage of the poem's crescendo. Though its lines literally identify the Nativity, the passage begins with a pointed reference to a section of Jean de Meun's *Le Roman de la Rose*, 7689–7764, that "concerns romantic love; the poet deliberately transforms its significance to the plane of divine love" (Andrew and Waldron 1979, note). Without losing the presence of human love or the image of an infant, yet gently inserting a divine presence, the poem expands its reach, rather than shifts its focus. Like the mathematical formula governing the size of its sections, which we shall see presently, the poem smoothly embraces ever larger dimensions of love. Not least, the crescendo under discussion accomplishes its ends without reference to the artificial border that separates the New Testament from the Old.

The third major division of *Purity* changes the subject very significantly. What began as images of husbands and wives eager to love and bring new life into the world, and then described three factors that thwart this kind of creation—advanced age, unproductive sexual practices, and the unavailability of partners—now concentrates on the moral condition of mankind, expressed symbolically as the "overriding of categories," to use Spearing's description, "the use of sacred vessels for profane purposes, that is the real impurity and that unleashes God's destructive anger" (1980, 303).

In this third major division, however, there is more to the poet's strategy than identifying a variety of categories whose boundaries are compromised. Near the end of *Purity* the poet brings to conclusion a biblical episode that has been unfolding for nearly four-hundred lines, but also instructs readers regarding how the entire poem is to be read. It is the foreboding scene where an unattached hand, "Þe fyste with þe fyngeres þat flayed þi hert, / Þat rasped renyschly þe woȝe with þe roȝ penne" (1723–24), writes three words on the wall of Baltassar's banquet hall. The surrounding narrative has been describing how Baltassar came to power as the most glorious leader his people had ever known, yet let himself be overcome first by false, gilded idols, then by fleshly excess, and at length by vainglory (1339–60). Among his many affronts to God his colossal, disrespectful banquet attracts most of the poet's attention, for here Baltassar displays both pride in his debauchery and blasphemy in his gall, as his concubines desecrate vessels once venerated by Solomon. Much attention is lavished on the beauty of these vessels and especially on the significance of the great candlestick which

> watz not wonte in þat wone to wast no serges,
> Bot in temple of þe trauþe trwly to stonde
> Bifore þe *sancta sanctorum*, þer soþefast Dryȝtyn
> Expouned His speche spiritually to special prophetes.
> (1489–92)

The entire episode underscores the filth of everything associated with Baltassar: his beliefs, his fleshly indulgence, and the use to which he puts sacred vessels. The prophet Daniel, summoned to interpret the handwriting on the wall, reads its three words in the light of all this history, understandably interpreting them as a comment on Baltassar's reign:

> *Mane* menes als much as "Maynful Gode
> Hatz counted þy kyndam bi a clene noumbre,
> And fulfylled hit in fayth to þe fyrre ende."
> To teche þe of *Techal*, þat terme þus menes:
> "Þy wale rengne is walt in weȝtes to heng,
> And is funde ful fewe of hit fayth-dedes."
> And *Phares* folȝes for þose fawtes, to frayst þe trawþe;
> In *Phares* fynde I forsoþe þise felle saȝes:
> "Departed is þy pryncipalté, depryued þou worþes,

Þy rengne rafte is þe fro, and raȝt is þe Perses;
Þe Medes schal be maysteres here, and þou of menske schowued."
(1730–40)

Daniel's interpretation—that the kingdom had reached the limit of its days, was found wanting, and would be destroyed—turns out to be a true prophecy. That very night, the scriptural source goes on to record, Darius the Mede defeated Baltassar and assumed his throne (Dan. 5:31).

These three words and Daniel's interpretation of them, we should not fail to realize, are two very different things. Not that Daniel falsifies. But he elaborates, expands the neutral meaning of the words until they have dire significance for Baltassar. The words are literal, concrete; their interpretation is subjective. Most of the exegetical attention given to this cryptic passage concentrates on the subjective interpretation of the three words, leaving their literal meaning unremarked. If we look at the literal words, however, independent of their location in Baltassar's hall and separated from their agreement with subsequent history, we recognize the appeal they hold for the poet of *Purity*. The Hebrew renders the three, probably Aramaic words written on the wall thus: מ ב א (transliterated as "mane" in the Vulgate, meaning position, number), תקל ("thecel," to weigh), and פ ר ס ("phares," to divide).[6] These words are almost identical, though in a different order, to the famous passage in the Book of Wisdom (11:21), discussed above in chapter 1, where God is said "to have ordered all things in measure, and number, and weight" ("sed omnia in mensura, et numero, et pondere disposuisti"). While the passage from Daniel certainly renders a fitting judgment on the reign of Baltassar, further proof that all things given to filth contradict the divine plan and will suffer accordingly, it also instructs the reader to give special attention to the mathematical and geometric basis, the "clene noumbre" (1731), of the divisions and sections of the very poem in which it appears. That the ultimate credit for this precision belongs to the divine geometer has been carefully anticipated by an earlier passage explaining that Christ breaks bread cleanly and precisely, without the aid of knives (1101–8).

A reader may already have suspected that the principles of numerical construction determine the shape of *Purity*. As noted in chapter 2, the total length of *Purity* is far from arbitrary. That it exceeds 1800 lines by the same number of lines that mark *Pearl*'s excess, that is by twelve, is unlikely to be coincidence. Similarly the ratio of *Purity*'s length to *Pearl*'s, minus these signature excesses, that is 1800 to 1200 or 3 : 2, is entirely too clean, too artful, too suggestive of one of the most pleasing musical harmonies, a fifth, not to have been planned. Further, in a manuscript where the first and last of four poems exceed a stanza count of 100 by one stanza to achieve the 25th prime number, 101, it does not seem arbitrary that the total number of sections in *Purity* should exceed the most frequently cited number in the manuscript's duodecimal system—that is, 12—by one section to achieve the 5th prime number, 13. While these correspondences may strike some readers as unrelated, coincidental, a glance at the specific lengths of these thirteen sections discloses so many numerical curiosities that all doubt about authorial intention vanishes. Several of these curiosities surface as soon as the possibility of numerical construction is raised.[7]

(1) Section 1 has 124 lines; sections 2 and 3 together also total 124 lines. For an equal number of lines, therefore, the sections are 1 : 2, or what musicians would call an octave tonally, a duple rhythmically.

(2) Sections 1 through 4, totaling 344 lines, are structurally repeated in sections 5 through 8, which also total 344 lines. Thus the first eight sections can be perfectly halved with respect to lines as well as sections for a ratio of 1 : 1.

(3) Sections 6 through 8 have the same number of lines, 204, as sections 9 and 10 together, for a section ratio of 3 : 2, a musical fifth.

(4) Sections 1 through 6 have the same total, 556, as sections 8 through 11, for a section ratio of 6 : 4 or 3 : 2, another fifth.

(5) Sections 1 through 7 have the same total, 600, as sections 7 through 11, yielding a section ratio of 7 : 5, a rational convergent for $\sqrt{2}$.[8]

(6) Sections 3 through 5 have 292 lines. Then, after the intervening 116 lines of sections 6 and 7, another 292 lines are in sections 8 through 10. This whole stretch of sections from 3 through 10 totals 700 lines, suggesting a conceptual block of two groups of 408 each, with the overlapping 116 shared between them. Moreover, $700 \div 408$ (1.71568 in modern notation) is very close to $12 \div 7$ (1.71428), a frequent medieval convergent for $\sqrt{3}$ (1.73205).

(7) The twelve sections from 2 through 13 segment their 1688 lines in a way similar to the segmenting of 3 through 10, as noted in (6). Sections 2 through 9 have 656 lines, as do sections 12 and 13. The intervening 376 lines of sections 10 and 11, if shared, would give two groups of 1032 lines each: §§ 2 through 11 and §§ 10 through 13. This ratio too, $656 \div 376$ (1.74468 in modern notation), is another convergent for $\sqrt{3}$.

(8) Sections 6 through 12 have exactly the same number of lines as the third fitt of *Sir Gawain and the Green Knight*, 872.

(9) Sections 8 through 13 have the same number of lines as *Pearl*, 1212. And the first major division (secs. 1–6, 556 lines), added to the third major division (secs. 12–13, 656 lines) also total 1212 lines, the same number as in *Pearl*.

As interesting as these observations may be, especially the several hints that the sections imply some symmetrical shape, they invite the charge of arbitrary game-playing, using line counts with no greater significance than words in a crossword puzzle. Such skepticism is potentially valid. Yet at some point in this litany of increasingly complex numerical correspondences the charge can no longer be taken seriously, especially when the correspondences increase significantly as the poem is tested for more complex computations. For *Purity* demonstrates many times the argument advanced in chapter 2, that the entire manuscript is arranged as a demonstration of the continuous ratio φ, that is 1.61803.

The first six sections of *Purity* form a natural unit, not only because they constitute all the sections governed by the first large initial, but because §§ 1 through 4, totaling 344 lines, are the mean in an approximate *phi* ratio between two extremes, §§ 5–6 totaling 212, and §§ 1–6 totaling 556:[9]

$$212 : 344 \approx 344 : 556 \approx 1 / \varphi$$

$$0.61627 \approx 0.61870 \approx 0.61803$$

A line total of 556 shows up again in sections 8 through 11, approximating a *phi* relation with exactly one-half of the poem (not counting the poem's signature of twelve extra lines):

$$556 : 900 \approx 1 / \varphi$$

$$0.61777 \approx 0.61803$$

Embedded within this highly significant second grouping of 556 lines, another proportion based on *phi* is evident in sections 8 through 10, whose totals are 88, 92, and 112, respectively.

$$112 \times \varphi \approx 180 \text{ (i.e., } 88 + 92 \text{ or §§ 8–9)}$$

$$180 \times \varphi \approx 292 \text{ (i.e., } 88 + 92 + 112 \text{ or §§ 8–10)}$$

$$292 \times \varphi \approx 472$$

Purity

Total lines in grouped sections

Cum. total	Section													
124	**1**	124												
			192											
192	2	68		248										
			124		344									
248	3	56		220		484								
			152		360		556							
344	4	96		292		432		600						
			236		364		476		688					
484	5	140		308		408		564		780				
			212		352		496		656		892			
556	6	72		256		440		588		768		1156		
			116		344		532		700		1032		1356	
600	**7**	44		204		436		644		964		1232		1812
			132		296		548		908		1164		1688	
688	8	88		224		408		812		1108		1620		
			180		336		672		1012		1564			
780	9	92		292		600		872		1468				
			204		556		800		1328					
892	10	112		468		756		1256						
			376		668		1212							
1156	11	264		576		1124								
			464		1032									
1356	**12**	200		920										
			656											
1812	13	456												

Figure 4.2

This last total, 472, though not precisely represented by one of *Purity*'s sections, is the arithmetic mean between §§ 2–7 (476 lines) and §§ 9–11 (468 lines). It is only four units smaller than the 476 measurement that will be shown in due course to contribute an extremely important dimension for the manuscript's design.

Figure 4.2 shows the number of lines in each section as well as the aggregate lines in any contiguous group of sections.[10] In addition to the divisions into extreme and mean ratio just noted, figure 4.2 reveals several other *phi* ratios. Sections 6 and 7 are in a *phi* ratio: $44 \times \varphi \approx 72$; $72 \times \varphi \approx 116$ (the sum of §§ 6 and 7). Sections 3 through 6 and 7 through 9 are also in a *phi* ratio: $224 \times \varphi \approx 364$; $364 \times \varphi \approx 588$ (the sum of §§ 3 through 9).

Still on the subject of ratios, the poem's arrangement of large divisions and smaller sections presents an interesting tension between a simple arithmetic ratio and the more complicated Divine Proportion. The central division of the poem (§§ 7–11) has 600 lines; the first division (§§1–6) together with the final division (§§12 and 13) total 1212 lines—the same size as *Pearl*—although this total can be considered 1200 by overlooking Bede's left-hand numbers, the extra twelve lines inserted to satisfy another rubric; and the entire poem has 1800 lines (again, discounting the extra dozen). Like the manuscript as a whole, which proceeds according to the Divine Proportion from the two medial poems, to the two extreme poems, and to the whole manuscript, *Purity*'s divisions reveal the same pattern, expanding from the center, to the extremes, and to the whole, according to a simple arithmetic progression, 600, 1200, 1800. The poem's sections, on the other hand, demonstrate the Divine Proportion, both an additive series and a constant ratio, making possible dramatic leaps to increasingly greater magnitudes, yet remaining a composite of what preceded. Moreover, an inverse relation between the sizes of the poem's divisions and the number of their sections leads to an intimation of infinity, that is, to the very thematic point its literal language advances. The sizes of the poem's three divisions increase from 556 to 600 to 656, while the number of sections in these divisions decreases from 6 to 5 to 2. If both trends were sustained, the magnitude would become infinitely large and the sections would be simplified to one, another way of attempting to represent divinity.

A graphic representation of the overlapping structure of items (6) and (7) above (83) leads in an interesting direction. Item (6) shows a magnitude of 700 lines segmented in three sections, such that the middle section represents an overlapping of the other two, as in figure 4.3.

Item (7) implies a similar design, though with different numeric values: two magnitudes overlapping to produce a third, as in figure 4.4.

The patterns represented in figures 4.3 and 4.4 show, initially, a familiar ancient and medieval poetic design (Batts 1969, 100), the recess pattern

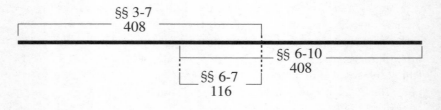

Figure 4.3

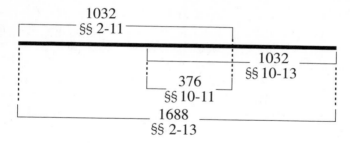

Figure 4.4

(ABCBA) or mirror pattern (ABC/CBA) of works like Catullus LXIV (Murley 1937), Boethius's *Consolation of Philosophy* (Scarry 1980), Old French narrative poetry (Robson 1961), and Chaucer (Condren 1999, 17–18). Of greater importance for our immediate concerns, however, is the fact that they look very much like any one of the diagonal lines constructing the pentangle in figure 2.12 and the line in figure 3.1, all of which represent the Divine Section. I do not suggest that the lines in figures 4.3 and 4.4 are divided into extreme and mean ratio. Nevertheless, if they were placed parallel to any one of the lines in figure 2.1 their ratios could be found somewhere in the triangle leading to the apex. Their visual representation thus leads us to a promising line of inquiry for which we must set our mathematical excursus aside, while a different but essential art form is illuminated. For the various subjects already on the table—a text, Scripture, Christianity, piety, artistic expression, geometry, *phi*, northern England—all converge on a single inevitable subject: early medieval insular bookart.

The Irish and English monks from the seventh through the tenth century have long been admired for enriching their religious texts with art of ineffable beauty.[11] The Book of Durrow, the Book of Kells, the Book of Mulling, the Lindisfarne, Echternach, and St. Gall gospels direct so much attention to their stylized figures, designs, and carpet pages that it is sometimes difficult to say whether the artwork embellishes the text or the text narrates the source of the artwork's enormous power. It is wrong, of course, to think of these as separate entities. While the gospel stories bring together God and Man in a chronicle of the life of Christ—a biography, as it were, from a remote place and distant past—the artwork depicting the Evange-lists, the geometrical designs, the crosses made of circles, the Chi-Rho fo-lios, and dozens of marginal drawings make the connection between God's creation and Man's place in it a palpable presence. Only in recent years have scholars begun to appreciate that the sophisticated mathematics gov-erning this bookart is based very precisely on the Euclidean and Timaean mathematics of God's creation, which subsequently unified the quadri-vium. Everything in these codices has been disposed according to "number, weight, and measure."

Robert D. Stevick (1994) demonstrates how a careful medieval drafts-man, equipped with no more than a compass and a straight edge, could produce every one of the exacting geometric proportions on which the codices mentioned above are based. Almost every one of these proportions is a derivative of *phi*. Even more astonishing, several complex Old English poems are constructed on the same principles, according to Stevick. That is, the line totals of the several sections in these poems correspond exactly to the line lengths produced by a book artist's typical geometric designs. I make no claim that these artists understood Euclidean geometry, though they may have. Nor is it necessary. Once it was recognized, perhaps by a single draftsman in the very early Middle Ages, that a diagonal across two adjacent squares is the key to constructing the Divine Section (see appen-dix 1), he and his successors could pass on to subsequent generations of artists the procedure for creating designs based on division into extreme and mean ratio, without ever discussing geometry in a theoretical way. Though there is no certainty that the specific grids, arcs, and diagonals Stevick proposes are the very ones medieval artists used to execute their artwork, his suggestions account for every detail in extremely complicated carpet pages and, with perhaps slightly less assurance, in every section length of *Andreas, Elene, Guthlac A,* and other Old English poems.

Although Cotton Nero A.x was produced several centuries after the flourishing of the insular bookart just alluded to, the following pages ar-gue that the divisions and sections of *Purity* precisely encode the underly-ing framework of a typical carpet page done in the manner of the early Irish and English artists. Indeed, the design follows a pure *phi* ratio, the very proportion that guided the artists of the Lindisfarne Gospels.

There is a strong probability that the author of Cotton Nero A.x spent most of his learned, pious life as a monk in a monastery or a canon in a priory.[12] Wherever he lived, he had access to a good library. If the dialect of the manuscript was the author's own dialect he may have spent his adult life in any one of the fifty religious houses in Shropshire, Staffordshire, and Cheshire, perhaps successively in more than one.[13] Nor may a northern county be ruled out, especially since, as a northwest midlander, his interests would have been oriented toward the north, perhaps to the cultural center at York, the ancestral home of Edward III who reigned until 1377.[14] The text contains a small hint that his family or his order sent him to a major center of learning for his education. The prayer uttered by Jonas in the belly of the whale, perhaps alluding to the excesses of scholasticism, substitutes the word "maystres" (*Patience* 329), the usual term for university lecturers, for the Vulgate's indefinite "qui" (Eldredge 1979, 92). If this substitution does contain an autobiographical reference, we may assume that he was instructed in the quadrivium and the mathematics on which it was based.

An educated northern cleric, capable of creating Cotton Nero A.x, could not have failed to be familiar, as well, with that area's great codices surviving from an earlier age, gospel books that were considered religious and artistic treasures, often associated with a revered saint who was connected in some way with their origin. Let us remember that the earliest manuscript of Vitruvius's extremely important, ten-volume *De architectura*, MS Harley 2767, was made "at Jarrow (or Wearmouth), to which Ceolfrid brought manuscripts from Italy" (Vitruvius 1.xvi). This would have occurred even before Archbishop Theodore of Canterbury in the 690s sent an Italian manuscript of the Latin Vulgate as exemplar for the Lindisfarne Gospels. Both of these works, the Vitruvius and the Lindisfarne Gospels, are deeply indebted to the concept of proportion, especially the proportions inherent in number theory (Vitruvius 1.3.1; Stevick 1994, 102–16). And both codices would also have been well known and still available in the fourteenth century, when the *Pearl*-poet was acquiring his education and, later, planning what was undoubtedly the major work of his life.

The most famous of all these codices, the Lindisfarne Gospels, long associated with St. Cuthbert who died a mere decade before it was written, was housed continuously in Northumberland and Durham from its composition in 698 through the accepted date of the *Pearl*-manuscript in the last quarter of the fourteenth century. Its successive locations were Lindisfarne itself, where it was made, Chester-le-Street, where it resided from 883 to 995 to be safe from Vikings, and finally, after a four-month stay at Ripon, permanently at Durham where it presumably remained until the

Dissolution of the monasteries (1536–40). The codex may have been taken back to Lindisfarne from time to time, in particular in 1367, as some slight evidence suggests (Brown 1960, 25). Thus, its location during the fourth quarter of the fourteenth century was a short journey from the probable district that produced the author of Cotton Nero A.x. It is virtually impossible, then, that the educated person we are imagining, living in the northern half of England during the fourteenth century, would not have known this famous codex. Whatever individual careers the Lindisfarne Gospels and the *Pearl*-manuscript may have had during the fourteenth century, some time after the Dissolution they found a common home in the Cotton Collection, now in the British Library.[15]

If the bookarts that had been so highly developed among the Irish and Anglo-Saxons from the seventh to the tenth century remained in the culture, at least in general knowledge if not in actual practice, by being handed down from generation to generation, as the Anglo-Saxon poetic form with only slight alteration survived in Middle English as alliterative poetry, it is likely that the author would also have known something of the craft of planning a carpet page based on Euclidean geometry. Only one further conclusion is necessary and the strategy for Cotton Nero A.x is in place. Let us assume, finally, that the *Pearl*-poet, mindful that number unites all things in the universe, made an imaginative connection between the one ratio in mathematics whose terms continually expand toward infinity and the one path (as he saw it) that leads from the Old Testament to the New Testament, and from the New Testament to salvation for all eternity. Having made this connection, he may then have resolved that the mathematical ratio of the Divine Section would be his governing rubric. Following a well-attested medieval tradition, he might also have wanted to incorporate his design in the shape of the manuscript, as Leon Baptista Alberti less than a century later would arrange green marble courses in the façade of Santa Maria Novella, Florence, to display the mathematical ratios governing the design of portions of that church (March 1996, 61–62; 1998, 193–95). *Purity* would be the *Pearl*-poet's display of the mathematical ratio governing the design of his entire manuscript, not merely an "ornament," but part of the manuscript's "beauty," to use Robert Tavernor's dichotomous terms (1991, 11–12).

When the author of Cotton Nero A.x began his ambitious project, he would have planned to produce *Purity* in three stages. First, he would already have settled on the lengths of the four movements in the whole manuscript to produce a *phi* ratio suggesting a continuous progression to infinity and eternity: [1200 (*Pearl*) + 2500 (*Sir Gawain*)] ÷ [1800 (*Purity*) + 500 (*Patience*)] ≈ φ. In other words, he knew from the beginning that *Purity* was to have 1800 lines. Next, he would have drawn a carpet-page design, a kind of template needed to show him the total number of lines to give to each section of his poem. Then, finally, he would have composed the poem by fitting the biblical episodes he intended to retell into various sections so that the number of lines in each section would correspond to the length of a particular line in the geometric design he had just drawn. This assumption of a three-stage construction implies that the carpet design was a means to an end. The completed poem would be that end. But in fact, from the poet's perspective, a major reason for composing *Purity* was undoubtedly to set out the geometric blueprint governing the entire manuscript. That is, *Purity* is the means and the carpet design is the end. What follows now is an attempt to recreate the author's probable process of construction, to imagine the choices he made as he was generating this blueprint. The design about to be presented, though only an hypothesis, coincides with so many of the poem's dimensions that, if this is not the actual design the author laid out, it must be close to it.

If the *Pearl*-poet followed the methods of the book artists before him, as Stevick claims certain Old English poets did for their poems (1982, 48–53), he would have begun by constructing a frame and then shifting to the central point of interest within the frame. Since this central point of interest for the *Pearl*-poet would not have been a visual portrait of an Evangelist or of a saint known by name, as it was in the Lindisfarne Gospels, but instead the very poem itself, we shall assume that he followed the initial procedures for constructing the other frequently represented full-page design: a geometric design, similar to those which represent a stylized cross, for example, folios 94v, 138v, and 210v of the Lindisfarne Gospels.[16] All geometric carpet pages were constructed from a simple square, laid out on *x* and *y* axes, perpendicular to each other and crossing at their midpoints. From this square—let us call it the "underlying square" whose construction is step (1)—were erected (2) a framing rectangle, (3) an enclosing square, (4) a circle, and (5) a cross of varying designs. For step (1) the only significant variable was the size of the underlying square, from which everything else proceeded. Normally this size was determined by the width of the available folio, minus an appropriate amount for left and right margins. In this case, however, the size was predetermined by the poet's overall plan to give *Purity* 1800 lines plus an extra 12. But it is obvious that the author disregarded the extra 12 lines in constructing his design, for the resulting dimensions produced from an underlying square with 1812 units on each side do not correspond to a single section of *Purity*, other than the overall dimension of 1812. If we assume a basic dimension of 1800, however, perfect correspondences appear between the dimensions of the resulting geometric design and the number of lines in almost all of the sections of his poem. These correspondences strongly suggest that the design proposed here may actually have been the one used by the poet.

The poet undoubtedly began as described by Stevick (1994, 6), whose persuasive explanations I follow in figure 4.5. He first drew a horizontal

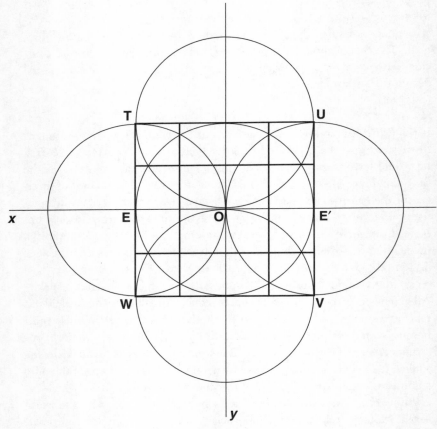

Figure 4.5

line (the *x* axis in figure 4.5), marking off a segment equal to 1800 units (EE') and bisecting the measured segment with a perpendicular *y* axis. It is of no importance what units are used—centimeters, inches, feet—as long as the same increments are maintained throughout. A circle is then drawn with center at O and circumference passing through E and E'. This circle therefore has a radius of 900. Four more 900-radius circles are drawn next, with centers at the first circle's 12, 3, 6, and 9 o'clock points where it intersects the *x* and *y* axes. The intersections of these four circles define the corners of the "underlying square" WTUV. That is, the 9 o'clock circle intersects the 12 o'clock circle at the center of the figure and at point T; the 12 o'clock circle intersects the 3 o'clock circle at the center of the figure and at point U; and so forth. By constructing two horizontal lines through the four points where the 12 o'clock and 6 o'clock circles intersect the center circle, and extending these lines to reach the sides of the "underlying square"; then by constructing two vertical lines through the four points where the 9 o'clock and 3 o'clock circles intersect the center circle, and similarly extending these lines to reach the top and bottom of the underlying square; the resulting figure will be a grid of 16 squares of 450 units on each side, all contained within the underlying square of 1800 units on each side.

If this were step (1) in what would be a rectangular carpet page in a codex, suitable to contain the portrait of a saint or a stylized cross, this underlying square would be extended at the top and bottom, through the use of some proportion derived from the underlying square, probably the Divine Proportion, to complete step (2). Although we have no evidence that the poet had in mind a golden rectangle for the overall design *Purity* encodes, he may have wanted the geometric design of this second poem in the manuscript to fit one of the golden rectangles discussed in chapter 3, the internal *phi*-related rectangles contained within the dodecahedron implied by the shape of *Pearl*. Nevertheless, since this speculation has no effect on the central point of interest, if the poem actually did represent a folio in a codex, we will dispense with the extension and the framing rectangle in order to move on to the next step.

Step (3), the enclosing square, is constructed by using a derivative of the proportion selected in step (2), the step which we are omitting from this discussion. Although the early insular book artists used many different proportions,[17] the one which obviously governs *Purity* is the Divine Section, as we have seen. This is the very proportion that governs the carpet pages of the earliest and most famous example of insular bookart, none

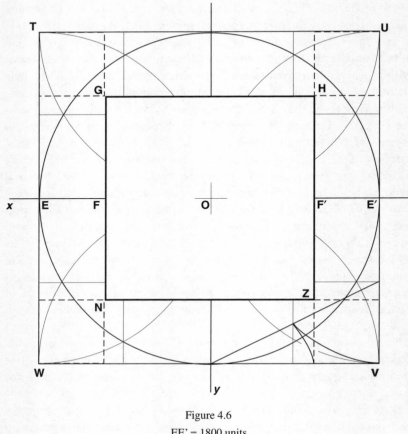

Figure 4.6

EE' = 1800 units

$$\frac{TU}{GH} = \varphi$$

other than the Lindisfarne Gospels. To derive the Divine Section needed to complete step (3) for the figure we have been constructing, use any two adjacent squares of the original 16, shown in larger scale at the lower right corner in figure 4.6 and explained in appendix 1. Executing this procedure eight times—two procedures for each corner—positions the dotted lines whose intersections define the four corners of the enclosing square NGHZ. Each side of the enclosing square now stands in relation to a side of the underlying square in a φ ratio. That is, TU : GH = φ : 1. When dimensions are substituted, the equation looks like this:

$$\frac{1800}{GH} = \frac{1.61803}{1}$$

This yields a dimension of 1112 for GH. If we now examine various lines, we see that segments EF and E'F' on the *x* axis measure 344 each, the same dimension as sections 1–4 and 5–8 of *Purity*. Segments FO and F'O measuring 556 each are equivalent to sections 1–6 and 8–11.

Figure 4.7, at twice the scale of figure 4.6 but reflecting the same proportion, isolates the design that fits snugly within the enclosing square shown in figure 4.6. The area within this enclosing square, intended for the

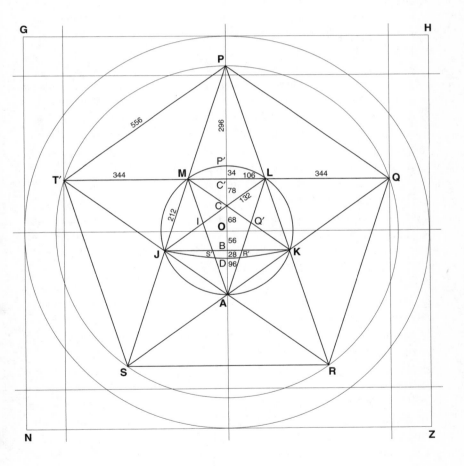

Figure 4.7

design's main point of focus, would normally have been given further em-
bellishment by the construction of a circle, as is evident on three of the
Lindisfarne Gospels' cross-carpet pages, 94v, 138v, and 210v. Much trial-
and-error demonstrates that the poet was working with two circles, one
having a radius of 180, the other a radius of 476. Both of these dimensions
show up in *Purity:* Sections 8 and 9 total 180 lines, and sections 2 through
7 total 476. Let us assume that the poet began with the smaller of these two
circles, although the argument would be unaffected if he began with the
larger circle.[18] The circle with a radius OA, measuring 180, is now fitted
with a pentangle—using a method to be discussed presently—whose
apexes are at A, J, M, L, and K in figure 4.7. Why a pentangle, rather than
some other shape? Because no other shape tested produces the correspondences with *Purity*'s sections. Nor does any other shape have as intimate a
connection with *Pearl* and *Sir Gawain* as a pentangle/pentagon does.
When these apexes are connected to complete pentagon AJMLK, the center of the design is complete and a blueprint is now available for the size of
nearly every section in *Purity*. The inscribed pentagon has sides measuring
212 (sections 5 and 6). The diagonals of this pentagon, while forming a
pentangle, measure 344 (sections 1–4), segmented by *phi* into 212 (sections 5–6), 132 (sections 7–8), and 80. That is, JL = 344; JC and IL = 212
each; CL and JI = 132 each; and IC = 80.

Returning to pentagon AJMLK measuring 212 on each side, we notice
that when the sides of this pentagon are extended in both directions, they
meet other extended sides to form a larger pentangle with apexes at P, Q,
R, S, and T'. Each of the five lines of this larger pentangle is divided into
extreme and mean ratio by the inner circle: T'M = 344, ML = 212, and LQ
= 344. Connecting the apexes constructs pentagon PQRST' with each side
measuring 556 (sections 1–6 and 8–11). And when this larger pentangle-
pentagon is circumscribed, the resulting circle is found to have a radius OP
of 476 (sections 2–7).

These correspondences between the dimensions of a geometric figure
and the line count of sections in a poem, while perhaps persuasive in suggesting that the two are related, does little to show how the poet actually
constructed his geometry. In particular, the positioning of a pentangle
within a circle poses great problems, especially for one who lacks, as the
fourteenth century apparently did, a protractor to measure angles. To solve
this problem the author apparently began by plotting several check points
to insure accuracy. Knowing that the radius of the circle is 180, he would
have been able to use standard Euclidean geometry to calculate the length

of the pentagon's diagonals at 344, cut into mean and extreme ratio giving segments of 212 and 132, respectively.[19] He might then have begun at point A, where the y axis intersects the circle, and drawn an arc of 212 radius to intersect the circle at J and K. To ensure accuracy he might have used a second, unrelated method. It is possible to move a line of length 344 (i.e., the length of the pentagon's diagonal) along the radius line AO, at right angles to it, moving away from A toward O, and keeping the midpoint of the 344 line on the y axis, until the two ends of this 344 line intersect the circumference of the circle at J and K. The distance this line must move along the vertical diameter (the original y axis) is indicated by segment AB. He would now have three points of the pentangle: A, J, and K. The Pythagorean theorem offers yet a third method for computing the shortest right-angle distance, measured on a diameter, between the circumference of a circle and a diagonal of an inscribed pentagon. Knowing the dimensions of two legs of right triangle AJB in figure 4.7 (AJ = 212; JB = one-half of 344, or 172), the poet would also have been able to compute the third. All three methods yield the same dimension for segment AB, 124. This is precisely the number of lines in *Purity*'s section 1. The remaining distance BO to the center of the circle is therefore 56 (section 3 of *Purity*). The crucial point C, the only point, other than A, where diagonals intersect on the vertical axis, measured from O, is 68 units (section 2 of *Purity*). Drawing lines from J through C to L, and from K through C to M, locates the final two points of the pentagon. All five of the pentangle's apexes are now located and pentagon AJMLK can be drawn.

One additional check for accuracy is still available. The extensions of JM and KL intersect the y axis at P. Line OP measures 476 (sections 2–7); both JP and KP measure 556 (sections 1–6 and 8–11). Using P as center, PJ as radius, an arc from J to K will intersect OA at D. If all procedures have been performed accurately, AD will measure 96 (section 4).

Only one dimension has not yet been discussed. It is the smallest of the three segments of line JL, namely IC, which measures 80. This is exactly the distance, measured on a radius, between the circle surrounding pentagon PQRST' and the outermost circle in figure 4.7. In view of the many correspondences already noted, one might think it strange that *Purity* has no section measuring 80. But the poet did not have to know the radius of this circle, since it is the inscribed circle within the enclosing square shown in figure 4.6. In other words, its radius is 556, indicated in figure 4.6 as OF and OF'. This radius is exactly 80 units greater than the 476 radius OP in figure 4.7. These two circles might better be viewed, therefore, as a framing ring outlining the design contained within the enclosing square.

Though we have referred to the first four sections of *Purity* as checks for accuracy, it is probable that they were intended to be directions. They measure the first four steps in constructing, within a circle of radius 180, a pentangle and its associated pentagon, geometric designs of great importance for *Pearl* and *Sir Gawain*. Much more significant, the expanding relation between a pentagon, a pentangle that grows from it, another pentagon surrounding the pentangle, and still another surrounding that pentagon, ad infinitum, echoes perfectly the main thematic strategy of the manuscript's literal lines that draw a direct line from the Old Law, through the New Law, and ultimately to eternal salvation (cf. Morse 1978, 133–34).[20]

The pentangle is not the only figure on Gawain's shield, however. Complementing this Old Testament symbol associated with Solomon, the knight has as well an image of the New Testament's Blessed Virgin on the inside of his shield. If the thematic content of the manuscript thus points to a combination of the Old Testament and the New Testament, it is logical to assume that the figure encoded by *Purity*'s geometric design would also contain some combination of the Old and New Testament. Solomon's "endless knot" obviously represents the Old Testament. To discover the shape and meaning of the New Testament's symbol, we must turn to the next poem in the manuscript, the poetic recreation of the story of Jonas.

5

Patience

Like the poem that precedes it in the manuscript, *Patience* paraphrases a part of the Old Testament in unrhymed, four-line units. Its difference from *Purity*, however, may be greater than its similarity. Most noticeably, the poet limits himself here to a single book of Scripture, the Book of Jonas, instead of arranging in an elusive way a number of disparate passages from several books, as seems to be the case with *Purity*. In this poem, therefore, the poet reflects more noticeably than in the other poems of the manuscript one of the disconcerting conditions that characterize humanity. Limited to only the story of Jonas, yet free to expand and emphasize certain of the book's details rather than others, the poet demonstrates in *Patience* the insoluble combination of predestination and free will under which every Judeo-Christian was understood to spend his life.[1] To notice more readily what particular details in his source the poet chooses to highlight, it will be useful to have parallel summaries of the two texts.[2] Each new section is indicated in *Patience* by the appearance of a decorated initial letter.

Book of Jonas (Vulgate)
48 verses in 4 chapters

Patience
531 lines in 5 sections

Section 1, 1–60 (60 lines). Intro: the 8 beatitudes, a focus on patience and poverty, and a claim that it does no good to grumble against God. If He sends you to Rome on an errand, go. Didn't Jonas rebel once, to no avail? I'll tell you his story, if you'll wait a while.

Chapter 1:1–16. On hearing God's command to journey to Ninive and preach there, Jonas flees by taking a ship bound from Joppa to Tharsis. A storm arises. Jonas is ejected (v. 15). The remaining sailors fear for their safety and make vows to the Lord.

Section 2, 61–244 (184 lines). Jonas hears God's command to preach in Ninive but objects, sails for Tharsis. A storm nearly destroys the ship. A wise man says a miscreant on board is causing this storm. Everyone responds to muster, except Jonas whom they rouse from sleep and drag topside. The lot falls to Jonas as the one causing the gods' displeasure. When questioned, Jonas admits he is the one whom God is punishing. They try to row away from the storm, to no avail. They toss Jonas overboard. The storm stops. A wind takes the boat to shore where the sailors convert to Jonas's God. A forewarning that no one would believe the rest of Jonas's story, if it weren't for holy writ.

Chapter 2:1–4. A fish swallows Jonas, keeping him in its belly for 3 days and 3 nights. Jonas prays to the Lord: You heard me when I cried out of the belly of hell. Now I am cast into the sea. Hear me.

Section 3, 245–304 (60 lines): Jonas is swallowed by a whale and lies for 3 days and 3 nights in its gut, which happens to stink like the devil. He sleeps. An equation is explicitly drawn between his earlier sleep in the bottom of the boat and this sleep in the belly of the whale.

(Cont'd. 2:5–11) Jonas's prayer sincerely declares that the Lord is all-powerful and that he, Jonas, is abject. Though worried about his physical safety, this is not Jonas's complaint. He simply expresses his belief that, though cast out of the sight of God, "I will see thy holy temple again."

Section 4, lines 305–408 (104 lines): A long prayer by Jonas to God, sincerely declaring his sorrow, his belief in God and God's omnipotence, and his promise never again to disobey (lines 305–36).

Chapter 3:1–10. Jonas arrives in Ninive, predicts that the city will be destroyed in 40 days. The city mends its ways and worships the Lord. The Lord takes compassion on the city, does not destroy it as He earlier said He would.

(Cont'd; §4, 337 ff.) God bids the whale to deliver Jonas to the shore near Ninive. Obediently proceeding to Ninive, Jonas begins to preach that God will destroy the city. The people then repent and God withholds His wrath.

Chapter 4:1–11. A two-part conversation between Jonas and God. The first part ends with the question, "Dost thou think thou hast reason to be angry?" Jonas moves to a hill overlooking the city, builds a hut. A miraculous woodbine grows overnight, yet withers the next night. The second conversation begins with the same question, now associated with the woodbine: "Dost thou think thou hast reason to be angry for the ivy?" God then makes the connection between the ivy, for which Jonas did not work, and the city of Nineve where there are more than 120,000 people.

Section 5, lines 409–531 (123 lines). A sorrowing Jonas argues with God. You said you'd destroy Ninive. That's why I left for Tharsis. They would have killed me. Now God answers: Is it right for you to object to any deed I have done or ordained for you? Jonas, miffed, moves to a hill, builds a hut. God grows a woodbine for him. While Jonas sleeps, yet again, it withers overnight. God makes the sun blaze, bringing discomfort to Jonas. A third time Jonas asks for death. But God rebukes him: you did nothing to tend the woodbine. I made it, I can take it away. Should I punish a people who have come to call Me their King and their Lord?

After looking at these two texts, which echo each other rather closely in spite of their differences, one might ask what subject they are meant to explore. The question is not as odd as one might initially think. If their main subject were only the prophet Jonas, as the scriptural title Book of Jonas seems to announce, a reader would wonder why this subject has no resolution. Jonas apparently fails to benefit from his experience, behaving at the end of the story exactly as he does at its beginning. The story says nothing of his future life; it leaves him sitting at his hut on a hill, bereft of the woodbine he had so briefly enjoyed. Yet Jonas occupies center stage throughout both versions, a surprising prominence if he is not the main subject of either the scriptural account or the Middle English poem.

A key to this attention is surely the contrast between the effort made by everyone and everything throughout the poem and Jonas's lassitude, named *acedia* in the Middle Ages and the subject of considerable modern commentary.[3] His most frequent acts are flight and sleep, obvious symbols of not working at his tasks. He does nothing about God's commands, except try to hide. By contrast the sailors work at the storm by trimming their sails, discarding baggage to lighten their ship, and trying to discover the miscreant whose presence may be causing the storm. The whale receives Jonas, works its way through the sea, and delivers him up on the strand at Ninive. The Ninivites work at their morality, when they hear Jonas preach God's word. Even God sets a divine example with his work, giving orders to Jonas, controlling the sea and the whale, and sending Jonas to the Ninivites, not to mention how hard he works at trying to save Jonas. But Jonas fails to see in all these scenes the powerful lesson they carry for him. Unlike the sailors, the whale, and the Ninivites, who work hard at their tasks, Jonas resembles more closely the woodbine later in the book, withering from inactivity, as he sleeps and pathetically believes that the death he says he longs for will bring relief. Similar to what he did at the beginning of the poem, at its end he withdraws to a hilltop to sleep yet again. Angry that God did not destroy Ninive, as predicted, Jonas apparently believes in a wrathful God who would turn his back on a repentant Ninive, yet fails to realize that if in fact God were as wrathful as Jonas wants him to be, he would not have let Jonas survive his two rebellions. In the death of the woodbine, grown by God and killed by him to make a point, may be found the most ominous prediction of what may lie in Jonas's future.

Though, indeed, Jonas shows no progress or growth at all, it would be incorrect to think that the story seeks only to emphasize Jonas's unwillingness to accept God's power over him. On the contrary, Jonas does understand God's omnipotence, for he sees it demonstrated over and over again governing four different levels of creation: (1) inert nature, when a violent storm suddenly troubles the sea and subsides just as suddenly; (2) living nature, when a woodbine miraculously grows to maturity overnight and perishes the next day; (3) animal nature, when a whale swallows Jonas whole and delivers him to Ninive three days later; and (4) human nature, shown as an intimation of what might befall man—physical destruction in a storm, condemnation to hell as portended by the stench of the whale's belly, abandonment by God as the woodbine is abandoned, and utter loss of body and soul, as might have befallen the citizens of Ninive. Having once acknowledged to the Tharsis-bound seamen God's power over all (206–8), as well as his own guilt in disobeying God and bringing on the storm as punishment (209–10), Jonas repents again by expressing a sincere prayer while trapped in the belly of the whale:

"Now, Prynce, of Þy prophete pité Þou haue.
Þaȝ I be fol and fykel and falce of my hert,
Dewoyde now Þy vengaunce, þurȝ vertu of rauthe;
Thaȝ I be gulty of gyle, as gaule of prophetes,
Þou art God, and alle gowdez ar grayþely Þyn owen.
Haf now mercy of Þy man and his mysdedes."
(282–87)

He follows this with an abject, yet remorseful quotation from Psalm 68:

"Careful am I, kest out fro Þy cler yȝen
And deseuered fro Þy syȝt; ȝet surely I hope
Efte to trede on Þy temple and teme to Þyseluen."
(314–16)

Words spoken in extremis, to be sure. They succeed nevertheless in obtaining Jonas's swift deliverance, when the whale "hym sput spakly vpon spare drye" (338). Despite the clarity of this lesson, by the time Jonas's next crisis occurs he has already forgotten the lesson that should have been painfully present forever in his mind. We look to him in vain for the kind of sustained repentance the Ninivites apparently display, although if the scriptural writer and his Middle English follower had chosen to let their story remain with these Ninivites they too might have shown the same brief attention span we find ludicrously evident in Jonas. In this respect

Jonas may accurately represent the whole of mankind, for all too easily we recognize in him the typical actions of fallen man.

It is much more difficult to understand God's tolerance of Jonas, perhaps because mankind has never seen such conduct, nor would embrace it themselves or recommend it to others. For both the scriptural account of Jonas and the Middle English *Patience* mainly convey God's willingness to endure what for anyone else would be intolerable treatment. We should not forget that the cognate Latin deponent verb *patior* has a force much stronger than "endure with patience," coming closer to the kind of endurance that approaches suffering. Standard medieval theology teaches that God too suffers, when his creatures fail to carry out his will, at least as much as Jonas would have suffered, had he proceeded directly to Ninive and risked the possible anger of the Ninivites. The great revelation of *Patience*, then, is not the anguish Jonas feels as he seeks to avoid, and then to carry out, God's command, or his failure to learn from his trials. Rather, the story's sustained focus is God's infinite patience with Jonas (cf. Spearing 1970, 78–79).

Here lies the sharpest difference between Cotton Nero's two paraphrases of the Old Testament: In *Purity* a terrifying God punishes those who fail to carry out his will, pervert his plan for sustaining the human race, and desecrate his vessels. In *Patience* there is no limit to God's tolerance and mercy, as he observes in man one relapse after another, yet grants him a new beginning after every breach of his will and penitent plea for another chance. *Purity* records the effects of God's judgment, as if everyone depicted in it had already lived out his life and were now being given the eternal reward he earned. *Patience* follows a life in progress, as anyone reading or hearing the poem must realize that his own life is yet to be settled, and as the poet himself must have realized of his life too as he was composing his poem. Taken together, *Purity* and *Patience* provide, therefore, an indication of the thematic strategy of the manuscript. After *Pearl* depicts both the temporal and the eternal aspects of the whole universe, the remaining three poems progressively complete a circle by returning to—one might more correctly say "growing into"—that total conception. *Purity* shows an omnipotent God who punishes forever those who refuse to accept him. *Patience* reveals a compassionate God who means to instruct man. And *Sir Gawain and the Green Knight* follows a mortal who accepts this instruction as he works his way from a temporally oriented world to a spiritually focused future. The manuscript, then, incorporates two schemes, one a linear progression, showing mankind experiencing life as the passage of time, the other a composite of all time, a coherent representation of all creation as a wonderfully organic reality sprung from the mind of God.[4]

The frequent observation among some Christian exegetes, that divine justice progresses "from Old Testament vengeance to New Testament grace" (Citrome 2001, 260), does not seem to hold here. If Jonas had been orchestrating Ninive's fortunes and recording its history for Scripture, he might have placed its story in Genesis, where God's sudden vengeance would have made a foreboding prophet superfluous. But the vengeful God whom Jonas expects to see does not appear. Instead, the God who does appear tolerates Jonas beyond reason. What is most surprising of all, this compassionate God comes, paradoxically, not from the New Testament, but from the Old. Instead of inserting a New Testament episode depicting compassion, of which there are many, the *Pearl*-poet chooses another Old Testament story for this second poem about the ancient world. After depicting God's awful justice in *Purity*, he narrates a story about his infinite mercy in *Patience*, implicitly contradicting the notion that "one of the oldest and most familiar antinomies of Christian thought and symbolism [is] the opposition of Ecclesia and Synagoga, the New and Old Testaments, grace and law."[5] It is a mistaken assumption that God somehow changes from one era to the next, when this imagined difference may only testify to a shift in perception by those who record their testimony. Consistent with fourteenth-century doctrine, the *Pearl*-poet accurately represents these different perceptions as a perfectly natural expansion of the old law into the new. The two laws are not in opposition, but in concert. The Old Testament's New Jerusalem, to which the *Pearl*-maiden has been elevated, is none other than the heaven for which the New Testament's parable of the vineyard (cf. Matthew 20:1–16; *Pearl* 497–588) allegorizes a means of attainment. Cotton Nero's transition from *Purity* to *Patience* explores the theological mystery of how a God of infinite justice can simultaneously be a God of infinite mercy.

As raptures about springtime's fresh verdure tell more about an observer than about nature's awakening vitality, which in fact has not waned, the *Pearl*-poet contrives a subtle mathematical transition from the first half of his manuscript to the second half to suggest a growing awareness of divine attributes present from the beginning. In chapter 2 we remarked a series of expansions that contribute to the form of Cotton Nero A.x, parallel to the expansion from the tetragrammaton to the pentagrammaton. Johann Reuchlin prepares for a second discussion (1983, 350; trans. 353) of how the four-letter sign for Jaweh, YHVH, expands to the five-letter Hebrew name of Jesus, YHSVH, by associating two subjects whose juxtaposition has immense significance for the manuscript we have been studying. Simon, Philolaus, and Marranus, the three participants in Reuchlin's dialogue, have been discussing the possibility of working "miracles not only with letters and figures but also with words and songs" (351). Philolaus then responds to Simon by describing the occasion on which Antiochus, facing a battle against the Galatians, dreamed that Alexander instructed him to issue his soldiers an emblem of health as a watchword in the impending battle. Through this sign Antiochus was promised victory. The sign was "a triple triangle which forms a pentagram" (353)[6] and which contains at its intersections, according to Reuchlin, the Greek letters ὑγιΘα (health), the symbol Θ standing for the diphthong ει (Huntley 1970, 30).[7] (See plate 3 for a facsimile copy of page 350 in Reuchlin where this design and the next to be discussed appear in the margin.) This "triple triangle" is, of course, the design that we have been calling the pentangle throughout this study. What makes this passage in Reuchlin especially intriguing is not the triple triangle alone, for this symbol was revered since well before the Pythagoreans, but the thought it triggers in the mind of the next speaker in Reuchlin's dialogue. The significant part of the passage is printed in Reuchlin's Latin at lines 20–24 (350). Quoted here is the translation of Martin and Sarah Goodman, located three pages later in the same book:

> MARRANUS: It is surely relevant to mention the "Sign of God," as they used to call the Cross at that time, which appeared to Constantine the Great at the very hour of midday and in the presence of his whole army. It appeared on high, inscribed in Latin letters, with the words: "In this conquer." And Constantine did conquer with this sign, and was then chosen as Emperor and saluted to the applause of the Roman people, and was named the most invincible of all emperors. (353, lines 17–23)

As the symbol in the margin of plate 3 indicates, this is the famous Chi-Rho symbol, indicating the first two Greek letters of Christ's name on the one hand, and on the other a stylized representation of the cross. In this chapter on *Patience* and the following on *Sir Gawain* I will suggest that the

DE ARTE CABALISTICA

illis uera loquar) oīa ea fidei pótius tribuūt, quanq̃ & orōnibus nōnulla
eſſe inſitā poteſtatē opinant.Dicūt em atq̃ credūt cp orō fidei ſaluabit in-
firmū,neq̃ aliter idonei Cabaliſte ſentiūt,q pariter affirmāt opatiōes mi
raculoſas ex ſolo deo,& ab hoīs fide pēdere.Mēdaces igit & ſtultos eſſe ſ
los ,pnūciāt q ſoli figurę,ſoli ſcripturę,ſolis lineamentis,ſolis uocibus aere

M fracto natis,tātā miraculorū uim & poteſtatē cōcedāt,ut teſtat Rabi Moy
ſes ægyptius in libri pplexorū primi capite lxxii.Ad hæc nō ſolū,inqt Phi
lolaus,Hebreorū Cabaliſte ſed etiā Grecorū pſtātiſſimi multū ſignaculis
& ſigillis fidei tribuerūt.Antiochus em cognomēto Soter cū eſſet in expe-
ditiōe cōtra Galatas uiros fortes & militū innumerabili cōcurſu munitos,
pliū difficillimū cōmiſſurus,qñ iā ut de eo Lucianus ſcribit τὸν πυκάς ἐχε
Ταὸ ἱλπίλας.noctu uidit p ſomniū aſſiſtere ſibi Alexādrū,iuberecp,ut mi
litib, ſuis ante pugnā pro bellica teſſera ſignaculū q̃ddā ſanitatis ediceret,
p q̃d ſibi cōtingere uictoriā pollicebat.Id erat eiuſmodi q̃ in ueſtibus inſi-
gnirent,ut idē Samoſateſis de cōpellationis errore notauit ξι•πλοῦν ξί•ηυη

Αἰαχύλωι τὸ πυπάγγεμμον.i.Triplex triāgulus inter ſe qnquilinçaris. Antiochus aūt ſigno to leuato mirabile aduerſum Galatas nactus eſt uictoriam.
Egoipſe,ptecto illud pētagoni ſymbolū ſçpe in Antiochi argētea moneta.
pcuſſum uidi,q̃d reſolutū in lineas oſtēdit uocabulū ὑγίε.i.ſanitas.An nō

in rē erit,Marranus inqt,id q̃d Magno Cōſtātino q̃ndā dei ſignū (ut tūc
appellabāt cruce) in ipſa meridiei hora corā oī exercitu ſupne apparuit la
tinis līis inſcriptū ſic,In hoc uinçe.Et uicit qdē Cōſtātinus eodē ſignaculo,
atcp tūc plauſu populi Romanorū Impator lectus ac ſalutatus,oīumcp im

N patorū inuictiſſimus ſuit cognoīatus.Quātū igit ualuerūt ſigilla & ſigna-
cula teſtes erūt ſummi uiri,Iudeis Machabeus,Grecis Antioch⁹,Romanis
Cōſtātinus.Nec te fallit,Simō q̃d de Chriſtianis paulo ante loquutus es.
Nā ea gente nihil ſub hoc ſeculo eſt in opificio ſignorū,characterū & uo,
cū admirabilius,q figura crucis & noīe Ieſu ſiſtūt maria,uētos mitigāt,ſul
mina repellūt.Eſt pterea charactere illo & effigie crucis nihil etiā fortius,
& in piculis nihil magis ſalutiferū,quanq̃ nōn aliā (ut libere fatear) ob rē
niſi cp ueri Saluatoris ſymbolū extāt,ſicut uobis dei ſymbolū eſt nomē il
lud Tetragrāmaton.Quodcp Cabaliſte poſſunt in noīe ineffabili cū nup
a te mōſtratis ſigillis & charagmatis,id multo ualidiore modo poſſunt fi-
deles Chriſtiani p nomē I E S V effabile.cū ,pprio ſignaculo crucis,cū ſe
arbitret nomē tetragrāmatō lōge recti⁹ ,pnūciare in noīe יהשוה ue
ri Meſſihg,ad hoc citāt. id q̃d in Midras Thillim ueſtri ſcripſerūt אמר

ר׳ יהושע בן לוי בשם ר׳ פנחס בן יאיר
מפני מה מתפללין ישראל בעולם הזה ואינן
נענין על ידי שאינן יודעין בשם המפורש

.i.Dixit Rabi Ioſue fili⁹ Leui allegādo magiſtrū Pinhes filiū Iair.Propter

cross is a prominent symbol in Cotton Nero A.x and that the combination of the pentangle from the Old Testament era and the cross from the New Testament era constitute a major geometric design informing the whole manuscript. This is an hypothesis, of course, not subject to independent verification. But unlike the speculations regarding the identity of the author and his audience, which rely on the scant social evidence of late-fourteenth-century England, the speculation advanced here regarding geometric symbols may be measured by numerical evidence in the actual text of Cotton Nero A.x. Readers can judge whether or not these correspondences are sufficiently numerous to gain assent.

Paralleling the divinely engineered expansion of the *Pearl*-manuscript, evident when the 2343 lines of the medial poems *Purity* and *Patience* constitute an almost precise *phi* ratio with the 3743 lines of *Pearl* and *Sir Gawain* at the manuscript's extremities, a lesser, humanly engineered mathematical transition from the first half of the manuscript to the second half achieves the same kind of expanded association of thoughts that Marranus demonstrates in Reuchlin's dialogue, when he associates a five-pointed star with a symbol of Christ. Where the first Old Testament poem, *Purity*, is organized in a four-unit metrical form, and remains within a duodecimal system, as announced by its 1800 basic lines and by its signature of twelve extra lines to indicate its key, *Patience* seems to grow from a four-based system into a five-based system. It has a four-line metrical form, but arranges this form into a basic 500 lines with a signature of 31, the 10th prime number in the Middle Ages. A glance at the parallel columns comparing the Vulgate's and the *Pearl*-poet's accounts of Jonas, printed at the beginning of this chapter, similarly suggests a conscious effort to expand Scripture's four chapters into the poem's five sections. The poet makes this conversion not only by adding the introductory section 1, for which Scripture has no counterpart, but also by redistributing Scripture's verses. The 16 verses of Scripture's chapter 1 parallel the 184 lines of the poem's section 2, while Scripture's chapter 4 is recreated in the 123 lines of section 5. But the two middle chapters of the Vulgate are distributed in an odd way between sections 3 and 4 of the poem. The first four verses of chapter 2 expand into the whole of section 3 of the poem, while the remaining seven verses of chapter 2, plus all ten verses of chapter 3—a total of seventeen verses—appear as the 104 lines of the poem's section 4.

Where the Book of Jonas combines the scenes in the belly of a fish with those in which a prayer for deliverance may also be heard, the *Pearl*-poet apparently wanted to emphasize the striking difference between these two scenes. Likening the fish's maw to the stench and filth of hell, the three days of Jonas's repose there allude to the punishment that the God of justice might mete out to Jonas. The sincere prayer from the prophet, by contrast, calls upon the mercy that this same God might bestow. This fundamental opposition suggests the preclusive results that mankind's moral decisions produce, a contrast made more stark by the poet's placing them in successive sections, especially when Jonas's deliverance implies that the latter will always overwhelm the former. These small rearrangements promote the belief that the shape and size of the several sections of *Patience* may be as artfully planned, though perhaps according to a different design, as the plans governing *Pearl* and *Purity*.

The placement of decorated initial letters in *Patience*, at lines 1, 61, 245, 305, and 409 reinforces this belief. They divide the poem's 531 lines into five sections of 60, 184, 60, 104, and 123 lines. Sections 2 and 4, where the line totals exceed prominent round numbers by four extra lines, draw attention to the twenty-three lines by which section 5 also exceeds an even one hundred. These four extra lines in section 2, four more in section 4, and twenty-three in section 5, add up to the poem's 31-line signature, the 10th prime number, the significance of which is explained in chapter 2. If the line totals of these sections are diminished by these amounts—not by removing lines, but by imagining these same lines to include the poem's "signature" and therefore to be disregarded when turning to the numerical design that the signature governs—all five sections have highly significant round numbers—60, 180, 60, 100, and 100, respectively. In addition to suggesting a graduation from the duodecimal system (60, 180, 60) to the decimal system (100, 100), four of these sections represent the approximate dimensions of a divine rectangle measuring 60 x 100.[8] The remaining dimension, 180, signals the scale in which this rectangle may be found, namely the scale of the first pentagon/pentangle discussed in chapter 4, a circumscribing circle of radius 180, equal to the combined lengths of sections 8 and 9 of *Purity*.

The hypothesis advanced in chapter 3 suggests that a dodecahedron and its three inscribed rectangles are either the symbols of, or symbolized by, *Pearl* and the three poems that follow it in Cotton Nero A.x. That *Pearl* visits both heaven and earth, while *Purity*, *Patience*, and *Sir Gawain* remain on the two-dimensional planes of time and space, reinforces the parallel with the fifth Platonic solid for the former and the dodecahedron's internal planes for the latter three. Now each of these planes is a golden rectangle. If we assume that an edge of the originating dodecahedron is 12 units, we can determine the dimensions of its inscribed rectangles by applying the Pythagorean theorem and other proportions well known to the Middle Ages.

Length	23
Width	14
Diagonal	27

None of these dimensions agrees with anything we have seen thus far. If, however, we compute the dimensions of these rectangles, after expanding the original dodecahedron three times, as described in appendix 2, interesting numbers emerge.

Length	401
Width	248
Diagonal	472

Although this width is exactly the combined total of sections 1, 2, and 3 of *Purity*, the diagonal is a more important dimension. Since the diagonal of these rectangles is equal to the diameter of a sphere inscribed in the dodecahedron we have been discussing, one which has been expanded three times from the original dodecahedron measuring 12 on each edge to produce one measuring 212 on each edge, the radius of this sphere (one-half the diameter) would be 235.745, rounded to 236. This magnitude is the precise sum of sections 4 and 5 of *Purity*.

Up to this point in our discussion every dimension that has been found to correspond to the line count of a section, or sections, in *Purity* also corresponds to a known property of a dodecahedron: the edge of a pentagonal face; the edge of an inscribed icosahedron; the golden rectangles within a dodecahedron; and so forth. The dimensions of *Patience* are a different matter, since the two 60s and the two 100s in the sectional dimensions of this poem are nowhere to be found in the sections of *Purity*, which has otherwise provided a reliable mathematical blueprint for the manuscript. For this reason we may assume no more than that the rectangular dimensions implied by four of the five sections in *Patience* express a ratio only, not literal dimensions.

But what if they *are* literal dimensions, perhaps not for their own significance, but for something else to which they lead? Confirmation that such a plan may have been in the poet's mind is not far to find, for the diagonal of a 60 x 100 rectangle is 116.6, which is not only the approximate sum of sections 6 and 7 of *Purity*, but the precise length (as precisely as it can be measured by modern dividers) of the horizontal x-axis that lies within the pentagon described in chapter 4, CQ'R'S'I (figure 4.7, reproduced here as figure 5.1). We are forced to measure this line segment ourselves, rather than rely on the equations of Pythagorean geometry, since the line in which this dimension appears does not figure in ancient or medieval discussions of the fifth Platonic solid. This segment of the horizontal axis gains enormous significance when pentagon sides IS' and Q'R' are extended to intersect at point A in figure 5.2. The resulting irregular polygon AICQ' appears to be a knight's shield, a shape of the greatest importance for Cotton Nero A.x. That this is not simply a fortuitous coincidence, but actually part of the poet's design, seems likely. For the extended horizontal axis meeting the edges of the next larger pentagon AJMLK in figure 5.3, when measured by modern dividers, is extremely close to 308, the

Figure 5.1

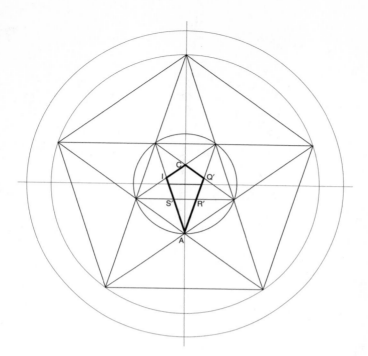

Figure 5.2

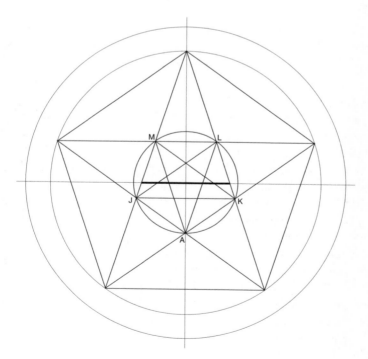

Figure 5.3

Figure 5.4

combined total of sections 4, 5, and 6 of *Purity*. From a modern perspective this particular pentagon has an unfamiliar upside-down appearance.

Two of the sides of this new pentagon, when extended to meet at P in figure 5.4, produce yet another knight's shield, AJPK, similarly in an up-side-down view. A further expansion along the horizontal x-axis, extending this segment until it meets the sides of pentagon PQRST' in figure 5.5 reveals a dimension of 800, the combined total of sections 7–12 of *Purity*, and producing another shieldlike polygon, T'PQ and a fourth point (not shown) at the intersection of extended lines T'S and QR.

Although this expansion along the x-axis may seem arbitrary, not at all based on proven theorems of geometry, it produces extraordinary mathematical beauty. Each expansion creates an almost precise demonstration of the Divine Section. Since the expansion under discussion here originates at the central point of the entire design and occurs in two directions that mirror each other (actually it expands in omni-directions in a three-

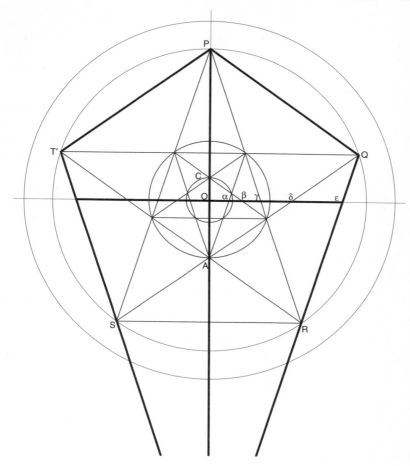

Figure 5.5

dimensional solid but is treated here in a single plane to simplify discussion), we need only consider one direction. Segment Oα is one half of 116, or 58. Segment αβ measures 36. Thus these two segments are in a *phi* ratio. As Heath makes clear in his discussion of the Pythagorean understanding of the five regular solids (Heath 1921, 158–62), successive expansions of a pentagon inevitably produce *phi* ratios *in corresponding lines of the pentagon itself.* It is remarkable, therefore, that this *phi* ratio along the horizontal axis in figure 5.6 does not appear in corresponding lines. Further expansion to γ, δ, and ε creates several more *phi* ratios such that Oα, αβ, βγ, γδ, and δε are all in a *phi* series.[9]

It should be obvious by now that the horizontal lines we have been discussing, especially since they appear successively within shapes that resemble the shield of a medieval knight, is none other than a representation of the horizontal beam of the cross of Christ, the same object to which Marranus refers in Reuchlin's dialogue. Reuchlin imagines a Chi-Rho design, whereas the encoding in *Patience* seems to imply a conventional cross. It is entirely logical, then, that a vertical line would be drawn through the center of the shield, coinciding with the y-axis of the entire design, to add an image of a vertical beam and thus to complete the cross of Christ. Nor does this vertical beam stand apart from the mathematics controlling the entire design. If the innermost circle—even smaller than the one with which we began—has a radius OC measuring 68, the vertical beam of its cross, multiplied by φ^2, leads to the circumference of the next larger circle, whose radius OA is 180, as the vertical beam of this new shieldlike shape points to the circumference of the next larger circle, with radius OP of 476 units.[10]

Let us pause here to consider a possible objection, that no evidence has been produced to suggest the presence of a shield in *Patience*, much less a cross depicted on it. This is certainly true. But we cannot ignore the abundant evidence that the manuscript comprises four related poems and that as a result no individual poem can be isolated from the others. A knight's shield will shortly be the focus of two whole stanzas in *Sir Gawain and the Green Knight* (619–69). As to the second part of the objection, that there is no evidence of a cross on a shield, the question might better be turned around. What chance is there that a knight of Arthur's court, featured in a medieval romance, would *not* have a cross depicted on his shield? None. Indeed even Ross G. Arthur, a scholar discussing the meaning of Gawain's pentangle, not the shield on which it is depicted, associates a cross with a shield. After suggesting that the pentangle has multiple meanings, the Trinity, truth, and so forth, he cautions: "By placing such a device on Gawain's shield, the poet is not claiming that Gawain is God, any more than the cross on a crusader's shield means that he is the cross" (Arthur 1991, 223).

Seemingly lost in the forest while looking for the Green Chapel, Gawain makes the sign of the cross and prays to it for help, "He sayned hym in syþes sere / And sayde, Cros Kryst me spede" (761–62). Immediately thereafter he makes the same sign of the cross three times, "Nade he sayned hymself, segge, bot þrye / Er he watz war in þe wod of a won in a mote" (763–64). Whether these explicit references give the cross sufficient

Plate 4. MS Brit. Lib. Cotton Nero D.iv. Folio 94 verso (The Lindisfarne Gospels). Reproduced by permission of the British Library.

prominence or not is beside the point. A cross is a constant presence in the poem and, as I am suggesting here, in the design that gives shape to the manuscript.[11] Most significantly, the very proportion that enabled the *Pearl*-poet to plan and execute Cotton Nero A.x, namely the Divine Proportion, was the proportion used by the artists of the Lindisfarne Gospels to produce five carpet pages depicting stylized representations of the cross of Christ. While all of these depictions follow a plan based on the Divine Proportion and a circle positioned at the center from which the design expands, one of these pages, folio 94v, the cross-carpet page introducing the Gospel according to St. Mark, shown as plate 4, makes this circle explicit in the design's final form.

The intricate mathematical expansion, from what appears to mortal eyes as a design on a shield to a complicated equation leading to the apparent threshold of infinity, and from the pentangle associated with Solomon to the cross associated with Christ, suits perfectly the most important theme of the manuscript's literal language. Imagined as a figure inscribed on each of the three divine rectangles within a dodecahedron, and expanding from this solid's center with each expansion of a pentagonal side into a new pentangle, and from this new pentangle into a new pentagon, until infinity seems within man's grasp, the cross of Christ has been everywhere present from the beginning. The poet's composite design thus draws upon and integrates the three great traditions enriching his age—(1) ancient Egyptian, Babylonian, and Greek mathematics, (2) Hebraic monotheistic wisdom, and (3) Christian theology.

We turn now to the final poem in the manuscript, the most celebrated of the four, *Sir Gawain and the Green Knight*, which synthesizes everything discussed thus far, yet accomplishes the remarkable task of bringing all these esoteric disciplines and beliefs to the service of Arthurian romance, or as the poet himself might have thought, the remarkable task of adding Arthurian romance to the esoteric disciplines that both demonstrate and explicate the providential plan.

Sir Gawain and the Green Knight

Consistent with the most pervasive theme of the first three poems in Cotton Nero A.x, *Sir Gawain and the Green Knight* explores the difficulty man has reconciling the immediate, often transitory concerns of a life lived day-to-day with other, competing concerns that arise from immutable values, concerns that are impervious to the shifting needs of a given moment. Its method, however, is very different from that of the preceding poems. *Pearl's* symbolic confrontation, scarcely different from a debate between body and soul, sifts its material in a kind of moot-court whose most serious judgment returns its plaintiff to the dross of normal life. *Purity*, concerned in part with lives untroubled by moral scruple and punished accordingly, shows catastrophes that are inconceivable, set in times and places that are unimaginable. And *Patience* portrays nothing so much as an errant child, never in danger of real punishment, continually in need of rebuke, as he struggles toward social maturity and spiritual understanding. Only *Sir Gawain and the Green Knight* has familiar temptations of the flesh, terrifying dangers to body and soul. As a result, the range of potential consequences awaiting Gawain has immediate resonance for every audience, but especially in the fourteenth century when violence was a frequent and palpable reality. Here the contest between relative values and absolute values acquires the terms of an enforceable contract requiring Gawain to stand, apparently helpless, before almost certain death. This account of Sir Gawain's most famous adventure in the whole of the Arthurian cycle turns the immediate dangers of life as it is actually lived into a surrogate court for the spiritual dangers that threaten all humanity for all eternity.

The poem's central character, Sir Gawain, while at first seeming more accessible and less enigmatic than his rival the Green Knight, remains by the poem's end as puzzling as his adversary. Though often seen as a thoroughly self-conscious, articulate hero, Gawain fits this description only to a limited extent. The claim ceases to be true at just that point where Gawain's self-consciousness and his reality fail to coincide. Certainly Arthur's nephew knows he is a mortal being, subject to all the pain and suffering descendants of Adam and Eve are heir to, but his awareness of these limitations may be more rhetorical than real, as his first speech's artful tissue of formulaic remarks suggests:

> I am þe wakkest, I wot, and of wyt feblest,
> And lest lur of my lyf, quo laytes þe soþe.
> Bot for as much as ȝe ar myn em I am only to prayse;
> No bounté but your blod I in my bodé knowe.
>
> (354–57)

This and other well-turned speeches may be more self-revealing than self-conscious. What readers recognize in these words, indeed in the entire speech from line 343 to 361, is not only its transparent meaning—of course Gawain doesn't believe what he is saying—but the more troubling self-satisfaction of its speaker, confident that his words confirm his reputation as the best of all possible knights. They suggest Gawain's most serious problem—nothing heinous, of course, or even scandalous, but a blemish nonetheless: a confidence that his language can rise to any occasion, concealing from him that he is by nature a fallible mortal. His verbal skills, particularly when dissembling, are more highly developed than his ability to examine the connections, or lack of them, between his words and his thoughts, or his words and his works. To appreciate this point Arthur's court must be subjected to the kind of searching examination the Green Knight has traveled to Camelot to conduct, not the kind that contributed to the reports he has obviously heard:

> þe los of þe, lede [i.e., Arthur], is lyft vp so hyȝe
> And þy burȝ and þy burnes best ar holden,
> Stifest vnder stel-gere on stedes to ryde,
> Þe wyȝtest and þe worþyest of þe worldes kynde,
> . . . .
> And þat hatz wayned me hider.
>
> (258–61, 264)

"Rude," some critics say of this first appearance of the gome "al grayþed in grene" (151), yet this belief too may be inaccurate. The word would only be appropriate if a person's conduct and the locale or occasion where this conduct is displayed were in sharp disagreement. If a young man at a funeral does *not* dress and act like an old one, to adapt Burrow's figure, he is rightly called rude, because the event itself calls for ponderous movement. We have a very different situation here, where the Green Knight strongly suspects that Arthur's court may not be what its four-teenth-century reputation assumes it to be. The whole point of the Green Knight's mission is to discover whether the stories he has heard of the Round Table and the boasts its knights make of themselves bear any rela-tion to reality. His very presence seriously questions whether the verbal reports of Arthur's court are based on anything substantial, or whether these warriors foreshadow the tinsel knight Tennyson saw, singing "Tirra lirra" by the river. Are the burg and its burnes only *held* to be highest? Or is this what they really are? Until these questions are resolved, the Green Knight's decorum cannot be judged; it may indeed be rude, if the court is found worthy, or it may be appropriate, if the court's reputation is un-founded. Several details described early in the romance give some weight to the Green Knight's doubt that anything substantial lies behind the mer-riment, the gift-giving, the dancing, and even the praying and the atten-dance at Mass this Christmas season in Camelot.

There is, of course, some truth to Burrow's point about decorum (1965, 5), supported by a motto found in Froissart:

Seiés jolis devant la gent
Et servés Dieu privéement;
Chantés et volunters jués
Que papelard ne resemblés.

[Be always gay before people
And save Our Lord for the steeple;
Sing eagerly and play with zest,
Not as if the pope were your guest.][1]

But references to the central purpose of the feast are missing—as if at a birthday party no one referred to its honored guest—making one wonder if the full import of the Christmas season is anywhere present in the thoughts of those we see and hear. Most revealing of all, when the sud-denly intruding Green Knight states his challenge in line 287 no one re-sponds for what must be an embarrassing length of time, "If he hem stowned vpon fyrst, stiller were þanne / Alle þe heredmen in halle, þe hyȝ and þe loȝe" (301–2). Finally, in a sad indictment of his knights, Arthur himself rises to answer the Green Knight's challenge. Forty lines elapse before Arthur himself takes the Green Knight's axe in line 326 and fifteen more before Gawain begins his speech in line 341, certainly long enough to give the "heredmen"—the word emphasizes their role as warriors (cf. OE *here*, "army")—a chance to defend the Round Table. The irony of a king longer in tooth than those banqueting with him, yet quicker to assume battle mode than a whole hall full of "hearty" knights, apparently moves Gawain to action. Not action yet, however, for he first finds it necessary to give the fulsome, overly elegant preamble noted above—the emphasis is on "amble"—before relieving his uncle of the axe (368) and preparing to swing at the intruder. If this unfolding scene typifies the conduct of the Round Table, the Green Knight's suspicions may have a truthful ring. Camelot seems to hover between cowardice, seen in the shameful silence that forces the king to act for the court, and hollow knighthood that values the symbols and appearances of valor and courtesy above their substance—even when confronted with a dire event.

This indictment is not leveled at Gawain and his fellow knights alone. Arthur too contributes to the general impression that Camelot is filled with lightweights. The intruder's unambiguous assurance that he comes "in pes and no plyȝt seche" (266), confirmed by a bob of holly in his hand (206) and the absence of battle armor on his body (268–71), makes no impression on Arthur, who responds immediately to this request for a Christmas "gomen" (273) as if he had not heard the man's literal words:

> "Sir cortays knyȝt,
> If þou craue batayl bare,
> Here faylez þou not to fyȝt."
> (276–78)

Again the knight insists his visit is peaceful, "Nay, frayst I no fyȝt" (279). This time, however, his statement of neutral curiosity about the character of the Round Table, given moments earlier, becomes a distinctly negative judgment, goading the court by giving his opinion of the knights arrayed before him:

> "Hit arn aboute on þis bench bot berdlez chylder.
> If I were hasped in armes on a heȝe stede,
> Here is no mon me to mach, for myȝtez so wayke."
> (280–82)

The Green Knight's shift to blunt speech must be attributed to a combination of Arthur's inability to comprehend the stranger's plain language and the inexplicable reluctance of his knights to leap for the Green Knight's axe before Arthur takes it. These are, after all, the only events that take place between the Green Knight's noncommittal observation and his taunti. second opinion.

The specific accusations leveled against Arthur's knights, that they are beardless children and weak warriors, had been anticipated by the casual way in which the Green Knight asks for their leader, "Wher is . . . Þe gouernour of þis gyng?" (224–25). While this inquiry does not exactly have the force of "Who's the boss of this mob," the cognate relation of *gyng* and Modern English "gang" suggests the direction in which his thought is taking him.[2] The poet, too, reveals his own opinion of Arthur, just before the king takes his seat for the banquet, by calling him childish, despite his seniority, and claiming he has a short attention span, apparently not for this occasion alone, but in general:

> Bot Arthure wolde not ete til al were serued;
> He watz so joly of his joyfnes, and sumquat childgered.
> His lif liked hym lyȝt; he louied þe lasse
> Auþer to longe lye or to longe sitte,
> So bisied him his ȝonge blod and his brayn wylde.
> (85–89)

Though it is tempting to minimize the import of these words or even take them as a compliment, their true significance is verified at the Green Knight's beheading when the assembled knights, consistent with Arthur's "childgered" demeanor, treat the grisly head rolling on the floor as if it deserved no more respect than a ball on a playing field:

> Þe fayre hede fro þe halce hit to þe erþe,
> Þat fele hit foyned wyth her fete þere hit forth roled.[3]
> (427–28)

The king's first words, after the Green Knight retrieves his head, mounts his horse, restates the terms of the contest, and gallops away from Camelot, surprisingly do not call an immediate meeting of his council to plan a response to this mysterious intruder, but rather address to Guenevere a patronizing speech trivializing the event, reducing it to one of the things to be expected at Christmas. Perhaps the king wishes merely to allay the court's fear. Yet his single phrase of reassurance, "demay yow neuer" (470), draws less of his energy than his eagerness to tuck into his victuals, "Neuerþelece to my mete I may me wel dres, / For I haf sen a selly I may not forsake" (474–75). The poem spends six more lines on the dainties and merriment of the feast, before the concluding wheel of the first

hints at the importance of all these details for a court that
of their full significance:[4]

wel, Sir Gawan,
ϸat ϸou ne wonde
ıre for to frayn
Pat pou natz tan on honde.

(487–90)

One is reminded of Chrétien's *Le Chevalier de la Charrette*, where a not
dissimilar scene occurs at the beginning of the narrative (1992, lines 31–
172). There Arthur, though just informed that an intruding knight holds
captive large numbers of his subjects and intends to fight an appointed
champion for custody of the queen, turns to what he must believe is the
more important business of dissuading his seneschal from resigning. A
seneschal, let us remember, was in charge of banquets. Granted, the Old
French romance has a breezier tone than *Sir Gawain and the Green
Knight,* and may even be a thoroughgoing send-up. But does not Arthur
do the same thing here?

Whether Gawain's speech in this opening fitt is consistent with Arthur's
and the court's conduct may remain uncertain and in any case depend on a
total interpretation of the poem. It is possible, nevertheless, to see in these
scenes the beginning of a sharp contrast between the Green Knight and
Gawain that will become more pronounced as the poem proceeds (cf.
Schmidt 1987, 158–59). Most notably, their senses of the relation between
language and meaning are entirely different, one a model of unambiguous
direct address, the other a monument to hypotaxis and indirection. When
the Green Knight wants to know whether the reputation of the Round
Table is based on fact or fancy, he simply asks the question straight out:
Are you beardless children, or do you measure up to your reputation? But
when Gawain asks that the Green Knight's challenge be assigned to him,
he first pays attention to decorum, not decorum regarding the blow he will
deal to the intruder, but on whether it is proper to vacate his place at the
table to approach the king and leave the queen unattended. Style is still on
his mind when he assures all within hearing that it is indecorous for so
lofty a one as Arthur to answer the challenge, however able the king would
be to the task. He dwells next on danger, but again indirectly, claiming that
if a life is to be sacrificed his own would be little loss. And finally, though

he is the first to ask this favor, this indiscretion should not be charged to the court.

Perhaps all this circumlocution masks fear, giving Gawain some pretense to occupy him, in order to banish from his mind the awful business that awaits. Yet much later in the poem, as he languishes at Bertilak's castle and faces little danger of this sort, evasiveness still dominates his speech. Disingenuously wondering why his host's wife has stealthily entered his chamber, Gawain certainly knows that, by permitting the lady to slip quietly within the curtains of his bedstead while he pretends to be asleep and then pretends to awaken, he will soon be calling upon the power of his speech to maintain a delicate balance between courtliness and chastity. With a touch of hubris, he gives no hint of doubt that his speech will match the task: "Bot ȝet he sayde in hymself, 'More semly hit were / To aspye wyth my spelle in space quat ho wolde'" (1198–99).

The stark contrast between these two main characters is evident in more fundamental ways than in their sharply contrasted modes of speech. A. C. Spearing advanced our understanding of how they might best be viewed by suggesting that the Green Knight brings to the poem the kind of heightened awareness that a typical central consciousness might provide in a Henry James novel, while Gawain parallels such a novel's main figure. Aping James's own layered prose, Spearing says that "the poet seems to have intended in his hero a character such as James, with the wisdom of hindsight, saw that the hero of his early novel *Roderick Hudson* ought to have been" (1970, 233). While any appeal to Henry James risks the logical fallacy of *ignotum per ignotius*, especially when drawing upon a work written relatively early and thus little known to all but specialists, the important contribution here is in seeing that the Green Knight and Gawain, together, constitute a kind of totality similar to the combination of a Jamesian hero (Roderick Hudson) and the gifted central consciousness who witnesses this hero's adventure (Rowland Mallet).

This useful observation makes us realize that the two title roles in the poem are diametric opposites who together might comprise a single splendid specimen. Everything a reader learns of the Green Knight pertains to action, what is yet to be tested at Camelot; Gawain's usual mode is thought, precisely what we miss most in the Green Knight's spare words. The great difference, however, between a Jamesian sensibility and a medieval sensibility makes all the difference. True enough, the Green Knight's motives are never laid bare, at least until the very end of the poem. But there is an apparent openness to his actions, similar to that of his speech, that makes Gawain's conduct seem almost duplicitous. No emblem on the Green Knight's shield or elsewhere even remotely suggests the complex fusion of ancient learning, Hebraic tradition, and Christian faith evident in the designs of Gawain's shield. Yet the Green Knight may reflect more effectively than Gawain the cultural ideals these emblems symbolize. It is not at all misleading, then, to think of the image of the Green Knight, with head severed from his body, as an apt symbol of Gawain's imbalance, or at least of the imbalance the Green Knight suspects: all outward form, disconnected from the kind of critical intellection that would distinguish between *trawþe,* a concept close to eternal truth, and the artful intellection associated with mere form that Gawain has in abundance.

The medieval poem does not, of course, merely contrast one character, driven by the usual enticements, customs, and ambitions of his age, and another able to intuit the sensibilities, motives, and tastes of the same age, yet preferring the genuine to the garish, as James's stories do. Rather it brings together, in what may at first appear to be adversarial contact but later as collaboration, one knight driven by the worldly values and pressures of his age and another knight who is absolutely certain that these values and pressures must be governed by interior values—courtesy in one context, morality in another, *trawþe* overall. The Green Knight has complete faith in the supremacy of the spirit over the flesh, otherwise known as the immortality of the soul, captured dramatically in the bizarre scene in which his severed head topples to the ground, but does not cause his death. Gawain's inability to grasp the significance of this scene, to understand that "*clannes* and *cortaysye* (along with three other virtues) form part of a moral continuum subsumed under *trawþe*" (Horgan 1987, 310), causes all his later grief.[5] Habitually acting as if his perfection rests in his worldly powers, especially his powers of speech, yet conscious at some fundamental level that such power can never transcend mortality, he is utterly unprepared for his ultimate trial in fitt 3 at Bertilak's castle.

A knight setting out on a quest would have little reason to suspect that the objective he seeks includes more than the stated terms of the challenge. At Arthur's court the Green Knight asked straightforwardly for someone—anyone—willing to "strike a strok for anoþer. . . . I schal bide þe fyrst bur as bare as I sitte. . . . And I schal stonde hym a strok . . . A twelmonyth and a day" (287–98). That there be no misunderstanding, Gawain gives the knight his name and repeats the terms of the agreement:

'Gawan I hatte
Þat bede þe þis buffet (quatso bifallez after)

And at þis tyme twelmonyth take at þe anoþer
With what weppen so þou wylt—and wyth no wyȝ ellez
　　　On lyue.'
(381–85)

However much readers of the poem—especially those familiar with medieval literature's fondness for scenes inserted for the sake of exposition, despite their seeming irrelevance[6]—may suspect that the events of the third fitt are crucial to Gawain's future, nothing in his exchange with the Green Knight would make him think he owed his courteous adversary anything more than an appearance at the appointed time to receive a return blow. Hence the "action" of the plot suggests that fitt 3 stands apart from the poem's main concern. If fitts 1, 2, and 4 press relentlessly toward the conclusion of the sequence that begins when the Green Knight shatters the merriment of Arthur's court at Christmastide, the third fitt has the feel of an interlude, a departure from care, a respite before the obligations of a knight's honor take Gawain to his ominous meeting at the Green Chapel. The structure of the poem proves otherwise.

Historical details prominently featured at the beginning of the poem appear again at the end, but in reverse order to suggest a deliberate mir-

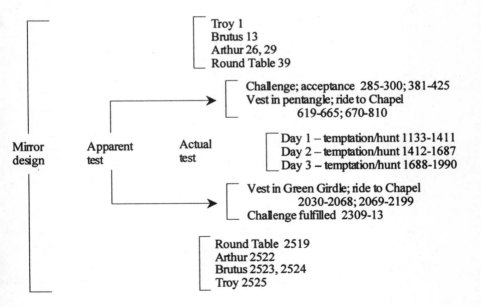

Figure 6.1

rored pattern. The design governing the whole of *Sir Gawain* (see figure 6.1) follows suit, drawing unmistakable attention to the very center of the scheme, the scenes in fitt 3, where the lady of the castle daily tempts Gawain while her lord takes to the forest for three days of hunting. This is not to suggest that Gawain's obligation to keep his appointment at the Green Chapel has less importance than his obligation during his stay at the castle to conduct himself properly—whatever that may mean. It does imply, however, that the virtues tested in private, where no mortal but an insistent lady can observe him, reveal his character more tellingly than those tested in public, where many knights—those of the Round Table and the Green Knight himself—hear him swear to keep his appointment in a year and a day and will know if he fails at his word. The questions prompted by the earlier scene at Arthur's court may reasonably be asked again in fitt 3: Does Gawain's eagerness to keep his reputation unblemished exert on him more pressure than his desire to make his beliefs and actions match this reputation?

As with everything else in Cotton Nero A.x, the relative sizes of a poem's parts adumbrate its thematic meaning.[7] Like *Purity*'s method for establishing divisions and sections, *Sir Gawain* too employs a scheme of decorated initial letters of three sizes. The first line of the poem shows a decorated *S*, the first letter of *Siþen*, extending eight lines down into the text, but also spilling the equivalent of two lines up into the space at the top of the leaf. This first decorated initial letter marks both the beginning of the poem and the beginning of the first fitt. Fitts 2, 3, and 4 beginning at lines 491, 1126, and 1998, respectively, are marked by decorated initials standing six lines high. Finally, five more decorated initials, each with a height of three lines, mark lines 619, 763, 1421, 1893, and 2259. If these decorated initials beginning all nine sections, not just those that begin the four fitts, contribute to the poem's aesthetic design, we may assume a distribution into fitts, sections, and lines as shown in figure 6.2.

In a manuscript exceptionally attentive to mathematics it is highly significant that the number of stanzas in fitts 1, 2, and 4 are very nearly identical, while the stanza count in fitt 3 is much larger. A reader might suspect that the poet planned to give approximately the same size to the three fitts that advance the beheading game and a different size to the fitt that serves as an interlude. But this explanation is inconsistent with the assignment of sections. Although the third fitt has 37 percent more lines and 42 percent

Fitt	I		II			III		IV	
stanzas	21		24			34		22	
lines	490		635			872		534	
Section	1	2	3	4	5	6	7	8	9
stanzas	21	5	6	13	11	19	4	11	11
lines	490	128	144	363	295	472	105	261	273

Figure 6.2

more stanzas than the second, it has the same number of sections. More likely, the poet used mathematics to emphasize several different thematic threads, one related to the number of fitts, another to the number of sections, another to the number of stanzas, and yet another to the number of lines. Freed from having to adhere to a fixed number of lines in each of *Sir Gawain*'s stanzas, the poet had the kind of flexibility such a plan needs.

An examination of the stanza count for each fitt in relation to every other fitt reveals an extremely significant detail. The first and third fitts are in a nearly perfect Divine Proportion, exceeding *phi* by only 0.00102:

$$34 \div 21 = 1.61904$$

The subtle link thus forged between the first and third fitts suggests that the values the Green Knight came to Camelot to examine, as found in knights he described with disdain, will be tested more closely in Bertilak's castle during fitt 3 than at the Green Chapel during fitt 4 for which a golden link cannot be established. Moreover, the principle of expansion in the Divine Proportion implies that the matter being tested in the third fitt is commensurately greater than the object of investigation explicitly announced in fitt 1.

While the Divine Proportion, though a mainstay of medieval higher learning, may lie beyond a modern reader's frame of reference, not even our medieval counterparts would have had to make the connection on their own between the poem and higher learning. They would have been pointedly directed to the Divine Proportion by the two whole stanzas that give prominent attention to the pentangle on Gawain's shield (619–69), stanzas whose double reference to red and gold (619–20, 663) nicely "mimic, in their opening and closing lines of verse, the very pattern of endless self-enclosure which [a pentangle's lines] betoken" (Schmidt 1987,

147–48). We recall from chapter 2 that a pentangle cannot be constructed without recourse to the mathematical principle of division into mean and extreme ratio. The poet seems to have known that readers of his manuscript might not realize that the mathematics of the pentangle reveals the machinery of his manuscript; therefore he made it more explicit by giving this shape a prolonged focus in the poem.[8] The first of the two stanzas describing the pentangle is even marked for special attention by a decorated initial, the first of the group of five decorated initials that stand three lines high. This stanza and the next (except for the wheel at lines 666–69) cover the final moments of Gawain's presence in Arthur's court, for immediately thereafter "He sperred þe sted with þe spurez and sprong on his way" (670).

One of the most significant features of the Divine Proportion, its expansion to ever greater magnitudes that nonetheless retain the same proportion (see chapter 2), finds verbal expression in the famous catalogue of "five fives" that the points of Gawain's endless knot represent: five wits (that is, senses), five fingers, five wounds of Christ, five joys of the Virgin, and five virtues. While the mathematics of the pentangle expands in size only, progress among these five groups moves to higher orders of being, from passive to active, from earthly to spiritual. Equally significant, this listing of five fives expands seamlessly—another endless knot—to higher levels of being, like the examples of ontological expansion in a single stanza of *Pearl*, where nature elevates an inert grain of sand to a gemstone and a statue receives literal life as Galatea. In *Sir Gawain* each group of five retains the properties of its predecessor, while ascending to a new dimension. The five senses register impressions in an entirely passive process, whether or not one wills these impressions to arrive or to be registered. The five fingers and the entire physical being that they obviously represent, though an integral part of the sentient process, require a positive decision of the will, an act that rises above that of the purely passive senses. The five wounds of Christ bridge the fleshly and the divine since, like any wounds, they afflict mortal flesh yet here mark the body of Christ.[9] The five joys that line 647 says "þe hende Heuen Quene had of hir Chylde" originate and remain in the mind, though they are inspired by physical circumstances and to this extent retain contact with the fleshly realm.[10] Finally, the five virtues or habits of will (*fraunchyse, felawschyp, clannes, cortaysye,* and *pité*) join a motif of circularity that has been a continuing feature of the entire manuscript. Nurtured through repeated acts in the extended world, virtues are entirely abstract, yet serve as guides for further expression in the same extended world, and thus complete a circular movement.

These important stanzas describing Gawain's pentangle and what it signifies nestle between two five-stanza sections, ostensibly unrelated to each other, but in fact linked through their similar relation to this pentangle. A subtle parallel is drawn between the passage of seasons through a year, which precedes Gawain's arming, and the passage of the knight through Logres, Wales, and Wirral, which follows it. What begins with descriptions of human activity in the context of winter—a yearning for tales that are slow to begin, a reference to men in their cups, and an admission that the merriment such cups produce often ends more quietly—shifts smoothly to a meditation on the passage of seasons. By selecting verbs normally associated with human activity, the poet artfully invests the year with more than the temporal and vegetative properties it actually possesses. Yule and the year "ouerȝede" (500), followed by a Lent that "fraystez" (503) for meat and a weather that "þrepez" (504) with winter. Following a summer that clothes in green its grounds and groves, and listens to noble notes in the wood, winter returns to wrestle (525) with the sun and to warn itself (or someone) to grow ripe (or ready) for the coming need.[11] Everything that once was green now turns gray and "al rypez and rotez þat ros vpon fyrst" (528).

If the graying of the earth were not enough to make clear that the subject is as much Man as it is the yearly cycle, a pointed allusion to Psalm 89:4 places Man's graying in the context of Judgment and the eternity that lies beyond, "And þus ȝirnes þe ȝere in ȝisterdayez mony" (529). More complex than a mere statement that everything in nature is fixed to a cycle, the conflation of vegetative nature and human nature demands that we understand the distinction between the two as well as their similarities. They both share the ripening, graying, and rotting of the physical realm. But nature's regeneration resurrects only the same seasons of many "ȝisterdayez," whereas man's regeneration replaces the physical realm with a spiritual eternity, like the mathematics of the Divine Proportion that expands a pentangle through ever larger dimensions toward a spatial infinity.

Whether Gawain forgets that this different regeneration awaits him, as the passing seasons and the unspoken condolences of the court remind him that he shares nature's decline but not her rebirth, is partly answered by the poem's description of his journey in the stanzas immediately following his vesting in the pentangle. We hear only of hunger, loneliness, depression, enemies, and cold. References to God are either formulaic (692, 702, 724) or in one instance pure litotes as it imagines God as a fellow to pass the time with along the way, "no gome bot God bi gate wyth to karp" (696). Although these frightful experiences are diametrically opposed to the elegance and finery at Camelot, both extremes allude to the same continuum implied by the pentangle's Divine Proportion, the opulent and the sparse, the mild and the savage, the infinitely great and the infinitely small. Not until the passing days place Gawain in extremis, the very condition Jonas found in the belly of a whale, does he make what seems to be a sincere prayer of supplication. The implications of this prayer, and especially whether memory of its efficacy will last long in Gawain's mind, are discussed below. Meanwhile, let us consider what follows the conclusion of this arduous journey in search of the Green Chapel.

For suspense, excitement, artful repartee, and skillful interleaving of visceral hunting in the fields and subtle preying in the boudoir, few scenes from any age equal the brilliant scenes at Bertilak's castle. Critical discussion has never doubted that Gawain errs on his third full day at the castle. Nor does anyone challenge that his most obvious error is his deliberate concealment from Bertilak of a green girdle he receives from the lady of the castle and fails to exchange with his host as required by the agreement in stanza 45. A prior error may have been committed by accepting the green girdle in the first place, although no critical consensus has emerged regarding what this error might be. As we saw in *Pearl*, where a crucial stanza (745–56) advances that poem's thematic design at the very point where its divine cut is located, so too in *Sir Gawain and the Green Knight* the numerical design of the scenes at Bertilak's castle leads to an understanding of Gawain's error.

The distribution of lines among these three days, and particularly their parallel divisions into four parts, achieve subtle proportions that guide us to the poem's meaning. Each day is very carefully divided into the same four parts: (1) the lord of the castle leading the first stage of each day's hunt; (2) Gawain being tempted at the castle; (3) the concluding stage of the hunt; and (4) the festivities at the end of the day when Gawain and Bertilak exchange gifts. I divide these scenes according to the event being described, often marked by an aural signal, rather than at stanza divisions.

First Day

	First Hunt Scene	Temptation Scene	Second Hunt Scene	Evening at Castle	Total
Scene	1a	1b	1c	1d	
Inclusive lines	1133-1178	1179-1318	1319-1364	1365-1411	
Total lines	46	140	46	47	279

Figure 6.3

As a result their inclusive lines differ slightly from A. Kent Hieatt's (1970, 128). On the first day, for example, where Hieatt counts the first hunting scene from the beginning of the fitt, I omit the first seven lines because the scene seems to me to begin at line 1133 where the lord of the castle arrives to lead the hunt to the forest. For the same reason I conclude the second hunting scene at the sound of the horn (1364), reckon the succeeding division to begin with the next line when attention shifts to Gawain at the castle rather than five lines later, and mark its end when "Vche burne to his bedde busked bylyue" (1411), one line before the cock crows the next morning. Other departures from Hieatt are similar.[12]

Figure 6.3 shows the relative sizes of these four scenes during Gawain's first day at Bertilak's court. One notices a certain balance in the way the scenes that advance the agreement between Gawain and Bertilak, scenes 1a, 1c, and 1d, have very nearly the same number of aggregate lines (139) as scene 1b (140), which from Gawain's perspective lies outside both this recent agreement and the one made a year ago. This kind of balance seems appropriate. Behaving as honorably in the castle as Bertilak behaves in the forest, Gawain can be justly proud of neither insulting his host with dishonesty, nor offending his hostess with discourtesy while yet resisting her unambiguous invitation:

'Nay forsoþe, beau sir,' sayd þat swete,
'Ʒe schal not rise of your bedde. I rych yow better:
I schal happe yow here þat oþer half als

And syþen karp wyth my kny3t þat I ka3t haue.

. . . .

　　3e ar welcum to my cors,
　　Yowre awen won to wale.'[13]

(1222–25; 1237–38)

After a certain amount of study, however, a curious arithmetic progression emerges, when the whole day is compared to its first half and its second half:

$$(1a + 1b + 1c + 1d) : (1a + 1b) : (1c + 1d)$$

$$279 : 186 : 93$$

$$3 : 2 : 1$$

This continuous arithmetic ratio may also be thought of as musical proportions. The ratio 3 : 2 : 1 produces a string ratio composed of an outer twelfth, 3 : 1, divided into lower fifth, 3 : 2, and upper octave, 2 : 1. For example, the fifth would be produced by the chord from C to G, followed by the octave from G to G'. All three of these intervals are concords going back to Boethius: *diapente cum diapason* or twelfth, *diapente* or fifth, and *diapason* or octave (Bower 1967, 55, 413). The proportions among the lines on this first day imply a musical harmony perfectly suited to Gawain's having resisted the temptation to compromise his values.

On the second day Gawain again finds himself subjected to serious temptation, and again he rejects the lady's entreaties, though with a response more suggestive of the boar being hunted by Bertilak this day, than the elegant doe and hind he hunted the day before. To the lady's professed disappointment that he has not taught her the subtleties of love, especially since her lord is away (1534), the knight responds with words that come close to accusing her of a sordid past:

Bot to take þe toruayle to myself to trwluf expoun
And towche þe temez of tyxt and talez of armez
To yow, þat (I wot wel) weldez more sly3t
Of þat art, bi þe half, or a hundreth of seche
As I am, oþer euer schal in erde þer I leue,
Hit were a folé felefolde, my fre, by my trawþe.

(1540–45)

As shown in figure 6.4, the relative lengths of these scenes, too, scarcely draw attention, since they look similar to those of the first day: the total is

Second Day

	First Hunt Scene	Temptation Scene	Second Hunt Scene	Evening at Castle	Total
Scene	2a	2b	2c	2d	
Inclusive lines	1412-1468	1469-1560	1561-1618	1619-1687	
Total lines	57	92	58	69	276

Figure 6.4

almost identical; scene 2b is again much larger than the others while scenes 2a, 2c, and 2d are close to each other in size. Despite these similarities, every number has changed. The proportion, however, remains identical to the proportion of the first day, another continuous arithmetic proportion producing a musical fifth and an octave. Now, however, the common factor is 92, the line total of scene 2b, the proportion taking shape as follows:

$$(2a + 2b + 2c + 2d) : (2a + 2c + 2d) : 2b$$

$$276 : 184 : 92$$

$$3 : 2 : 1$$

That the common factor has now shifted to scene 2b where Gawain is tempted, whereas the common factor on the first day was shown in the conclusion of the hunt and the exchange of gifts, emphasizes that Gawain's behavior has replaced the hunt and its social aftermath as the most important activity transpiring in Bertilak's world.

The arrangement of scenes on this second day has, as well, a subsidiary concord produced by a highly unusual string, more expansive than the harmonious chord we have already seen. The common factor here is 23:

$$(2a + 2b + 2c + 2d) : (2a + 2c) : 2b : 2d$$

$$276 : 115 : 92 : 69$$

$$12 : 5 : 4 : 3$$

Third Day

	First Hunt Scene	Temptation Scene	Second Hunt Scene	Evening at Castle	Total
Scene	3a	3b	3c	3d	
Inclusive lines	1688-1730	1731-1893	1894-1923	1924-1990	
Total lines	43	163	30	67	303

Figure 6.5

It is intriguing that the proportions that include 5 as one of their magnitudes, namely 12 : 5, 5 : 4, and 5 : 3, show up on this second day. These five-based ratios do not occur in Pythagorean intonation, although they are showcased in the musical theory of the Renaissance. I say "intriguing" because they suggest the poet chose intervals especially pertinent for *Sir Gawain and the Green Knight*, a poem based very decidedly on fives. The outer interval 12 : 3, or 4 : 1, called *disdiapason* or double octave and recognized from antiquity on, though unattested in the polyphonic music of the fourteenth century as far as I know, provides further potential evidence that the poet is exploiting musical harmony to advance the manuscript's thematic content. This second day's proportions, while remaining as harmonious as those of the first day, expand to include a wider range of tones, as the manuscript's use of a single Old-English poetic line expands to a rubric encompassing four poems, and as the geometry of the Divine Section permits any *phi*-related line segments to expand to infinity.

The scene divisions of the third day are an entirely different matter. In fact, they produce no recognizable proportion. (See figure 6.5.) With scenes 3a, 3b, and 3d showing prime numbers in their line totals, it is impossible for any meaningful proportion to emerge, either in the integer series or in the prime series (43 is the 13th prime, 163 the 37th, and 67 the 18th). As music, the day's totals produce nothing but cacophony. As geste, the day itself yields nothing of value. In the field Bertilak takes only the ignoble fox, "For I haf hunted al þis day and noȝt haf I geten / Bot þis foule fox felle—þe Fende haf þe godez!" (1943–44).

These mathematical proportions in fitt 3, while never appearing in the explicit language of the text, nevertheless point more effectively to Gawain's error than do the regrets he expresses later at the chapel when the Green Knight reveals himself as Bertilak and explains that the three swings of his axe—one dodged, the second halted, and the third a mere graze—are related to Gawain's behavior during the three days he rested at the castle. Referring to the last of these days, the Green Knight gives only a vague statement of Gawain's fault, "At þe þrid þou fayled þore, . . . here yow lakked a lyttel, sir, and lewté yow wonted" (2356, 2366). It is certainly clear that Gawain was wrong to conceal from his host the green girdle that rightfully should have been exchanged. But the more problematic question about *lewté* remains: To what, precisely, is Gawain disloyal? The knight himself proves a doubtful authority on the subject when he thrice blames himself for *cowardyse* and *couetyse* (2374, 2379–80, 2508), adding at even greater length that "þurʒ wyles of wymmen [he] be wonen to sorʒe" (2415). There is not the least evidence for any of these explanations. His merely seeking out the Green Chapel is proof enough of his bravery. And if he thought that evidence of cowardice may be seen in his flinch at the Green Knight's first swing of the axe, he would be wrong again, since that swing and the dodge that reacts to it are related to the first day's temptation, where Gawain successfully resists a dangerous assault with artful dodging. Of avarice he is even less guilty:

> Ho raʒt hym a riche rynk of red golde werkez,
> Wyth a starande ston stondande alofte,
> Þat bere blusschande bemez as þe bryʒt sunne;
> Wyt ʒe wel, hit watz worth wele ful hoge.
> Bot þe renk hit renayed and redyly he sayde,
> "I wil no giftez, for Gode, my gay, at þis tyme;
> I haf none yow to norne ne noʒt wyl I take."
> (1817–23)

As for the "wyles of wymmen" and the seductive enticements this phrase usually conjures, Gawain may well be the most "fautles freke on folde." Not once does he even consider the pleasurable opportunity presented to him, much less act upon it.

Gawain's unpersuasive explanations aside, the poet has embedded in the numerical design of fitt 3 a clear indication that the knight's action on the third day brings disharmony to the scene. A brief remark that Gawain makes better than he knows, explaining to Bertilak that he will always wear the green girdle "in syngne of my surfet" (2433), gives a hint of how this disharmony expresses itself in the thematic progress of the poem. Although *surfet* as a word may be as elusive as the green girdle is as a symbol, Cawley and Anderson (1976) translate it as "fault" and Andrew and Waldron (1979) as "transgression." The *OED* does list these variants as the second of eight possible meanings, citing as its first authority this very line in *Sir Gawain*, but these broad translations ignore the sense that the other seven meanings share, the more usual fourteenth-century meaning, "excess, superfluity; excessive amount or supply of something" (*OED*, senses 1, 3, 4, etc.). If the poem's mathematics parallels its thematic meaning, the disproportions of the third day produce cacophony in the social sphere, as Gawain's *surfet* conveys imbalance in the moral sphere.

Whether Gawain passes accurate theological judgment on himself—that the stain of sin is permanent, "twynne wil hit neuer" (2512)—may be moot in the light of evidence that the knight is completely exonerated, a reading based on evidence that David Aers conveniently summarizes (1997, 95–97). From a purely ontological consideration, however, if the phrase "permanently stained" refers to original sin, the judgment is absolutely correct; Gawain is indeed a mortal man, subject to the same limitations of the flesh that everyone experiences. His failure, then, is his reluctance to acknowledge his mere mortality, that he is *by nature* imperfect. The fault is a slight one, as the Green Knight himself says (2362–68), but Gawain's failure to realize he has such a fault violates the ordered structure of the universe by subtly elevating himself above the sphere of humanity—an excess, a pride, a *surfet* perhaps greater than the *felix culpa* of original sin. True enough, Gawain is permanently stained with sin, but it is none of the culpable sins he tries to attribute to cowardice, greed, or woman. It is the unacceptable (to him) sin of being mortal, a stain he gave no earlier evidence of acknowledging with sincerity.

The remark made by the Green Knight, noted above, may now be more readily understood. The failure of loyalty the Green Knight alleges of Gawain was immediately evident when the Virgin Mary's own knight, as he is called, placed greater faith in the magic of a green girdle to keep him from harm than in Christ who had protected him well to this point. The efficacy of prayer had been made clear to Gawain earlier when he was lost in "a forest ful dep" (741) and in need of a fit place to attend Mass the following day, Christmas morn:

> "I beseche Þe, Lorde,
> And Mary, þat is myldest moder so dere,

O sum herber þer heʒly I myʒt here masse
Ande Þy matynez tomorne, mekely I ask,
And þerto prestly I pray my Pater and Aue
    And Crede."
  He rode in his prayere
  And cryed for his mysdede.
  He sayned hym in syþes sere
  And sayde, "Cros Kryst me spede."

Nade he sayned hymself, segge, bot þrye
Er he watz war in þe wod of a won in a mote
. . . .
A castel þe comlokest þat euer knyʒt aʒte,
Pyched on a prayere . . .
(753–64, 767–68)

This recent demonstration that the cross of Christ has the power to pitch a castle on a prayer[14] should have convinced Gawain that prayer and the faith it implies could see him through any travail, either in Bertilak's castle or at the Green Chapel. For readers of Cotton Nero A.x this sudden appearance of Bertilak's castle should confirm what was dramatized in *Patience* when Jonas was granted deliverance from the belly of a whale immediately after making a sincere prayer to God (305–36). Nevertheless, instead of calling upon *Cros Kryst* a second time, he places desperate faith in the alleged magic of a pagan symbol, erring spiritually by turning away from his most effective protector in the past. This lapse of faith is a greater fault than the error it begets in the sphere of human relations, his concealing the girdle from Bertilak and failure to exchange it with him as required by agreement. Schmidt puts the point precisely, "His failure is the result of inadequate faith . . . an inadequate understanding of the precise action dictated by a robust faith in the sufficiency of God's grace" (1987, 164). The spiritual and social harmony sustained during the first two days disappears on this third day.

    The disharmony of Gawain's failures of faith and courtesy receives greater emphasis by contrasting sharply with the wider numerical design of fitt 3 and of the poem as a whole. The chart at figure 4.2 in chapter 4 shows that sections 6 through 12 of *Purity* have the same number of lines, 872, as fitt 3 of *Sir Gawain*. The subdivisions of fitt 3 also appear uncannily in the section totals of *Purity*, underscoring yet again that the second poem in the manuscript acts as the blueprint for the entire mathematical design. The fitt begins with a large decorated initial letter at line 1126, indicated by

Fitt III, lines 1126-1997

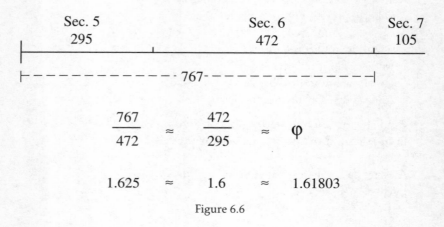

Figure 6.6

the large vertical stroke in figure 6.6. Two more decorated initial letters, approximately one-half the size of the initial at the beginning of the fitt, appear at lines 1421 and 1893, shown here by two small vertical strokes. The three quantities embraced by these decorated initials—the 295 lines from 1126 to 1420, that is, section 5 of *Sir Gawain* (cf. sections 6–9 of *Purity* with 296 lines), the 472 lines from 1421 to 1892, that is, section 6 (cf. *Purity*'s 476 lines in sections 2–7), and the aggregate 767 lines of sections 5 and 6 (cf. 768 lines in sections 2–10 of *Purity*)—constitute a nearly perfect Divine Section, as shown in the last line of figure 6.6.[15] While the activity of the human figures in Bertilak's castle has been creating mundane divisions, as we have seen, this elegant counterpart, unlikely to be disturbed either by Gawain's transgressions at Hautdesert or Jonas's dereliction in *Patience*, implies that a more artistic craftsman is evidently overseeing the wider harmony of the universe.

Confirmation that the poem contains implicit references to this divine artificer, consistent with the poem's most important motifs, may be found, again, in the numerical design of the poem. Since every Divine Proportion implies a golden rectangle, one would be understandably tempted to assume that the Divine Proportion created by sections 5 and 6 would define such a rectangle. Its dimensions would be either 767 x 472, or 472 x 295. But this assumption would ignore section 7, the 105–line segment of the line in figure 6.6. By adding section 5 (295 lines from 1126–1420) and section 7 (105 lines from 1893–1997), which together total 400 lines, a more promising rectangle begins to take shape. A dodecahedron whose pentagonal faces can be circumscribed by a 180–radius circle has internal golden rectangles measuring 401.27 on their longer sides and diagonals measuring 472.12. This, then, is the golden rectangle defined by fitt 3. It completes this final poem's contribution to the overall design of the manuscript, which seems to call for a dodecahedron to represent the three-dimensional universe and three planes within this dodecahedron to receive three different histories enacted on the two-dimensional surface of the earth. That the poet did not choose to accomplish this purpose by simply dividing fitt 3 into two sections of 400 and 472 lines implies that a different objective was sought. The extended hypothesis of this study holds that this additional objective is the encoding of the cross of Christ, which the poet begins to construct by dividing the smaller of these two numbers, 400, into 295 and 105.

Before proceeding to this final reach of the poet's strategy let us recall two details discussed in previous chapters to see how they merge in *Sir Gawain and the Green Knight*. First, the entire manuscript comprises a Divine Proportion: the two medial poems constitute the lesser extreme of 2343 lines; *Pearl* and *Sir Gawain* represent the mean of 3743; and the 6086 lines of the entire manuscript complete the proportion by displaying the greater extreme. Second, all four poems in the manuscript respond in various ways to the appeal Gawain himself makes to the cross at lines 762–63. *Pearl* describes a procession leading to the Lamb; *Purity* gives prominent attention to the birth of Christ; *Patience* shows God's infinite mercy, a divine attribute usually associated with Christ; and *Sir Gawain*, in addition to showing its hero appealing to the cross in 762–63, identifies the wounds Christ suffered on the cross as one of the five fives signified by the pentangular emblem on his shield.

The Divine Proportion is often expressed as a rectangle whose sides are in a *phi* relation. Since the numerical design of the manuscript reveals this proportion twice, it can be illustrated with two rectangles, as shown in figure 6.7. The poet seems to have been drawn to the smaller of these two rectangles, representing *Pearl* and *Sir Gawain* vertically, *Purity* and *Patience* horizontally, whereas the larger rectangle represents *Pearl* and *Sir Gawain* horizontally and the entire manuscript vertically. The dimensions of the smaller rectangle permit an easy arrangement of an image of the cross, shown in figure 6.8.

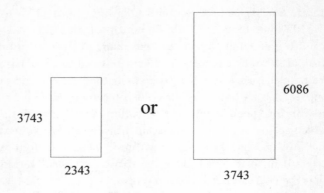

Figure 6.7

While there can be no certainty regarding the poet's actual design for *Sir Gawain and the Green Knight*,[16] short of discovering an historical record, the claim that the sizes of the poem's fitts and sections encode an image of Christ's cross rests on a theme that is undeniably present in the poem as well as in the dimensions of several of its sections. The four major parts, or fitts, of *Sir Gawain*, unlike the whole manuscript, do not fit as easily into a cross design as do the four poems in the manuscript. Only fitts 1 and 3 are in a *phi* ratio—and only when their stanza-counts are compared, not their total lines. If, however, we consider the fitts and sections of *Sir Gawain* in the same way we came to understand the divisions and sections of *Purity,*

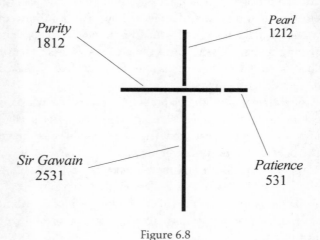

Figure 6.8

that is, as detailed instructions for creating a design, we shall see that instructions for a design emerge from this poem too. The opening section of fitt 3, that is, the poem's fifth section extending from the major initial at line 1126 to just before the decorated initial in line 1421, totals 295 lines. If we turn again to the manuscript's blueprint in chapter 4 (i.e., figure 4.7), we see that the distance between the inner and outer circles, measured from P' to P, is 296. This is the same measurement as A'A in figure 6.9. It differs from the number of lines in the opening section of fitt 3 of *Sir Gawain* by only one unit. Consequently the succeeding section in *Sir Gawain*, section 6, becomes immediately pertinent, for its total number of lines, 472, is almost exactly the measurement of the outer circle's radius OA'. In chapter 4 we labeled this radius 476, shown as radius OP in figure

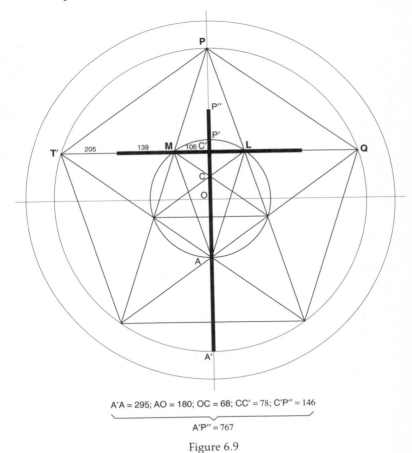

A'A = 295; AO = 180; OC = 68; CC' = 78; C'P" = 146

A'P" = 767

Figure 6.9

4.7, equal to sections 2–7 of *Purity,* noting at the same time that there may be a four-unit error in this measurement.[17]

As the first two sections of *Patience* announced a magnitude of 60 constructed on a scale defined by a circle of radius 180, so the first two sections of fitt 3 in *Sir Gawain* (i.e., sections 5 and 6) serve the same purpose. Section 5, measuring 295, indicates the distance from A' to A. Section 6 identifies the scale on which A'A will equal this measurement, namely the particular stage in the pentangle's expansions when an enclosing circle has a radius of 472. If these two *phi*-related dimensions[18] are also added together, as occurs when the two unequal segments of every Divine Proportion expand to its next expression, they produce a magnitude represented by the broad, vertical line in figure 6.9, reaching an undetermined, freestanding point, labeled P'', located somewhere between P and P'. I suggest that the author imagines this line as the vertical beam of the cross of Christ, which also stands free. The total length of this broad vertical line in figure 6.9 is 767, only one unit less than the number of lines in sections 2 through 10 of *Purity.* It happens, not coincidentally, to be the exact amount by which radius OA' must be extended to equal 1239, the radius of the next expansion of the pentagon/pentangle design the poet has been using throughout the manuscript.[19] Appendix 3 explains the mathematics the poet may have used to calculate these expansions. I list here the sizes of the various segments of A'P'':

$$A'A + AO + OC + CC' + C'P'' = 767$$

$$295 + 180 + 68 + 78 + 146 = 767$$

Determining the size and location of the cross-beam to complete the construction of the cross depends on a different kind of reasoning. Of the four poems in the manuscript only two—*Purity* and *Sir Gawain and the Green Knight*—employ an irregular system of decorated initials of different sizes to indicate major and minor blocks of text.[20] *Purity* has three main divisions and thirteen sections; *Sir Gawain* has four fitts and nine sections. In all this complicated assignment of lines to divisions and sections, fitt 1 of *Sir Gawain* is unique. Though it is a major division, it has no small decorated initials indicating internal sections. Since many of the sections in *Purity* are related to measurements along the vertical *y*-axis, we may tentatively infer that fitt 1, without internal sections, indicates measurement on a horizontal line. Still to be determined is where on the vertical axis these 490 horizontal units should be placed. Among the existing horizontal lines in figure 6.9, only T'Q crosses the vertical axis at a point indicated by a dimension in *Sir Gawain*. The distance from the center O of the figure to point C', where T'Q crosses the vertical axis, is two units greater than the number of lines in section 3 of *Sir Gawain:* OC' measures 146; section 3 has 144 lines. If the cross-beam were assumed to have a thickness of 4 units, then the 144 units indicated by section 3 would be the exact measurement from the center of the medallion at O to the *bottom* of the cross-beam.

Apart from section 3 in figure 6.2, the remaining sections 1, 2, and 4 of fitts 1 and 2 present a puzzle. It is unclear why sections 2 and 4 almost exactly duplicate the number of lines in fitt 1: 128 + 363 = 491. A similar arrangement appears in the first three sections of *Purity*, where the 124 lines of section 1 equal the 68 and 56 lines of sections 2 and 3. But these figures, 124, 68, and 56, reveal significant dimensions of the geometric figure implied by that poem. And 124 by itself equals one-fourth the size of *Purity*'s sections 3 through 8. No such correspondence is discernable for these dimensions in *Sir Gawain*. Nor can an explanation be found in the resulting segments of the cross-beam when it is centered on line T'Q. Line LM was shown in chapter 4 to measure 212, half of which is 106 for segment C'M. The remaining length of the outer segment of the cross-beam would then be 139, and the distance from the outer tip of the cross-beam to point T', or to point Q for the other half of the beam, would be 205. None of these quantities seems to have a role in either the thematics of the poem or the measurements of the geometric figure we have been working with.

There is, however, one persuasive correspondence between the poem's thematics and the size of fitt 1, and consequently between the poem and the cross-beam of Christ's cross. We noted above that the number of lines assigned to the day on which Gawain shows a failure of *trawþe* in Bertilak's castle, while Bertilak himself hunts a "foule fox" (1944) in the wood, totals 303. By itself this number has some slight promise, since it is one of the factors of the 1212 lines in *Pearl,* and can itself be factored by 101, the number of stanzas in both *Pearl* and *Sir Gawain*. Although its divisions into that day's four distinct parts, as noted above, do not produce the pleasing musical proportions of the first two days, this is not to say that the third day has no role in the overall strategy of the poem. For if 303 is multiplied by the proportion that organizes the entire manuscript, in other words by the Divine Proportion, it produces the exact number of lines in fitt 1 and, if that fitt contributes to the geometric design suggested here, the exact size of the cross-beam of the cross of Christ:

$$303 \times 1.61803 = 490.26$$

The cross always implies a double significance, both a symbol of Christianity, including the faith Christians repose in Christ, and an image of how Mankind habitually treats God's Incarnation. An oft-repeated image in Christian tradition assumes that every transgression, however minor, offends God and helps to crucify Christ anew. The numerical association of the third day of Gawain's sojourn at Bertilak's castle, when he violates both his faith in God and his covenant with his host, with the cross of Christ, which is an integral part of the geometric design of Cotton Nero A.x, makes inescapable the conclusion that Gawain's conduct on his third day in Bertilak's castle offends the moral order. However subtle his *surfet* may be in leading to a failure of *trawþe* toward God and man, in some slight way Gawain has helped crucify Christ anew.

The poem, therefore, takes a circuitous route we have seen before. Like the Dreamer in *Pearl*, Gawain arrives by the last stanzas of the poem at that uncertain terrain between this life and the next, between his confidence that his recent sojourn gave him ultimate insight and earned God's favor, and the suspicion—in many a reader's mind if not in his own—that such self-assurance may place that favor in jeopardy. That he is ashamed of his conduct at some level, there can be no doubt. But this proper response fades behind the bitterness that blames his mad folly on the "wyles of wymmen" (2415) and the scent of *surfet* that equates him with Adam, Solomon, Samson, and David, men whose similar betrayal by women he hopes will mitigate his own:

> "And alle þay were biwyled
> With wymmen þat þay vsed.
> Þaȝ I be now bigyled,
> Me þink me burde be excused."
> (2425–28)

Bertilak attempts gently to correct Gawain's thought that the stratagem engineered by Morgan le Fay was intended to test Gawain for cowardice and covetousness. In fact, as Bertilak explicitly says, it was conceived to test the court for pride (*surquidré*):

"[Morgan le Fay] wayned me vpon þis wyse to your wynne halle
For to assay þe surquidré, ȝif hit soth were
Þat rennes of þe grete renoun of þe Rounde Table."
(2456–58)

But this unambiguous explanation has no more staying power with
Gawain than the efficacy of prayer has with Jonas, or either has with humanity in general, lapsed as the race is by nature. Once he returns to
Camelot, the Gawain we observed at the beginning of the poem surfaces
again. Though we are told that he recounts to the court the whole of his
adventure, the only words quoted from the knight recall his first speech
(343–61), where language and its form seem to be the only truths. Here, at
the end of the poem, though his literal words are above reproach, the force
of the speech as a whole is unsettling:

"Lo! Lorde," quoþ þe leude, and þe lace hondeled,
"Þis is þe bende of þis blame I bere in my nek.
Þis is þe laþe and þe losse þat I laȝt haue
Of couardise and couetyse, þat I haf caȝt þare;
Þis is þe token of vntrawþe þat I am tan inne.
And I mot nedez hit were wyle I may last;
For mon may hyden his harme bot vnhap ne may hit,
For þer hit onez is tachched twynne wil hit neuer."
(2505–12)

While Gawain's admission of "vntrawþe" (2509) shows promise in ad-
mitting a fault he had not previously acknowledged and in apparently replacing his indictment of women a hundred lines earlier, the word remains
vague, in need of expansion and greater specificity. Most important, there
is no admission of pride in this speech. Indeed the knight repeats the empty
charges of "couardise and couetyse" (2508; cf. 2374, 2379–80) first introduced to emend Bertilak's observation that on the third day Gawain
"lakked a lyttel, . . . and lewté yow wonted" (2366). As a whole, the speech
is especially troubling for its cyclic recurrence of self-satisfaction, its implication that "nothing is, but saying makes it so" (to adapt another poet).
Bertilak and everyone at Hautdesert know well Gawain's blemishes. So do
the readers of the poem. The uncertainty, however, is whether Gawain
himself has come to understand his "blame," his "laþe," and his "losse," or

if he is doing no more here than giving a formulaic expression of humility that no one, certainly not the court at Camelot, really believes. And that little word "vnhap" (2509), so like the Dreamer's "happe" (1195) at the end of *Pearl*, has the effect of suggesting that both protagonists view the moral choices in their lives as a matter of chance. Far from diminishing either the Dreamer in *Pearl* or Gawain in the final poem, this inability or unwillingness to understand and admit the nature of their faults makes them painfully familiar.

Afterword

The implication of the highly wrought strategy we have been discussing, in which mathematics serves as a revealing analogue to metaphysical matters, might be stated in various ways depending on the context one wishes to emphasize. To a mathematician the conversion of a measuring system based on fours into a system based on fives requires the magic of an irrational number that leads to infinity if applied repeatedly. To a medieval theologian the New Law expands and enriches the Old Law through the advent of Christ, whose teaching, if continuously applied, in turn translates the New into eternal salvation. To a poet there is little difference, for his epiphany comes in recognizing the parallel between mathematics and theology and in realizing poetry's power to make palpable what would otherwise be ineffable. *Pearl* and *Sir Gawain and the Green Knight* have a foot in both the four-cornered world and the world that supersedes it. The duodecimal basis of the former, the four fitts of the latter, and the worldly concerns of both suggest the sphere of *Purity* and *Patience*. The 5^2 prime number of stanzas in both *Pearl* and *Sir Gawain*, the fifth Platonic solid suggested by the former, and the latter's pentangular emblem, five-line bob-and-wheel, and power of regeneration imply the abode of the *Pearl*-maiden. Above it all lies the manuscript's astonishing representation of elegant coherence. The profound congruence of the universe with man's theological and moral concerns, and with all that lies on his too-much-loved earth, unfolds before us with subtle simplicity. The disciplines of the quadrivium—arithmetic, music, geometry, and astronomy—have been drawing their lines unwaveringly toward the judgment on which will depend the eternity, not only of the characters described in its lines, but also of every reader humbled by this manuscript's exquisite beauty.

Appendix 1

Geometric and Algebraic Construction
of the Divine Proportion

However uncertain are the circumstances that led to the discovery of "division into extreme and mean ratio"—whether it predates the Pythagoreans, was contemporaneous with them, or was caused by the acceptance of incommensurability—its geometrical construction was well known to the medieval world. Mathematicians assume that the proportion was probably first demonstrated by a geometry of the Euclidean type, rather than by Babylonian quadratics. To find the Divine Section C on line AB in figure A.1, bisect AB and construct two adjacent squares. BD therefore equals one-half AB. Draw diagonal AD across these adjacent squares. With D as center and DB as radius, construct an arc to intersect AD at E. With A as center and AE as radius, construct an arc to intersect AB at C. Point C divides line AB into "mean and extreme ratio." The smaller extreme is CB; the larger extreme is AB; and the mean between them is AC. Stating the matter as the Divine Proportion satisfies two equations: (1) AB : AC = AC : CB; and (2) AC + CB = AB. The first of these equations may also be stated reciprocally, CB : AC = AC : AB, without changing the second equation.

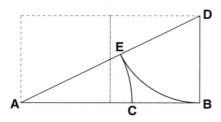

Figure A.1

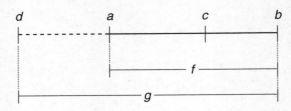

Figure A.2

Figure A.2 shows a unique feature of this continuous ratio. Since the first two terms (*ac* and *cb*) equal its third (*ab*), and since the larger segment *ac* has already been shown to be in a *phi* ratio with *ab*, a new term in the next larger demonstration of the Divine Proportion may be found by adding the larger segment (*ac*) to the whole line (*ab*) of the original figure. In figure A.2 let point *c* be the divine cut of line *ab*, making *cb* the smaller segment and *ac* the larger segment and also the mean between *cb* and *ab*. Extend *ba* to *d*, such that *ad* = *ac*. Another, larger demonstration of the

$$\frac{ab}{ac} = \frac{ac}{cb}$$

Let *ac* = x and *cb* = 1. Then *ab* = x + 1.

$$\frac{x + 1}{x} = \frac{x}{1}$$

$$x^2 - x - 1 = 0$$

$$x = \frac{1 + \sqrt{5}}{2} \qquad \text{[pos. solution]}$$

$$x = 1.61803$$

Figure A.3

Divine Section results. In the original solid-line demonstration of figure A.2 *ac* is the larger segment, or mean, in the *phi* ratio *cb* : *ac* = *ac* : *f*. By folding *ac* out, as it were, *ad* now becomes the smaller segment, *ab* the larger, and point *c* disappears in a new demonstration of the *phi* ratio: *ad* : *ab* = *ab* : *g*. And so on toward infinity, with the proportion always remaining constant.

The procedures for solving algebraic equations were well known to the Middle Ages, originally arriving in Europe in a Latin translation of al-Khwarizmi's pre-850 A.D. treatise *al-jabr*. The meaning of this tri-syllabic Arabic word presumably refers to the rule for changing signs when transposing, but its sound gave the West the name algebra (Boyer and Merzbach 1989, 227–30). If *ab* : *ac* = *ac* : *cb* in the solid-line portion of figure A.2, the value of *phi* can be found algebraically and then converted into a modern decimal (see figure A.3). Rearranging the equation, such that *cb* : *ac* = *ac* : *ab*, retains the proportion, but the solution for *x* would then be the reciprocal of *phi*: *x* = 0.61803.

Appendix 2

Construction of Three *Phi*-related Rectangles within a Dodecahedron, Using Medieval Mathematics, with an Assist from Modern Decimals

Every regular dodecahedron encloses three identical rectangles that intersect each other at right angles, sharing among them only the geometric center of the solid. The twelve corners of these rectangles (three rectangles x four corners each) touch the centroids of the twelve faces of the solid.

From Euclid it was known that a line between the centroids of any two adjacent faces constitutes the short edge of one of these inscribed rectangles. This edge is also an edge of the dodecahedron's dual, an icosahedron. From the same source the Middle Ages knew that the ratio of a dodecahedron's edge to the edge of its inscribed icosahedron is 2 : (1 + 3 / √5), in modern notation 1 : 1.17082. This short side of an inscribed rectangle is therefore 12 x 1.17082, or 14.04984.

Further, every dodecahedron has an inscribed sphere that, by definition, also touches the dodecahedron at its twelve centroids. The diameter of this inscribed sphere would therefore also be equal to the diagonal of these identical inscribed rectangles. Medieval mathematicians used the equation in figure B.1 for determining the radius, r, of a dodecahedron's inscribed sphere, although the fourteenth century would have used a fractional con-

$$r = \frac{\sqrt{(250 + 110\sqrt{5})}}{20} \quad x \quad \text{length of edge}$$

Figure B.1

vergent for the square root of 5.[1] Since the length of an edge has already been chosen as 12, the equation gives 13.36219 as the radius of the inscribed sphere of a dodecahedron measuring 12 on each edge.[2]

Since the radius of the inscribed sphere within this dodecahedron is 13.362, its diameter, 26.72439 (double the radius), is therefore the length of the diagonal of an inscribed rectangle. Two dimensions of the inscribed rectangle are now known: the short edge, 14.04984, and the diagonal, 26.72439. The long edge of the rectangle can now be found by using the Pythagorean theorem:

$$14.04984^2 + b^2 = 26.72439^2$$

$$b = 22.73312$$

These inscribed rectangles therefore measure 14.049 by 22.733. It is not surprising that the sides of these rectangles are in a *phi* ratio: 14.04984 x 1.61803 = 22.73306.

Chapter 5 discusses the dimensions of the three inscribed, *phi*-related rectangles in a dodecahedron that has been expanded three times from the initial dodecahedron which measured 12 on each edge. There are two ways of computing the dimensions of these three identical rectangles. It is highly instructive to examine both methods, for it is relatively easy to see that the poet used only one of these methods, the one that had the lesser opportunity for error.

Method 1. The initial dodecahedron, with edges measuring 12, produces internal rectangles of length 22.73312, width 14.04984, and diagonal 26.72439. To discover the dimensions of the rectangles in a dodecahedron that has been expanded three times from this initial dodecahedron, each of these measurements would be multiplied by *phi* six times, rounding off each result to prepare for the next multiplication, as shown in chapter 3, 65–66. This method of calculating gives length 411, width 254, and diagonal 487.

Method 2. Each edge of the initial dodecahedron measures 12. This dimension, multiplied by *phi* six times, yields 212 as the length of the edge of a dodecahedron that has been expanded three times from the original dodecahedron. Multiplying 212 by the equation for discovering the edge of a dodecahedron's dual, an icosahedron, produces 248.21. In addition to being the length of an edge of an icosahedron, this dimension also measures the short edge, that is the width, of the inscribed, *phi*-related rectangle in this expanded dodecahedron. The length is therefore 401.27. The diagonal would be computed from the equation for determining the radius of the dodecahedron's inscribed sphere. That equation produces a radius of 235.745, rounded to 236, doubled to measure the diagonal at 472.[3] Two of these dimensions are precisely echoed by the line lengths of sections in *Purity:* sections 1, 2, and 3 of *Purity* total 248. And sections 4 and 5 of *Purity* total 236, the precise measurement of the radius of the sphere inscribed in a dodecahedron whose sides are 212.

That method 2 gives dimensions almost identical to line totals in sections of *Purity,* a poem that has elsewhere proved a reliable blueprint for the geometric figure encoded by Cotton Nero A.x, whereas the dimensions produced by method 1 are two, three, and four units away from the closest totals in *Purity,* strongly suggests that the poet used method 2 to calculate the size of the inscribed rectangles in the dodecahedron from which he modeled his manuscript.

Appendix 3

The Poet's Successive Expansion of His Fundamental Design with Speculation about His Correction of an Error

Figure 6.9, based on figure 4.7 to which readers are referred for more complete annotations, shows three stages in the poet's expanding design, all related by the Divine Proportion. Each expansion requires a given dimension to be multiplied twice by *phi* in order to find the next larger corresponding dimension. For example, line CL must be multiplied by *phi* to determine, first, the length of line ML. Then ML must be multiplied by *phi* to determine the length of MP. This process can also be expressed by stating that a given line must be multiplied by φ^2 to find the next corresponding expansion; for example, CL x φ^2 = MP. The same process is true for all corresponding lines. In the case of radii, OC (the radius of a circle not actually drawn, but understood to circumscribe the innermost pentagon in figure 6.9) multiplied by φ^2 produces radius OP'. In turn, radius OP' multiplied by φ^2 produces radius OP, and so on.

Using a modern calculator it can be shown that, as the poet progressed to each larger stage, an increasing error was introduced. Because the dimensions of the figure shown within the circle of radius 180 (circle MJAKL in figure 4.7) show no errors when they are compared with section lengths in *Purity*, or very slight ones, we can conclude that he began to construct the design within this circle. Working outward from 180, toward the next larger circle, we calculate the next radius at 471.24379. But instead of using this precise magnitude for OP, he apparently understood this radius to be 476, sections 2 through 7 of *Purity*. If he had permitted this 476 to remain uncorrected, the next larger radius, measured from O to the intersection of T'S extended and QR extended (not shown in figure 6.9), would have been 1246.17803, or a little larger. But no such line count exists in *Purity*. Since the closest corresponding number in *Purity* is 1232, shown as the total of sections 2 through 12, we may conclude that the poet made a correction at some stage near the completion of this third expansion. If we work backward from 1232, we arrive at a magnitude of 470.57605 for line OP, an amount less than one unit smaller than the 471.24379 accurately calculated from the original radius of 180.

Glossary of Mathematical Terms
for the Nonmathematician

Arithmetic Mean. A simple average between a greater and a lesser magnitude. See *Proportion, Arithmetic.*

Commensurable. Two magnitudes are said to be commensurable if they can be compared according to the same measure. For example, 3/4 and 2/3 are commensurable because they can each be expressed in terms of twelfths, 9/12 and 8/12, respectively. Commensurable is a synonym for "rational," meaning the ability to be expressed as a *ratio.*

Cube. In geometry, a *regular polyhedron* with 6 square *faces.*

Cube Root. In mathematics, a positive *whole number* that, when raised to the third power (i.e., $n \times n \times n$), produces a whole number. The term cube root implies two numbers, the root and the cube; 13 is only a cube root if the number 2197 is also mentioned, otherwise it is just the number 13.

Decimal. A method (unavailable to the poet of Cotton Nero A.x) of expressing a quantity less than 1 by placing *digits* to the right of the *units column,* separated from the units column by a decimal point. If one digit is used, say .3, it signifies that 1 has 10 parts and that we are concerned with 3 of these 10 parts; if two digits, for example, .17, that 1 has 100 parts of which 17 are noted, and so forth. Decimals came into use in England in the sixteenth century, replacing *fractions* for most mathematical computations.

Repeating Decimal. An *irrational* decimal whose *digits,* appearing to the right of a decimal point, repeat according to a pattern that continues to infinity. For example, 1/7 would be expressed as 0.142857142857 . . . . Mathematicians usually express repeating decimals by placing brackets around, or a line over, the first appearance of the pattern: 0.[142857] or $0.\overline{142857}$.

Terminating Decimal. A *rational* decimal, that is, a *fraction* whose conversion to a decimal through long division results in a remainder of zero. To convert 5/8 into a decimal would yield the decimal 0.625. In lay terms, a terminating decimal is one that does not require a series of three dots to indicate ad infinitum.

Decimal System. The arithmetic system universally used in the modern world. As a base-10 system, it uses zero (to mean nothing) and *digits* 1–9. Adding one more item triggers an increase of 1 in the next column to the left, while causing a zero to be written in the original column.

Diagonal. A line connecting any two nonconsecutive angles of a *polygon.*

Digit. A written or printed symbol representing a number. In most modern cultures there are ten such symbols: 0–9.

Divine Proportion. The name by which the Middle Ages understood "division into extreme and mean ratio." See also *Phi, Golden Section,* and *Divine Section.*

Divine Section. A colloquial synonym for the *Divine Proportion, Golden Section,* and *phi* (q.v.). It calls attention to the specific point at which a line to be divided into mean and extreme ratio must be cut.

Dodecahedron. A regular *polyhedron* with 12 *pentagonal* faces, 20 vertices, and 30 edges.

Duodecimal System. References to this system in this book do not imply a strictly arithmetic system based on twelfths and twelves, as the phrase "base 12" would indicate. Rather, they refer to a custom of accepting as basic "round numbers" 12, 120, 1200, et cetera, and privileging the *factors* and multiples of 12.

Face. A flat surface of a *polyhedron.*

Factor. For purposes of this study, a factor is a whole number, other than 1 and the number itself, which can be divided evenly into another number. For example, 6 is a factor of 12; it is not a factor of 14. An exception: 1 is considered a factor of all *perfect numbers.*

Fraction. A *ratio* of two numbers expressing a quantity less than 1, written in the modern era with one number (numerator) above a horizontal line and another larger number (denominator) below the same line. For example, 4/5 signifies 4 parts of a totality divided into 5 parts. To facilitate certain kinds of mathematical functions, fractions occasionally give the appearance of having a numerator larger than its denominator, as 7/5. This actually signifies the whole number 1, implied by 5 of these 7 fifths, plus the fraction 2/5.

Golden Section. The name, borrowed from a famous passage by Kepler, signifying what mathematicians now know as *phi,* the name of the Greek letter φ. See also *Divine Proportion* and *Divine Section.*

Hexadic System. A counting system that conceives quantities as multiples of 6.

Hundreds Column. The third number to the left of a modern decimal point.

Icosahedron. As the third of five Platonic solids, an icosahedron has 20 equilateral triangular *faces,* 30 edges, and 12 vertices. It is the dual of the fifth Platonic solid, a *dodecahedron,* meaning that each of its twelve vertices touches the centroids of the twelve faces of a circumscribed dodecahedron.

Incommensurable. A magnitude is said to be incommensurable with another magnitude when a comparison of the two cannot be made according to the same measure. The term is also used as a synonym for *irrational,* meaning incapable of being expressed as a *ratio*

Integers. The set of *whole numbers* and, in the modern era only, their opposites, for example, -3, -2, -1, 0, +1, +2, +3. This book is not concerned with negative numbers.

Irrational. Incapable of being expressed as a fraction. See *Numbers, Irrational.*

Mean. A magnitude whose measurement lies between a greater and lesser magnitude according to a given *proportion.* See *Arithmetic Mean.*

Numbers

    Cube Numbers. The set of whole numbers produced by raising the set of integers to the third power (i.e., $n \times n \times n$).

    Feminine Numbers. One of the names that the Greeks gave to the set of even numbers.

    Fibonacci Numbers. An additive set of numbers, originally devised by Leonardo of Pisa (Fibonacci, son of Bonacci), in which each number is produced by adding the two previous numbers: 1, 1, 2, 3, 5, 8, 13, 21, 34, 56, 90, 146, ... As the series progresses, each number divided by its predecessor produces a quotient that approaches *phi,* alternately bracketing *phi* with greater and lesser approximations. See chapter 2.

    Figurate Numbers. Integers that can be represented by dots arranged into *polygonal* figures. The lowest rank of figurate number includes all the triangular numbers, because they can easily be visualized as forming a triangle. The first four triangular numbers, 1, 3, 6, and 10, form an arrangement of dots similar to a set of bowling pins. The first four pyramidal numbers are 1, 4, 10, 20. The first four square numbers are 1, 4, 9, 16. Under the influence of fertile ancient and medieval imaginations, the shapes of these arrangements of dots were also associated with the first four elements, and with the universe. But here opinions differed. While some assumed that 5 was the figurate number of the universe, others said that 10 served this purpose.

Irrational Numbers. Geometric magnitudes that cannot be expressed as mathematical *ratios*.

Masculine Numbers. One of the names that the Greeks gave to the set of odd numbers.

Perfect Numbers. The set of numbers whose *factors*, including 1 but not the number itself, equal the number itself. If the total is less, the number is called deficient, if greater, superabundant. An example of a perfect number is 6 because its factors, 1, 2, and 3, total 6. The next perfect number, 28, has factors of 1, 2, 4, 7, and 14, which total 28.

Prime Numbers. The set of *whole numbers* divisible only by themselves and 1.

Rational Numbers. Magnitudes that can be expressed as a *ratio a/b* where *a* and *b* are *integers* and *b* is not zero. More accessible for nonmathematicians: any number is rational if it is a *whole number* or a *terminating decimal.* For example, 7 and 3.4 are rational numbers; they can be expressed as 7/1 and 17/5, respectively.

Square Numbers. The set of *whole numbers* produced by raising the set of integers to the second power (i.e., *n* x *n*).

Whole Numbers. The set of numbers by which individual items are counted. Technically, any number that does not include a fraction or decimal.

Pentagon. A regular 5–sided *polygon* formed, among other ways, by connecting consecutive points of a *pentangle*.

Pentangle. A 5–pointed star formed, among other ways, by constructing the 5 *diagonals* of a *pentagon*. In the modern era this shape is often called a pentagram.

Phi or φ. In modern mathematics the symbol for 1.61803. . . . In geometry, the symbol for the division of a line into mean and extreme *ratio;* in algebra, the symbol for $(1 + \sqrt{5}) / 2$. *Phi* is the *irrational number* signifying the *continuous proportion* among 3 numbers that simultaneously satisfy two equations, $a + b = c$ and $a \div b = b \div c$. *Phi* is the only number whose *reciprocal* is itself minus 1. Thus, 1.61803 / 1 x 1 / 0.61803 = 1. See also *Divine Proportion, Divine Section,* and *Golden Section.*

Polygon. A closed plane figure formed by 3 or more line *segments.* A polygon is said to be *regular* when all its line segments and angles are equal.

Polyhedron. A solid (i.e., 3-dimensional) shape whose *faces* are *polygons.* A polyhedron is said to be *regular* when all its *faces* are congruent.

Proportion. An equation stating that two *ratios* are equivalent, for example, 5/10 = 1/2, or 5 : 10 = 1 : 2. For mathematical equations of the arithmetic, geometric, and harmonic proportions see chapter 2, note 17.

Arithmetic Proportion. An equation of two *ratios* when the second term in both ratios alters the first term by the same amount and in the same direction. Arithmetic proportions are usually written as a continuous series, for example, 3, 6, 9, 12. . . . When expressed as a series, each term is actually a middle term, though stated only once, instead of being expressed "three is to six, as six is to nine; six is to nine, as nine is to twelve; . . ." In any series of three terms in an arithmetic proportion, the middle term is said to be the *arithmetic mean* between the other two.

Continuous Proportion. An equation of two *ratios* where the second term of the first ratio is the same as the first term of the second ratio: $a : b = b : c; b : c = c : d;$ . . . . In both examples the repeated term is said to be the middle term. It is also the *mean* between the terms on either side.

Divine Proportion. The name by which the Middle Ages indicated "division into extreme and *mean ratio,*" always expressed as three terms in a *continuous proportion.* See also *Divine Section, Golden Section,* and *Phi* (φ).

Geometric Proportion. An equation of two *ratios* where the second term of each ratio increases or decreases the first term by the same rate. For example, the *continuous proportion* 3 : 9 = 9 : 27 or the noncontinuous proportion 9 : 3 = 300 : 100.

Harmonic Proportion. A consonance among three terms such that, where $c > b$ and $b > a$, the third term c exceeds the second term b by a certain percentage of c, which is the same percentage of a by which b exceeds a.

Ratio. A comparison of two *whole numbers,* for example, 4/5, or 4 : 5.

Rational. A magnitude that is less than 1 or lies between two *whole numbers* is said to be rational if it can be expressed as a *ratio* of two whole numbers. For example, 6.75 is rational because it can be expressed as 6 3/4 or as 27/4. The square root of 2 is not rational because it cannot be so expressed; mathematicians either leave it written as the symbol √2 or express it as a *repeating decimal,* 1.[414213].

Reciprocal. In mathematics, one of two numbers whose product is 1. For example, 2/3 x 3/2 = 1; 2/3 is the reciprocal of 3/2 and 3/2 is the reciprocal of 2/3. In geometry, the term generally means "in the opposite direction." For example, a line AB can be measured from A to B or from B to A. *Ratios* arising from such measurements are reciprocals of each other.

Reciprocals. Two numbers whose product is 1.

Regular. An adjective qualifying a *polygon* or *polyhedron*, indicating that all lines and angles of these shapes are equal.

Segment. A part of a line consisting of two endpoints and all points between these endpoints.

Sexagesimal System. A custom of visualizing quantities as multiples of 60.

Sphere. A solid (i.e., 3-dimensional) figure with all points the same distance from the center.

Square Root. Any number, whole or fractional, can be considered a square root in relation to the square it produces when this number is raised to the second power (e.g., n x n), provided the root is not an approximation. That is, the term "square root" implies two numbers, the root itself and the number it produces when squared. As it is used here, square root means any *whole number* that produces, when multiplied by itself, a whole number. Such numbers are often called "perfect squares."

Tens Column. The second number to the left of a modern decimal point.

Tetract (var. *Tetractys*). The first four integers and their mathematical properties, including their sum, 10, and the *whole numbers* lying between 4 and 10. See chapter 2, note 7.

Thousands Column. The fourth number to the left of a modern decimal point.

Units Column. The first number to the left of a modern decimal point.

x-Axis. The horizontal axis on a coordinate plane.

y-Axis. The vertical axis on a coordinate plane.

Notes

Chapter 1. Introduction

1. For the kinds of argument advanced throughout this book, as well as for matters of manuscript description and early provenance, the EETS facsimile edition (Gollancz 1923) is indispensable. The text quoted herein is that of Andrew and Waldron (1979).

2. Although the language of any manuscript may differ from the language of its author, if scribal intrusion is extensive, this does not appear to be a major problem with Cotton Nero A.x. But see the persuasive arguments of H. N. Duggan (Brewer and Gibson 1997, 233, 240–41) that, at least for *Pearl*, the poet and the scribe had slightly different dialects, the latter using a Cheshire dialect, the former speaking with the sounds of central or southern Staffordshire. In any case, in the absence of strong evidence to the contrary, this study assumes that the manuscript reflects the author's dialect, which has been placed by Angus McIntosh (1963, 5) in northeast Staffordshire or in southeast Cheshire. This assumption does not mean that I believe the author and the scribe were the same individual, although this is a distinct possibility. There is no more reason to think the poet was not the scribe than that he was.

3. There is no lack of speculation regarding the poet's identity. The most sustained proposal suggests that the poet was either connected to the Massey family or a member of it. See Greenwood 1956; Nolan and Farley-Hills 1971; C. J. Peterson 1974a, 1974b, 1977. In a series of publications Michael J. Bennett, an historian, has been advancing a different thesis, first claiming that the author was probably a Cheshire careerist, perhaps a clerk, living in London and writing for the court of Richard II (Bennett 1979, 1983; cf. Bowers 2001), then amending the proposal to leave the poet in Cheshire, though still writing for an aristocratic audience: "The likelihood must be that at least on some occasion during the king's time in the northwest midlands, the opportunity was taken to present to the court the finest poetry of the region, and *Sir Gawain and the Green Knight* was given an airing" (Bennett 1997, 90). While I do not wish to criticize these and other speculations about the author, for such work presents a wealth of knowledge about the history and people of the poet's dialect area and also testifies to the medieval author's con-

tinuing appeal, neither should we ignore that they rest on thin, or no, evidence. We must also consider that whatever moved the author to create his poetry may have been quite different in both time and impulse from the motives that produced the manuscript. A variety of ends—commerce, edification, instruction, commission—could have brought the project to a scriptorium, whereas the poet may have had only private aims.

4. The manuscript has none of the tell-tales indicating a collaborative effort in which a scribe, illuminator, and artist produce work to please someone else. Nor does it have miniatures that say things like *Adelricus me fecit*. These facts, along with the widespread belief that "the MS. is in one hand" (Gollancz 1971, 8; cf. Andrew and Waldron 1979, 16; A.S.G. Edwards 1997, 197), keep alive the possibility of an "onlie begetter," a poet who may also have been scribe, illuminator, and painter.

5. Judiciously summarizing the arguments for and against single authorship, Malcolm Andrew (1997) very decidedly favors the former. A persuasive, computer-aided, statistical study leading to the same conclusion, at least with respect to the manuscript's long alliterative lines (*Pearl* and *Sir Gawain*'s bob-and-wheel were excluded because their form is so very different from the rest of the manuscript), was conducted by Cooper and Pearsall (1988), who conclude that "the evidence we have presented offers the strongest support to the hypothesis that the three poems, *Sir Gawain and the Green Knight, Patience,* and *Cleanness* are by the same author" (385). But see McColly and Weier (1983), whose appeal to SNOBOL4 programs, chi-squares, z-scores, Poisson variates, and worse, lead to the following conclusion: "[T]hese results show that a quantitative and statistical analysis, at least at the present time, cannot verify the popular assumption of single authorship for the *Pearl*-poems" (65).

6. Critical appreciation of the language and thematic content of the four poems, but especially of *Pearl* and *Sir Gawain and the Green Knight,* has been growing almost exponentially. See, for example, the bibliographies by Malcolm Andrew (1979), Michael Foley (1989), Robert J. Blanch (1991), and in Brewer and Gibson (1997, 393–427).

7. Among the studies that increasingly suggest a thematic unity to the manuscript (cf. Johnson 1984; Davenport 1978), Blanch and Wasserman (1995, 6–8) succinctly summarize the historical continuum that is becoming the preferred unifying thesis (cf. Morse 1978, 129–99), but offer on their own "a premise to be extended and explored rather than a thesis to be proven. A collection of connected observations rather than an argument" (Blanch and Wasserman 1995, 1).

8. The mathematical underpinning of the universe, as noted throughout this study, is not to be identified with a "reductionist" theory of matter, understood by Barbour (1966) as "the attributing of reality exclusively to the smallest constituents of the world, and the tendency to interpret higher levels of organisation in terms of lower levels" (52). Nor is it related to "string theory" as advanced by scholars like Greene (1999).

9. Nor does numerical composition have anything to do with the kind of pattern poetry George Herbert exploits in "Easter Wings" and "The Altar," a genre studied by, among others, Dick Higgins (1987).

10. It would be arrogant to assume that medieval listeners and readers would not have counted lines or read with a straight edge and compass in hand, because modern audiences do not read thus. Whether audiences in the fourteenth century did, or did not, read with a mathematical sensibility is beside the point. The only pertinent question is whether there is enough evidence in the text to demonstrate that the author wrote in such a way. Moreover, it is illogical to think that an author of consummate skill, like the *Pearl*-poet, would simplify his work to suit the common denominator of a typical audience, as modern writers often do, when he might have been writing for entirely different eyes.

11. Cf. Batts (1969): "In creating these intricate patterns it mattered to the medieval poet not at all that his subtleties of composition—if indeed they may be called that—would never be appreciated by the audience or reader, any more than it mattered to the stonemason that the details of his carving on the spire of a cathedral would never even be seen once the scaffolding was removed. The universe was a divinely ordered and inspired harmony, and the poet was concerned to put into his work some small part of this order" (112).

12. Shepherd 1965, 100, quoting *The Defense of Poesy*. The following quotation is from March 1998, ix.

13. On whether this kind of critical inquiry can be fruitful, see the exchange among R. G. Peterson, S. K. Heninger, Thomas Elwood Hart, and Daniel Laferrière in "Forum" *PMLA* 92 (1977): 126–29, touched off by R. G. Peterson's earlier article (1976).

14. The Greek title is quoted by Ghyka (1977, ix); the translation is my own. It is not insignificant that Raphael's famous fresco *Causarum Cognitio* in the Vatican's Stanza della Segnatura, popularly named "The School of Athens" (see the frontispiece in D. H. Fowler 1987), positions Plato and Aristotle at the center of interest, with clusters of scholars and students in four distinct groups associated with symbols of the four quadrivial disciplines. Raphael's interpretation implies a direct line of mathematics from the ancients through the Middle Ages, down to the Renaissance.

15. The implication that this claim would demand a mathematical answer to the question of incorporeality versus corporeality can already be seen in an observation of Porphyry that Rashdall calls the central question of scholastic philosophy:

Next, concerning genera and species, the question indeed whether they have a substantial existence, or whether they consist in bare intellectual concepts only, or whether if they have a substantial existence they are corporeal or incorporeal, and whether they are separable from the sensible properties of the things (or particulars of sense), or are only in those properties and subsisting about them, I shall forbear to determine. For a question of this kind is a very deep one and one that requires a longer investigation. (1936, 40)

16. The seven liberal arts were divided into three language arts, known as the trivium (grammar, rhetoric, and logic), and four applied arts, called the quadrivium (arithmetic, music, geometry, and astronomy). Though Martianus was a compiler rather than an original thinker, according to Stahl, his *De nuptiis* has an ironic significance for modern readers:

> The marriage of the soaring and subtle Mercury, dear to classical poets and satirists, to a medieval personification of musty handbook learning represents the decay of intellectual life in the West during the later centuries of the Roman Empire. . . . The way of the popular handbook, as it is digested and made more palatable for each succeeding generation, is inevitably downward. *The Marriage of Philology and Mercury* is a milestone in that downward course. Martianus stands almost at the halfway mark of Latin traditions. His success in epitomizing classical learning in the liberal arts and in transmitting it to the Middle Ages makes him our best index to the course of deterioration. (1971, 231, 234)

17. Adelard of Bath (ca. 1080–post 1150) was the first to make Euclid available to the West. The complex question of how Euclid's *Elements* was transmitted to the medieval west has been thoroughly researched by John Murdoch whose findings are available in two places, the *Dictionary of Scientific Biography* (Murdoch 1980) and the published *colloques* of the *XIIe Congrès International d'Histoire des Sciences* (Murdoch 1968). See also Cochrane 1994; Haskins 1960; and d'Alverny 1982, 440–43.

18. R. W. Southern (1982) argues convincingly that Chartres' reputation as the principal center of scholastic activity in the twelfth century (cf. Klibansky 1939; Green 1956) has been greatly exaggerated, since "from the early years of the [twelfth] century Paris had far outstripped Chartres as a place of teaching and study, even in those areas of study which have been particularly associated with Chartres" (113). Whether the phrase "School of Chartres" appropriately signifies the educational center associated with the cathedral of that city, in particular with the four figures carved in the West Portal of that cathedral (ca. 1150), who represent allegorically the disciplines of the quadrivium, or should more appropriately be attributed to the Schools of Paris, does not matter to this study. There can be little doubt that the philosophy of Plato, and especially his account of Creation in the *Timaeus,* had a profound influence on the development of scholastic thought, the principles of which are remarkably consistent with those of the *Pearl*-poet.

19. Earlier than Curtius the most important study of number composition is Hopper (1938).

20. In a future study, based on a paper presented to the Biennial Congress of the New Chaucer Society in 2000, I hope to demonstrate that the *Parliament of Fowls* also encodes in its three sections and the poem as a whole the four proportions most revered in the Middle Ages, the arithmetic, geometric, harmonic, and divine proportions.

21. For pointing out to me this parallel between Shakespeare and Marlowe I am indebted to John Baker.

22. Obvious influences on Borges's thought include Georg Cantor, Bertrand Russell, Friedrich Nietzsche, Ludwig Wittgenstein, and others. See the chapter entitled "Borges: 'Algebra and Fire'" by Barbara M. Fisher (1997).

23. The terms "incommensurable" for the Middle Ages and "irrational" for the modern world, are interchangeable. Despite a layman's observation that 1.61803 and 0.61803 are different quantities, they are reciprocal ways of expressing the same proportion, indeed the only proportion whose reciprocal is itself minus 1. In the example from Virgil $144 \div 89 = 1.61797$, while $89 \div 144 = 0.61805$. These figures are extremely close to the irrational proportion known as φ and $1/\varphi$, respectively.

24. The dimensions of Solomon's Temple in 3 Kings 6 anticipate the arithmetic, harmonic, and geometric means of Nicomachus of Gerasa (for whom see chapter 2), while also demonstrating the four ratios of the musical consonances usually attributed to Pythagoras: a perfect fourth, 4 : 3; a perfect fifth, 3 : 2; an octave, 2 : 1; and unity, 1 : 1. See March (1998, 119–21).

25. I cite the Latin Bible (*Biblia sacra*) because it was undoubtedly the one used by the *Pearl*-poet. Four eras contribute to the background of these paragraphs: Solomon's reign, assumed by the Middle Ages to have been 600 years before the Greeks; the putative dates of composition of the scriptural texts describing his reign; the first or second century B.C., when the Book of Wisdom is thought to have been composed; and the late-fourteenth-century date of Cotton Nero. The *Pearl*-poet nevertheless seems only to have been interested in linking Sir Gawain and Solomon. The former displays on his shield a pentangle requiring sophisticated mathematics for its construction. The latter's famous statement about number, weight, and measure implies a knowledge of such mathematics. See chapter 6 for a discussion of the pentangle and its connection with Solomon.

26. The New Revised Standard Version translates "sapientiam et rationem" as "wisdom and the sum of things," a useful numerical contribution but limited to simple addition for its literal sense and therefore carrying only the force of a metaphor. The *Glossa ordinaria* does not discuss the matter. Nor is there commentary by Wycliffe whose Bible gives the translation "I cumpasside all thingis in my soule, to kunne, and biholde, and seke wisdom and resoun, and to knowe the wickidnesse of a fool, and the errour of vnprudent men" (1850, 3:64).

27. Cicero's musical context, extremely important for the manuscript studied here, is not apparent from the fragment quoted in Lewis and Short. Here is the full sentence and translation from the Loeb edition: "Hic est, inquit, ille, qui intervallis disiunctus inparibus, sed tamen pro rate parte ratione distinctis inpulsu et motu ipsorum orbium efficitur et acuta cum gravibus temperans varios aequabiliter concentus efficit" ["That is produced," he replied, "by the onward rush and motion of the spheres themselves; the intervals between them, though unequal, being exactly arranged in a fixed proportion, by an agreeable blending of high and low tones various harmonies are produced"] (Keyes 1970, 270, 271).

28. It is interesting that "arithmetic" and "rhythm" are related to the same Greek root, ῥεῖν (to flow).

29. Compare with the *Oxford Latin Dictionary* (1983, 3): "a proportion, relation," as in Vitruvius 3.3.7, "intercolumnia altitudinesque columnarum habebunt iustam rationem"; and the *Revised Medieval Latin Word-List From British and Irish Sources* (1965), "proportionate sum," recorded in 1324.

Chapter 2. Cotton Nero A.x

1. The visual dissimilarity of figure 2.2 to figure 2.1 disappears when it is understood that segment AC of figure 2.2 (the mean) represents the first and fourth poems in figure 2.1. The *Pearl*-poet's strategy here duplicates the strategy of Virgil in *Georgics I*, shown in the previous chapter at figure 1.1, where the mean between 144 and 55 is shown as the total of 37.5, the first section of the poem, and 51.5, the last section.

2. Menninger suggests further (157) that 12, perhaps originally meaning "ten [i.e., two hands' worth] and a little more," an excess of 1 for each hand, may then have become popular because it can be divided into quarters and thirds, all commercially useful fractions (1/4, 1/2, 3/4; 1/3, 2/3), whereas 10 can only be divided into halves and inconvenient fifths. Compare with Boyer and Merzbach (1989, 61).

3. Prime numbers are those that cannot be divided evenly by any number other than 1 and themselves. Though the modern world accepts 2 and (more rarely) 1 as prime numbers, medieval mathematicians, like their classical forebears, began the prime series with 3, since they considered "2 (the dyad) as being, not a number at all, but the principle or beginning of the even, just as one was not a number but the principle or beginning of number" (Heath 1921, 71). The first 25 prime numbers, as the fourteenth century knew them, are as follows: 3, 5, 7, 11, 13, 17, 19, 23, 29, 31, 37, 41, 43, 47, 53, 59, 61, 67, 71, 73, 79, 83, 89, 97, 101.

4. The sentiment expressed by the motto was well-enough known in fourteenth-century England for Chaucer to have used a close approximation in the *Prioress's Tale*, "Yvele shal have that yvele wol deserve" (7.632). According to Florence Ridley's note in *The Riverside Chaucer*, the underlying thought is ultimately traceable to the Old Law as codified in Scripture: "But if her death ensue thereupon, he shall render life for life. Eye for eye, tooth for tooth, hand for hand, foot for foot. Burning for burning, wound for wound, stripe for stripe" (Exodus 21:23–25). The fanciful suggestion that the presence of the Old French line suggests that *Sir Gawain and the Green Knight* was composed to honor the founding of the Order of the Garter is unconvincing. Indeed the tradition that the Old French expression was created while Edward III was dancing with a mistress at Calais (with Joan, Duchess of Kent, in another version) is very probably equally fanciful. According to legend, during the dance a garter fell to the floor, giving either the woman or the king an opportunity to stop the racy thoughts of onlookers by reciting this Old French proverb. Whether the incident happened or not, it is unlikely that the founding of the order had anything to do with the composition of the poem in Cotton Nero. The sash

worn by Knights of the Garter is blue. The patron saint of the order is Saint George. And the order's emblem is an eight-pointed star. None of these appears anywhere in the manuscript we are studying here.

5. In England during the late fourteenth century, Roman numerals would have been used rather than Arabic numbers. If the poet had written a number for these line totals, during the numerical planning stages of the manuscript, say, he might have written dxxxi and mmdxxxi, or something similar, rather than 531 and 2531. My phrase "the last three digits" is therefore technically incorrect, when "the last five symbols" would undoubtedly be more historical. Since quantities are more important to this study than the symbols conveying them, I feel justified in using modern notation to spare the reader as much as possible, in a book that may already be forbidding. In any case, the reversal of 531 into 135 is readily seen if the quantities are written in the convention medieval mathematicians apparently preferred (Menninger 1969, 50):

modern notation	531	135
fourteenth century notation	cc xx	cc xx
	v iii i	i iii v

6. In discussing this series of perfect numbers and the preceding one concerning the series 1–3–5, I have attempted to avoid confusion by treating 1 as if it were a number, whereas it would perhaps be more precise to say "the beginning of number, followed by the first three perfect numbers" and "the beginning of number, followed by the first two odd numbers." A perfect number is one whose factors, including 1 but not including the number itself, total the number they factor. For example, 6 is a perfect number, because its divisors, 1, 2, and 3, add up to 6. Similarly, 28 is a perfect number with factors of 1, 2, 4, 7, and 14, totaling 28. The divisors of 496 are 1, 2, 4, 8, 16, 31, 62, 124, and 248, which total 496. Since perfect numbers were associated with virtues (Masi 1983, 98 n. 39), there is a possibility that the poet saw a connection between "patience" and "prudence" (the fourth virtue in the cardinal series, faith, hope, charity, prudence, temperance, justice, and fortitude, and the closest in meaning to "patience"), and that he encoded the accretive numerical value of the first four virtues (1, 6, 28, and 496) in the total number of lines, 531, in the poem whose first word is "Patience."

7. The importance of the tetract ($\tau\varepsilon\tau\rho\alpha\kappa\tau\acute{\upsilon}\varsigma$) cannot be overemphasized. Signifying any group of four items, but especially the first four integers and their mathematical properties, including their sum and the whole numbers lying between 4 and 10, the tetract held special appeal for the Pythagoreans. On the one hand, it includes "the ratios corresponding to the musical intervals discovered by Pythagoras, namely 4 : 3 (the fourth), 3 : 2 (the fifth), and 2 : 1 (the octave)" (Heath 1921, 75–76). On the other, as the figurate number of the earth it includes so many unities—four seasons, four points of direction, four winds, four elements, four conditions (cold, hot, dry, moist), et cetera. In addition, it totaled the decad, the most complete number ($1 + 2 + 3 + 4 = 10$). There is no recognized kind of number that the tetract does not include: the beginning of number, 1; the first even, 2; the first odd, 3; the first prime, 3; the

first even square, 4; the first odd square, 9; the first cube, 8; the first two perfect numbers, 1 and 6 (Taylor 1962, 136–38). The progression in Cotton Nero A.x, from a four-unit basis to a five-unit basis, whether this progress leads from the first half of the manuscript to the second, or from the two medial poems, *Purity* and *Patience*, to the two poems at the manuscript's extremes, *Pearl* and *Sir Gawain*, may be viewed in one sense as a demonstration of the properties of the tetract, in particular as a progression from the figurate number of the earth, 4, to the figurate number of the universe, 5. This progression is elegantly symbolized in the foundation of all geometry, the Pythagorean theorem, $3^2 + 4^2 = 5^2$, where 3 symbolizes fire, air, and water, 4 symbolizes the earth, and 5 symbolizes the universe.

8. *Pearl's* 1212 lines are factored by 2, 3, 4, 6, 12, 101, 202, 303, 404, and 606. *Purity's* 1812 lines are factored by 2, 3, 4, 6, 12, 151, 302, 453, 604, and 906. *Patience's* 531 lines are factored by 3, 9, 59, and 177.

9. I do not accept the argument that *Purity* and *Patience* were written in four-line units and should only be viewed thus. The light ticks in the left margins of all the folios containing these two poems, which is the only evidence for such insistence, cannot be said to belong to the formal presentation of these poems' verbal structure. On the contrary, these marks belong to the vellum folios and may only have been guides to the scribe as he was copying from foul sheets.

10. The actual value of √2, written as a modern decimal, is 1.41421. The ratio 7 : 5, normally written in the Middle Ages as the fraction 7/5, was often used as a convergent for √2. That this convergent calculates to 1.4 in modern decimals—an error of .01421—indicates how much approximation a medieval mathematician was forced to rely on.

11. The discussion over the positioning of lines 510–12 of *Patience*, whether they should follow 515, as they are positioned in the manuscript, or appear three lines earlier, as Andrew and Waldron print them (1979, 205), following Gollancz's suggestion, has no bearing on the arguments advanced here. I do disagree, however, with the suggestion made by some, noted by Edwards (1997, 199), that these three lines do not belong in the text on the grounds that they disrupt the quatrain arrangement.

12. As a further possible indication of the poet's interest in primes, we should note that the total number of lines in *Sir Gawain*, 2531, happens to be the 369th prime number. That the poet was undoubtedly aware of the indivisibility of *Gawain's* total number of lines, though not perhaps that it is the 369th prime number, will be argued below.

13. Compare with Karl Menninger (1992, 154).

14. This formulation is taken from Huntley (1970, 48). For charm, elegance in discussing science, and exhilaration in describing the beauty of mathematics—on the very subject of this study—few works are more rewarding than Huntley's wonderful little volume.

15. This fallacy, long known to mathematicians, is best illustrated by using consecutive numbers in the Fibonacci series, which will be discussed later in the chapter. It can be avoided—that is, figures 2.4 and 2.5 will yield the same areas—only if the

dimensions are taken from an additive series that includes *phi:* 1, φ, 1 + φ, 1 + 2φ, 2 + 3φ, 3 + 5φ, ad infinitum.

16. As found in Euclid, Nicomachus, Pappas, and others, where c > b and b > a, an arithmetic progression satisfies the equation (c - b) ÷ (b - a) = c ÷ c; a geometric progression satisfies (c - b) ÷ (b - a) = c ÷ b; and a harmonic progression satisfies (c - b) ÷ (b - a) = c ÷ a. See: Heath (1921, 87); Boyer and Merzbach (1989, 56).

17. Luca Pacioli (1445–1514), better known to mathematicians as the author of the first printed work on algebra, *Summa de arithmetica, geometrica, proportioni et proportionalita* of 1494, and to others as the father of double-entry bookkeeping, published *De divina proportione* in 1509, a dissertation with figures attributed to Leonardo da Vinci. It has been handsomely reproduced in a 1956 edition. See Boyer and Merzbach (1989, 278–80), and Pacioli (1956).

18. The text of Campanus's remark, appearing at the end of prop. 10 of the *Supplement* to Euclid's *Elements,* usually called book 14, is taken from Otto von Simson (1989, 211 n) who quotes from "the Basel edition of 1537 by Chasles, *Aperçu historique sur l'origine et le développement des méthodes en géométrie,* p. 512." The translation is by Herz-Fischler (1998, 171).

19. Pacioli (1956, chap. 5) explains why he chose the title *De divina proportione,* quoted and translated by Herz-Fischler (1998, 171–72), summarized here.

20. Ackerman (1949), discussed by Otto von Simson (1989, 19). It is interesting that the argument was not over whether geometry should be the science controlling the design of the cathedral, but whether its unifying proportion should come from the square or from the equilateral triangle.

21. For an interesting, often witty, discussion of medieval education and how it "would simply have formed minds that were different from ours" (17), see Russell (1998, 6–53).

22. A diagonal, though popularly associated with four-sided figures, signifies a straight line connecting two nonconsecutive angles in any polygon.

23. For the prominence of mathematics in the quadrivium see Alison White (1981), John Caldwell (1981), and William H. Stahl (1971). The likelihood that the *Pearl*-poet had an education in the quadrivium is discussed later in this chapter.

24. It is significant that the poet passes over other numbers mentioned prominently by John: "7," noted 47 times; and "4," occurring 21 times, mostly referring to the "four living creatures" (i.e., the evangelists or "four calling birds" of the later Christmas carol).

25. All twelve of these pictures are conveniently reproduced by A.S.G. Edwards (1997).

26. On the various ways that man can see God spiritually, see the fine article by Theresa Tinkle (1988).

27. Reuchlin uses interchangeably and without comment the two forms of the Hebrew letter *vav* in his discussions of the word for God, YHVH and YHWH. Though Reuchlin was German and therefore more familiar with the Ashkenazi pronunciation *v,* his scholarly pursuits would undoubtedly have brought him into con-

tact with the Sephardic pronunciation w in the Near East. The different pronunciations have no effect on meaning.

28. Indeed the poet may have imagined the manuscript's dual dynamism in the context of a church. Let us recall that medieval churches, especially cathedrals, were laid out on an east-west axis, with their chancels at the eastern end. Cemeteries were usually situated behind the church, until the nineteenth century embraced the romantic movement's culture of death and created park-land cemeteries far from the daily haunts of the living, like Mount Auburn in Boston and Père Lachaise in Paris. The morning sun and its powerful iconography would literally reach a medieval cemetery first, then penetrate the church at its chancel end, cover its clergy, and finally reach the faithful in the nave who, now enlightened, would presumably progress toward the choir and beyond, the place of final rest at the end of their lives. A recent discussion of the modern world's shifting attitude to cemeteries, may be found in Garry Wills's popular as well as scholarly *Lincoln at Gettysburg*, 63–76.

Chapter 3. *Pearl*

1. In addition to other studies mentioned in this chapter, see Prior (1996), Stanbury (1991), and especially the subtle interpretation of the poem's first section by Nolan (1977).

2. Exceptions to the poem's concatenation are few. In section 8, where the final word of each stanza is "cortaysye," line 445 picks up only the first syllable, "The court of þe kyndom of God alyue," instead of the final sounds. And the first line of stanza 52, "Bot now þou motez, me for to mate" (613), echoes nothing of the final line of the preceding stanza, "For þe grace of God is gret inoghe."

3. Milton's *Lycidas*, lines 163–64.

4. Thorpe's full point is highly perceptive: "[A]lthough the physical act, the 'literal,' finds its fullest significance in our receptivity to the figurative meaning embodied within it . . . nonetheless this kingdom we experience in our sacramental labor is fully revealed to us only in and through that physical: the mundane acts of breaking and eating, of drinking the wine. We can distinguish literal and figurative, body and spirit, but to separate them is finally impossible, at least for us who dwell in a physical world. *Pearl* is in part about this danger: it is a poem composed mostly of talk that yet recognizes the fine irony of that fact" (1991, 30).

5. Compare with Blenkner (1968), who bases his study on the parallels between *Pearl* and Hugh of St. Victor, St. Augustine, St. Gregory, St. Bernard, and especially St. Bonaventure.

6. On the few occasions when "oyster" has been considered—and rejected by all but Donaldson (1972)—only the plural has been discussed. But -*ys* is a regular genitive singular ending in Middle English. Moreover, the appearance of "kyn" so often induces syntactic idiosyncrasies in Middle English that the genitive singular for "oyster" cannot be ruled out here. The objection that the word's short, unaccented second syllable would not rhyme with the long, accented syllables elsewhere

in the stanza overlooks the possibility of eye rhyme and the poet's not infrequent practice elsewhere. Compare with "cloystor" (969), where, as Donaldson notes (78), the accent must be pulled to the final syllable, and an unaccented *e* that would normally appear in the final syllable must be strained to a long *ū* sound in order to rhyme with "flōr," "bōr," "tōr," "fauōr," and "vygōur."

7. Sir Thomas Heath (1921, 91): "The actual method by which the Pythagoreans proved that √2 is incommensurable with 1 was doubtless that indicated by Aristotle, a *reductio ad absurdum* showing that if the diagonal of a square is commensurable with its side, it will follow that the same number is both odd and even (Arist. *Anal. pr.* i. 23, 41 a 26–27)." This association of Aristotle and incommensurables makes the word "propertéz" in line 752 entirely appropriate, for incommensurability was understood to be a property.

8. Several shellfish, notably the chambered nautilus, grow shells that very precisely follow mathematical equations. Another sea animal, the sea urchin, is known as "Aristotle's Lantern" (Ghyka 1977, 97). The phrase "an ordinary grain of sand" is proverbial. A zoologist friend informs me that a natural pearl is actually an oyster's protection against an intruding parasite.

9. This is scarcely the place to recapitulate the debate on "the continuum [a]s the fundamental structure of the physical world, whether it is a matter of space (point, line, surface, solid), movement (change of quality, quantity, or place), or time" (Eldredge 1979, 93), when the poems under discussion at most allude to the debate in metaphor. Nevertheless the extensive contributions to this subject by Aristotle, Thomas Aquinas, Robert Grosseteste, Thomas Bradwardine, Adam Wodeham, John the Canon, William of Ockham, Nicholas Bonettus, Albert of Saxony, and others strongly suggest that the question was widely available to anyone acquiring an education in the second half of the fourteenth century. The most complete discussion of the question is by Wolfgang Breidert (1970). But see also V. P. Zubov (1961) and Eldredge (1979). Of particular interest for this study are the remarks by Murdoch and Synan (1966) on Bradwardine's *Tractatus de continuo*, which they call "easily the most impressive work on the problem written at any time during the Middle Ages. His argument—one which tends to support Aristotle's denial of indivisibilism without qualification—is fundamentally a mathematical one. To begin with, the *Tractatus* is geometrical in form, modeled . . . on Euclid's *Elements*. Yet it is geometrical not merely in form, but in content as well" (221).

10. An alternate possibility involving a dodecahedron's "dual," an icosahedron, though appealing, must be rejected. (In this context "dual" means "mutually referential": by connecting the face centers, called centroids, of all adjacent sides of a dodecahedron an icosahedron is formed; conversely, by connecting the centroids of the adjacent faces of an icosahedron, a dodecahedron is formed.) An icosahedron has 20 faces and might therefore seem an appealing candidate to be represented by the 20 sections of *Pearl*. But there is no hint in ancient or medieval writings that an icosahedron is related to more than one of the four elements, namely water. As to the

other Platonic solids, the cube gave rise to the earth, the pyramid or tetrahedron to fire, the octahedron to air. But the sphere of the entire universe arose from the dodecahedron. (Heath 1921, 158–60, quoting Aëtius's attribution, 2.6.5, to Plato).

11. Heath 1921, 158–59; Boyer and Merzbach 1989, 84; Ghyka 1977, 44.

12. I am aware that a long, profitless discussion of tenor and vehicle could intrude upon this discussion at precisely this point. A modern critic would have a natural inclination to see the geometric shapes described here as symbols of the matter of the poems in the manuscript. In view of the medieval belief, however, that the Creator's first expression of virtue as essence took form as a dodecahedron (see the remark of Pacioli above on p. 63), it may be more appropriate to say that the extended world with which we are familiar is a symbol of this essence.

13. Although the Babylonian sexagesimal system included a highly advanced system of fractional notation, analogous to modern decimals, "the best that any civilization afforded until the time of the Renaissance" (Boyer and Merzbach 1989, 27), the English Middle Ages were very probably still encumbered with an awkward system of unit fractions. (But see appendix 2, n. 2.) For example, the modern 5.4 would have been expressed $5 + 1/3 + 1/15$ (Boyer and Merzbach 1989, 13).

14. The phrase "three 12-line stanzas" refers to *Pearl* only. But the 36 lines on each page have pertinence for *Purity* and *Patience* as well, where two light strokes in the left margin at every fourth line suggest that both of these poems were composed in four-line units. While this may be true of *Purity*, which would then be understood as having 453 such units, the same cannot be said of *Patience*, despite that poem's also having the same strokes in the left margin, for the 531 lines of *Patience* are not divisible by 4. It is highly likely, then, that these ticks in the margins of Cotton Nero A.x were only intended as guides, perhaps to help a scribe keep track of his place, as the custom of writing line numbers at regular intervals in modern texts is a guide to readers, with no bearing on the poet's conceptual structure.

15. Although A.S.G. Edwards indicates that *Pearl* begins on folio 41 (Edwards 1997), I follow here the marginal indications in the Andrew and Waldron edition that show *Pearl* beginning on "[f 39ʳ]."

16. That "Rolle never left Yorkshire, except as a student" (Connolly 1993, xvii; but cf. Marzac 1968, 22–25, who presents strong evidence for a six-year *séjour* at the Sorbonne from 1320 to 1326), and died in 1349, early enough for his writings to have been in circulation when Cotton Nero A.x was being created, make it entirely possible that the *Pearl*-poet was aware of the *Form of Living* and of its account of the five steps leading to mystical union. Moreover, the *Form of Living* is divided into twelve books, suggesting that Rolle, like the *Pearl*-poet, may have been influenced by principles of numerical construction. Though my reading of *Pearl* is consistent with Louis Blenkner's excellent article, "The Theological Structure of *Pearl*," especially in seeing progress toward a contemplative state, it develops rather differently from his. In contrast to the five steps I infer from Rolle, Father Blenkner quotes (Conley 1970, 231) the first sentence of the Rolle passage I print below to show the importance of rejecting the vanities of the world as a first condition for the contem-

plative life. One then proceeds, in Blenkner's interpretation, from cogitation, through meditation, and finally to contemplation.

17. The headings for these five steps come from Evelyn Underhill (1970, pt. 2, chaps. 2, 3, 4, 9, and 10). Various mystic systems show other formulations. The Neoplatonists identify three stages, the Sufis include seven, St. Teresa's nine steps divide Illumination into Recollection, Quiet, Ecstasy, and Rapt (Underhill 70–94). Underhill's five steps, while covering most other systems, closely parallel the progress Rolle describes.

Chapter 4. *Purity* (*Clannesse*)

1. To avoid inconsistency in the spelling of biblical names from the Old Testament, I have elected to use the form appearing in the Vulgate.

2. Drawing upon *Enchiridion* 117 for the three-age conception, and *De civitate Dei* 22.30 for the seven/eight-age conception, Morse summarizes: "Each [of the three ages is] characterized by a different law: the Age of Nature, when natural law prevails (the category under which the stories of the Flood and Sodom take place); the Age of the Written Law, when the law given to Moses prevails (the category under which the stories of Jerusalem and Babylon occur); and the Age of Grace, when the law of love instituted by Christ prevails (the category that includes all of Christian history, from Christ to the end in Judgment). . . . The other method . . . divided Old Testament history into six ages, marked by Adam, Noah, Abraham, David, a fifth figure chosen from the period of the Babylonian captivity, and Christ, who introduces the sixth age. The seventh age is doomsday. . . . The eighth age . . . the Last Judgment" (Morse 1978, 133–34).

3. The smaller decorated initials are all precisely three lines high. The larger initials are actually of different sizes. The decorated initial opening the poem at line 1 is eight lines high, matching the decorated initials at the beginnings of *Patience* and *Sir Gawain*. (The decorated P at the beginning of *Pearl* stands fifteen lines high, to indicate the beginning of the manuscript.) The initial at line 557 is four lines high, while the initial at line 1157 is five lines high, perhaps designed to be only four lines high to match the initial at line 557, but spilling over at its top into the blank line between 1156 and 1157.

4. Charlotte Morse (1978) has called attention to the separation of the damned from the saved as a controlling rubric for the poem as a whole. Initially introduced by the episode of the wedding feast, echoed by reference to the fall of the angels and the fall of Adam, this paradigm then defines, she argues, the context for all other episodes in the poem.

5. The miraculous birth of Christ is not to be confused with the Immaculate Conception, as many a modern reader is apt to do. The Immaculate Conception refers to the conception of Mary in her mother's womb, immaculate because Mary was uniquely exempted from original sin. The birth of Christ is called simply Virgin Birth. Whether Christ's human nature, as distinct from his divine nature, was similarly exempted from original sin, as his birth from the immaculate Virgin

would imply, or with the rest of humanity equally subject to original sin, as his baptism by John the Baptist implies, I leave to the scholastics of the medieval debating halls.

6. For the Hebrew text of these Old Testament words, see *The NIV Interlinear Hebrew-English Old Testament*, 4:458. For the range of meanings these words embrace, see Tregelles's edition of *Gesenius's Lexicon* (1979) and the Koehler and Baumgartner *Lexicon*. The Hebrew text has two linguistic idiosyncracies that should also be noted, whether semantically significant or not is yet to be determined: (1) The first word, מְנֵא, appears twice in succession in verse 25, מְנֵא , מְנֵא , "mane, mane," although only once in verse 26, where Daniel explains its significance for Baltassar. In the Vulgate the transliteration "mane" occurs only once in verse 25 and once in verse 26. Explanations for this odd double use in verse 25 of the Hebrew text include, among others, scribal error and an intended duplication that may accomplish for meaning what onomatopoeia does for sound, producing the notion of several numbers, or all numbers. (2) The third word, "phares," appears as the past participle, פַּרְסִין in verse 25, as it is read from the wall, but as the infinitive, פְּרֵס , in verse 26, where Daniel offers his interpretation. No convincing explanation accounts for either of these idiosyncracies.

7. In a groundbreaking study Donna Crawford (1993) has anticipated these remarks on the numerical proportions of *Purity*.

8. It is well to remember that medieval mathematicians could only approximate incommensurable magnitudes by using surrogate fractions, called convergents, for example, 7/5 for $\sqrt{2}$, 20/9 for $\sqrt{5}$, and 12/7 for $\sqrt{3}$, since a convenient decimal system had not yet developed (Boyer and Merzbach 1989, 61, 315–18).

9. As explained in previous chapters, the ratio known as φ produces expanding magnitudes leading to infinity. The same ratio can, of course, also lead to an infinitely small magnitude. In this case a number would be multiplied by the reciprocal of φ (0.61803; note that φ is the only number whose reciprocal is itself minus 1). Thus the total number of lines in the poem's first major division, 556 lines in §§ 1 through 6, when successively multiplied by the reciprocal of φ, reveal section totals through § 8:

$$556 \times 1 / \varphi \approx 344 \ (\S\S \ 1–4)$$
$$344 \times 1 / \varphi \approx 212 \ (\S\S \ 5–6)$$
$$212 \times 1 / \varphi \approx 132 \ (\S\S \ 7–8)$$

10. For the form of this chart, as well as for the connection between poetry and bookart to be discussed shortly, I owe a deep debt of gratitude to Robert D. Stevick, whose numerical analysis of the Old English poem *Elene* and geometrical analyses of early insular gospel books, taken together, explain the methodology that the *Pearl*-poet used to create *Purity*. For the former see Stevick 1982, for the latter, Stevick 1994.

11. One of the most prolific scholars on the subject is Jonathan J. G. Alexander (1992), whose thorough study of the craft of manuscript illumination contains a full bibliography. See also Stevick (1994) and the charming little book by Thomas Cahill

(1995), who explains with wit and delight the role of Irish monks in the preservation of learning during the early Middle Ages.

12. Notwithstanding that all suggestions about the author's life must be acknowledged as conjectures, the subjects of at least three of the poems in Cotton Nero A.x, and much of the atmosphere and activity in the fourth, *Sir Gawain*, strongly point to a religious life, rather than to the secular career that has been lately suggested (Bennett 1979, 1983, 1997; Bowers 2001). Moreover, the poet's almost obsessive preoccupation and genius with numbers and divinity point very strongly to an ascetic life in which there were fewer distractions than in a secular vocation.

13. The lists of monasteries in England by counties and orders throughout the Middle Ages in Roy Midmer (1979, 32–44, 352–65) suggest the author may have been a Benedictine at Tutbury or Burton upon Trent, or a Cistercian at Hulton or Dieulacres. If he was an Augustinian canon, whose priories were numerous in this area, he could have lived at Haughmond, Lilleshall, Ranton, Repton, Stone, or Trentham. He may even have been the canon at Lilleshall, who "wrote a manual for the guidance of parish priests" around 1400 (Midmer 1979, 198). The great historian of monastic life, Dom David Knowles (1955), covers the period when the author of Cotton Nero A.x would have been composing his poems. See also Colin Platt (1984).

14. The northernmost of the counties where the author may have resided include the Benedictine houses at Tynemouth, Jarrow, Monkwearmouth, and Durham. The last named monastery had an especially splendid library. If not a Benedictine, then perhaps he entered the Cistercian offshoot of the Benedictines, who had famous houses at Fountains, Rievaulx, Bylands, and Kirkstall.

15. *The Lindisfarne Gospels* (1960) is both the most complete study of the manuscript and the finest full facsimile, unfortunately only available in the largest academic libraries. More readily accessible is Millar (1923). Janet Backhouse (1981) has a fine brief study with full-color pictures of all the artwork in the manuscript.

16. In the Lindisfarne Gospels each of the four gospels begins with the same format: a portrait page, an elaborate geometric design representing a cross and usually called a cross-carpet page, and then a lavishly decorated incipit page. St. Jerome's letter to Pope Damasus, which opens the codex, has the same format, though it lacks a portrait page. Of the five cross-carpet pages, the *Pearl*-poet seems to have followed the designs for Mark (94v), Luke (138v), and John (210v), which are symmetrical on both the vertical and horizontal axes. The cross designs preceding Jerome's letter (2v) and Matthew's gospel (26v) follow a slightly different method. Though they have left-right symmetry, vertical symmetry is lost because the three horizontal modules intersect the four-moduled vertical axis at the second module from the top.

17. Stevick (1994, 281) lists three different proportions for the Book of Kells (convincingly demonstrated in his text [21–24, 227–33]): (1) 4 : 3; (2) √2 : 1, a diagonal to the side of a square; and (3) √3 + 1 : 2, derived from the hypotenuse of a triangle whose two other legs are the side and diagonal of a square.

18. Although we can never know precisely how the poet built his model, the most reasonable guess is that he began with the pentagon implied by the shape of *Pearl*, as

discussed in chapter 3. *Pearl's* five stanzas per section and twelve lines per stanza imply an original figure of five sides, twelve units per side. Now a pentagon expands to a pentangle when its sides are extended, as is often noted in the course of this book and explained mathematically in appendix 3. The points of this newly constructed pentangle, when connected, define the five points of a pentagon. This pentagon, in turn, can have its sides extended to form another pentangle, and so on, and on, toward infinity. If the Divine Proportion is applied to the original pentagon, measuring twelve units on each side, and the same operation is carried out six times, the result will be a pentagon, measuring 212 on each side, inscribed in a circle measuring 180 in radius. To carry out the computation eight times, with the rounding-off that medieval mathematics could not avoid, produces a pentagon within a circle measuring 476 in radius.

19. The author could have used Euclid 12, theorems 9 and 10, which show that the square of a pentagon side equals the sum of the squares of a hexagon side and a decagon side, when all three regular polygons are inscribed within the same circle. He would already know the hexagon side, since it is equal to the radius of the circle. The decagon side, too, would fall into place, since it is in extreme and mean ratio with the hexagon side, the hexagon side being the larger of the two. This yields 112 for the decagon side. Thus with two of the three terms known, the third, which is the pentagon side originally sought, is easily computed to be 212. He would also know from Euclid 13, theorem 8, that this dimension is the larger of the two φ-related segments of the diagonal of a pentagon inscribed in the same circle. And 212 multiplied by φ produces 344, the length of a diagonal of a pentagon inscribed within a circle of radius 180. The actual equation used in the Middle Ages would have been $S = r/2$ times $\sqrt{(10 - 2\sqrt{5})}$, requiring the substitution of the convergent 20/9 for $\sqrt{5}$.

20. Though Morse confines her discussion to *Purity,* the pattern she elucidates applies as well to the thematic development of the entire manuscript.

Chapter 5. *Patience*

1. The term Judeo-Christian usually appears as an adjective modifying an abstract term, like "tradition" or "culture." It is used atypically here to mean individuals in order to emphasize that every Christian in the fourteenth century as well as the modern world thinks of himself as synthesizing Hebraic and Christian beliefs. Christ was, after all, a Jew. Essential to medieval Christian thought was the belief that Christ, though the founder of Christianity, was also the Messiah, the culmination of Hebraic belief. The Book of Jonas, though an Old Testament story, embodies Christian belief as well as Hebraic.

2. Biblical chapters were not divided into verses until the sixteenth century. They are included here to facilitate a comparison of the Bible's chapters and the poem's sections and to show how the poet divided between his sections 3 and 4 material from chapters 2 and 3 of the Book of Jonas.

3. The classic study of acedia is by Wenzel. See also Lorraine K. Stock (Blanch, Miller, and Wasserman 1991, 163–75) who argues that acedia is the "poynt" of *Patience.*

4. The literary representation of a dual conception of time, both a linear progression as perceived by man and an organic whole known to God, echoes one of Chaucer's strategies, as I have advanced elsewhere (Condren 1999, 75, 247–52).

5. The quotation is taken from Sherman Hawkins's informative article on Chaucer's Prioress (Hawkins 1964, 605), which also references two important articles on the perceived tension between the old law and the new, Margaret Schlauch (1939) and Lewis Edwards (1958).

6. To a medieval mathematician the words "triple triangle" would have identified the pentangle we have been discussing throughout this study. Shown below, using coded lines for purposes of illustration, are two ways in which three triangles may be arranged to produce a pentangle. The figure on the left is the usual way "triple triangle" was understood in the Middle Ages, though the triangles in this case are missing their bases.

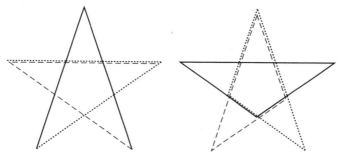

7. I print lowercase Greek here because Reuchlin's text uses the lowercase at line 19 of page 350 (plate 3). The similarity between the characters written in the notches of Reuchlin's pentagram on page 350 and the Greek word for "health" may be more readily seen if compared with uppercase Greek: ‘ΥΓΙΘΑ. The symbol Θ represents the diphthong EI in both upper- and lowercase.

8. At most, 60 x 100 only suggests a *phi* ratio. To increase precision, the poet could have begun his calculation with 60 for the shorter leg and determined the *phi*-related longer leg to be 97.0818. Conversely, beginning with one leg at 100, the other would be 61.803. But section lengths of 97 lines and 62 lines (rounding off the actual dimensions) would not emphasize the ratio. Nor would the closest compromise, 60.9957 x 98.69287, rounded off to 61 x 99. By electing to work with round numbers the poet made the proportion more noticeable.

9. According to my measurements, the pertinent dimensions are as follows: Oα and βγ = 58 each; αβ = 36; Oγ and δε = 152 each; and γδ = 94. The total length of Oε, then, is 398.

Diligent readers with a mathematical inclination will notice at least two instances of imprecision in my claims. First, 116.6 multiplied by φ^2 produces 305.26, not 308. And second, 398 doubled equals 796, not 800. Of course, the poet's precise method of computation may never be recovered. But given the medieval necessity of rounding off, if 116.6 is rounded up to 117, and then multiplied by φ^2, it produces 306.3, only

1.7 units less than the number of lines in 4, 5, and 6 of *Purity*. This small lack of correspondence at a magnitude of approximately 300 is about the same as the four unit lack of correspondence at a magnitude of 800. In the course of my own investigations of these poems I have been continually impressed by how my own frustrations at not finding precise correspondences between the poems of Cotton Nero A.x and the mathematics implied by *Purity* pale beside what must have been the far greater frustrations of the poet as he tried to create these correspondences. If indeed he was attempting to make these sections of *Purity* parallel the line segment I am suggesting, while working in a whole-number system, without modern calculators, an error of about one-half of one percent is greater testimony to his accuracy than to his misses.

10. The mathematical formula for the expansion of both the horizontal and vertical beams is identical. But since this expansion involves two steps (from pentagon to pentangle, and then from this new pentangle to a larger pentagon), the original dimension must be multiplied by *phi* twice, which is the same as multiplying once by φ^2. Thus, Oα times $\varphi^2 \approx$ Oγ. Similarly OC times $\varphi^2 \approx$ OA and OA times $\varphi^2 \approx$ OP.

11. The probability that the cross of Christ has prominence in the manuscript increases in the light of a recent article by David Aers. Arguing to restore to *Sir Gawain and the Green Knight* the Christian context in which it was originally composed, Aers provides a judicious corrective to the tendency to view the poem in cultural, courtly, and political terms, as expressed by R. A. Shoaf (1984), Jill Mann (1986), and Stephanie Trigg (1991): "Whatever the critical potential some of his poem's perspectives could have held for some late fourteenth-century readers brooding about the church, its alignments with the wealthy, its pastoral activities and its administration of penance, the poet himself chose not to actualize them" (Aers 1997, 98).

Chapter 6. *Sir Gawain and the Green Knight*

1. Burrow (1965, 5) quotes these lines from *Instructio patris regis ad filium Edwardum*, in K. de Lettenhove, *Oeuvres de Froissart* (1870, 542). The free translation is my own.

2. The more frequent meaning of *gyng* in Middle English is a simple retinue, implying neither praise nor disparagement. But as early as 1175 a deprecatory sense of "crew, rabble, rout" was developing. See *OED, Ging,* 3.c.

3. *Foin* is limited in the *OED* to a thrusting or poking with the point of a weapon, save for its appearance here in *Sir Gawain*, where its use as a metaphor, a thrusting with the feet, has the effect of showing extreme disrespect. A parallel with dribbling a soccer ball (football outside the U.S.) cannot be dismissed.

4. Each stanza of *Sir Gawain* concludes with a bob-and-wheel, a phrase referring to the five-line ending, a "round[ing] off by a line of one stress (the 'bob') followed by a rhyming quatrain (the 'wheel') of three-stressed lines, the second and fourth of which rhyme with the bob" (Andrew and Waldron 1979, 49).

5. A. D. Horgan suggests, in an earlier article on *Pearl* (1981), that *trawþe* and the modern word "faith" are interchangeable in both a biblical and theological sense.

6. The scriptural technique of inserting an explanatory gloss, like the parable of the vineyard to clarify the difference between temporal and eternal rewards, occurs more often in medieval literature than one might suppose. See my suggestion that Chaucer's *Friar's Tale* and *Summoner's Tale* are twin glosses underscoring a dimension of the *Wife of Bath's Prologue and Tale* that its teller may have concealed and its readers may have missed (Condren 1999, 114 ff.).

7. In addition to the several analyses cited elsewhere in this study, see also the ingenious discussion of the sizes of *Sir Gawain*'s sections, though reaching a different conclusion from the one offered here, by Michael Robertson (1982). Despite the appeal of his thesis, that the poem is organized in eleven-stanza sections, to make it work Robertson must not only present a convoluted argument but also assume that a decorated initial is missing from line 1690 (780).

8. Cf. Blanch and Wasserman who remark the poet's "overlong gloss of the pentangle, the very length of which calls into question the narrator's powers of judgment" (1995, 136).

9. The five Wounds of Christ venerated during the Middle Ages are in the two feet, two hands, and pierced side. It may be significant that medieval missals had a special Mass in honor of Christ's Wounds, believed to have been written by St. John the Evangelist. It was known as the Golden Mass and was indulgenced either by John XXII in 1334 or by Innocent VI in 1362, dates that very probably fell during the lifetime of the *Pearl*-poet. See Herbermann 1912, 15:715.

10. Lists of the five joys of Mary varied in medieval accounts. Though often listed as the Annunciation, Nativity of Jesus, the Resurrection, the Ascension of Jesus, and the Assumption of Mary into heaven, the "Five Joys" in the Harley Lyrics include the Epiphany and omit the Ascension of Jesus. The related Five Joyful Mysteries of the modern rosary are the Annunciation, the Visitation, the Nativity, the Presentation, and the Finding in the Temple. The specific joy does not matter for the present argument that joy—any joy—is a mental state triggered by some physical reality.

11. A. V. C. Schmidt sensibly argues that lines 521–22, "Bot þen hyȝes Heruest and hardenes hym sone, / Warnez hym for þe wynter to wax ful rype," refer to more than a time of year. In addition to their literal meaning of a harvest hurrying nigh, urging crops to ripen, they carry a message for Gawain, a "warning addressed by autumn. . . . 'Harden yourself, be mature and ready to face winter' (that is, death)" (1987, 153).

12. In view of the importance to my argument of each scene's specific length, I list here a comparison of Hieatt's divisions and my own. Although Hieatt shows five divisions, splitting the castle scenes at the point where the lady leaves the bed chamber, I list them here as a single scene to facilitate comparison. Long after working out these scene divisions I discovered a 1974 article by Hans Käsmann, whose scene divisions, I was comforted to learn, agree precisely with my own.

Scene	Hieatt	Condren
1a	1126–1178	1133–1178
1b	1179–1318	1179–1318
1c	1319–1369	1319–1364
1d	1370–1420	1365–1411
2a	1421–1468	1412–1468
2b	1469–1560	1469–1560
2c	1561–1620	1561–1618
2d	1621–1689	1619–1687
3a	1690–1730	1688–1730
3b	1731–1893	1731–1893
3c	1894–1923	1894–1923
3d	1924–1978	1924–1990

13. Andrew and Waldron may be even more gracious than Gawain here in suggesting that line 1237 means merely "I am pleased to have you here" (1979, 253 n). Indeed she is. Her words in lines 1237–38 literally mean, "You are welcome to my body, / Your own dwelling to choose."

14. *Prayere* appears twice in ten lines, once in line 759 referring unambiguously to a spiritual communication (traceable to L. *precarium*), and again in line 768 where it undoubtedly refers to an expanse of rolling land (cf. NE *prairie* < OF praiere, "meadow"). While the two words have entirely different etymologies, they are identical in the manuscript, although the final -e on the word in 759 is unnecessary. It is difficult to avoid concluding that the poet planned these proximate occurrences to increase the chances of ambiguity in 768, where the castle is literally pitched on a parcel of land and figuratively erected as a result of Gawain's prayer.

15. Two single-digit discrepancies and one four-digit discrepancy between sections in *Sir Gawain* and groups of sections in *Purity*, do not invalidate the possibility that the sizes of *Purity*'s sections refer to sections of *Sir Gawain*. Equalities between *Sir Gawain* and *Purity*, as between any geometric figure and a whole-number system measuring the figure, will inevitably be slightly off, especially since *Purity*'s verse form is based on four-line units. In any case, if the poet intended to use *Purity*'s sections as a blueprint for some of the sections in *Sir Gawain*, he seems only to have had fitt 3 in mind. *Sir Gawain* 5 = *Purity* 6–9. *Sir Gawain* 6 = *Purity* 2–7. *Sir Gawain* 5–6 = *Purity* 2–10. *Sir Gawain* fitt 3 = *Purity* 6–12.

16. The arguments of this study are offered as an hypothesis, of course, an invitation to each reader to determine whether the geometric designs proposed here correspond to enough of the formal schemes of the texts, and are sufficiently suggestive of the manuscript's thematic content, that to argue against the hypothesis would present a more difficult challenge than to accept it.

17. In chapter 4, 96, it was shown that an accurate expansion of one of *Purity*'s phi ratios produces a dimension of 472. That the poet used 476 instead of 472 does not invalidate the thesis, but rather suggests that, as he was working from the center of

the medallion toward its extremes, the whole-number system he was using introduced progressively greater errors. See appendix 3 for a related discussion.

18. Although I have been considering 295 and 472 "*phi*-related," as I believe the
poet did, they differ by a little more than the four–unit error we noted earlier. 295 x
$\varphi = 477$. But the poet's original circle of radius 180, multiplied by φ^2, does equal
approximately 472.

19. An error of two units will be detected if one tries to reconcile the additive
equation and the product of a *phi*-related proportion, although in theory these two
results are identical. If 767 is extended by 472, it totals 1239. But 767 x $\varphi = 1241$, not
1239. That the poet imagined an extension of 474, the arithmetic mean between 472
and 476, the two dimensions between which he seems to have been alternating for
the radius OP of his larger circle, suggests that he was attempting to correct his, as it
were, unwanted "precession."

20. The so-called "extra decorated initial" at *Pearl* 961, though calling irregular
attention to a block of text, as discussed on pp. 66–72, is not an exception to this
claim. Its size is the same as every other decorated initial in the poem. All other
decorated initials in *Pearl* regularly mark the beginnings of 5-stanza sections and
the lone 6-stanza section. The decorated initials in *Patience* indicate major blocks of
text, not major and minor blocks.

Appendix 2. Construction of Three *Phi*-related Rectangles within a Dodeca-hedron

1. Modern mathematics, computing as precisely as an irrational number permits,
gives the square root of 5 as 2.23606 . . . . Since decimals were not available to the
fourteenth century, a medieval mathematician undoubtedly used the convergents of
nonsquare numbers devised by Heron of Alexandria (Heath 1921, 2:51, 316–26;
March 1998, 65 ff.). I assume the poet would have used the most convenient fractional convergent for the irrational $\sqrt{5}$, namely 20/9 (which would produce the
modern decimal 2.22222 . . .). More accurate convergents were known, for example,
29/13 (2.23076 . . .) or 38/17 (2.23529 . . .), but these fractions have numerators and
denominators with which one cannot work easily in mathematical computation,
whereas 20/9 is much more convenient.

2. Modern readers curious about how a fourteenth-century English poet would
have written and solved the equation in figure B.1 will be disappointed to hear that
it is impossible for us to know. We cannot be certain which of three systems of
fractional notation he may have used—common, sexagesimal, or unit. If he favored
common fractions, we would still be uncertain whether he placed the numerator
below the denominator, as many medieval mathematicians did, or the reverse, as the
modern world does. In either case, he would not have drawn a line to separate them.
The sexagesimal system of fractional notation used by the Babylonians in
Mesopotamia, though superior in every way to common and unit fractions—in fact
identical in principle to modern fractional notation as decimals—is an unlikely pos-

sibility, because until the sixteenth century it was always and only used with the full sexagesimal system, a method that was not used at all in England in the fourteenth century. If he used unit fractions, preferred by Heron of Alexandria (fl. A.D. 100) and by most of Europe for at least a millennium after Heron, we can get a sense of how awkward the computation would have been: "In dividing 25 by 13 [Heron] wrote the answer as $1 + 1/2 + 1/3 + 1/13 + 1/78$" (Boyer and Merzbach 1989, 174). A sense of how daunting unit fractions must have been can be seen in a remark of Fibonacci in the *Liber abaci:* "The fraction 98/100 . . . is broken into 1/100 1/50 1/5 1/4 1/2, while 99/100 appears as 1/25 1/5 1/4 1/2" (Boyer and Merzbach 255). Of only one thing may we be certain, that the slow development of zero as a symbol—its general use in western Europe postdated the late fourteenth century—would not have prevented computations like the equation in figure B.1 from being carried out. The equation would undoubtedly have been written in Roman numerals, which do not use a symbol for zero. The last five fractions in the previous sentence would probably have been written ic/c i/xxv i/v i/iiij i/ij.

3. The dimension of this diagonal can also be confirmed by the Pythagorean theorem: $C^2 = 248^2 + 401^2$. This produces a diagonal of 471.49.

Works Cited

Ackerman, J. S. 1949. "'Ars sine scientia nihil est': Gothic Theory of Architecture at the Cathedral of Milan." *The Art Bulletin*, 31:84–111.

Adelhard of Bath. See Cochrane, Louise.

Aers, David. 1997. "Christianity for Courtly Subjects: Reflections on the *Gawain*-Poet." In *A Companion to the Gawain-Poet*, edited by Derek Brewer and Jonathan Gibson. Cambridge, England: D. S. Brewer.

Alexander, Jonathan J. G. 1992. *Medieval Illuminators and Their Methods of Work*. New Haven: Yale University Press.

Allen, Hope Emily, ed. 1931. *English Writings of Richard Rolle, Hermit of Hampole*. Oxford: Clarendon Press.

Allen, Michael J. B. 1994. *Nuptial Arithmetic: Marsilio Ficino's Commentary on the Fatal Number in Book VIII of Plato's Republic*. Berkeley: University of California Press.

d'Alverny, Marie-Thérèse. 1982. "Translations and Translators." In *Renaissance and Renewal in the Twelfth Century*, edited by Robert Benson and Giles Constable. Oxford: Clarendon Press.

Anderson, J. J. See Cawley, A. C., and J. J. Anderson, eds.

Andrew, Malcolm. 1979. *The Gawain-Poet: An Annotated Bibliography 1839–1977*. New York: Garland.

———. 1997. "Theories of Authorship." In *A Companion to the Gawain Poet*, edited by Derek Brewer and Jonathan Gibson. Cambridge, England: D. S. Brewer.

Andrew, Malcolm, and Ronald Waldron. 1979. *The Poems of the Pearl Manuscript*. Berkeley: University of California Press.

Arthur, Ross G. 1991. "Gawain's Shield as Signum." In *Text and Matter: New Critical Perspectives of the Pearl-Poet*, edited by Robert Blanch, Miriam Youngerman Miller, and Julian N. Wasserman. Troy, N.Y.: Whitston Publishing Co.

Augustine, Saint. 1950. *The City of God*. Trans. Marcus Dods, D.D., with an introduction by Thomas Merton. New York: Random House.

———. 1964. *On Free Choice of the Will*. Trans. Anna S. Benjamin and L. H. Hackstaff, with an introduction by L. H. Hackstaff. New York: Bobbs-Merrill.

Backhouse, Janet. 1981. *The Lindisfarne Gospels*. London: Phaidon Press, Ltd.

Barbour, I. G. 1966. *Issues in Science and Religion*. London: S.C.M. Press.

Barrow, John D. 1995. *The Artful Universe: The Cosmic Source of Human Creativity*. New York: Little, Brown and Co.

Batts, Michael S. 1969. "Numerical Structure in Medieval Literature." In *Formal Aspects of Medieval German Poetry: A Symposium*, edited by Stanley N. Werbow. Austin: University of Texas Press.

Baumgartner, Walter. See Koehler, Ludwig, and Walter Baumgartner, eds.

Beaujouan, Guy. 1982. "The Transformation of the Quadrivium." In *Renaissance and Renewal in the Twelfth Century*, edited by Robert L. Benson and Giles Constable. Oxford: Clarendon Press.

Bennett, Michael J. 1979. "*Sir Gawain and the Green Knight* and the Literary Achievement of the North-West Midlands: The Historical Background." *Journal of Medieval History* 5:63–88.

———. 1983. *Community, Class and Careerism: Cheshire and Lancashire Society in the Age of Sir Gawain and the Green Knight*. Cambridge: Cambridge University Press.

———. 1997. "The Historical Background." In *A Companion to the Gawain Poet*, edited by Derek Brewer and Jonathan Gibson. Cambridge, England: D. S. Brewer.

Benson, Larry D. 1965. "The Authorship of *St. Erkenwald*." *Journal of English and Germanic Philology* 64:393–405.

Benson, Robert L., and Giles Constable, eds., with Carol D. Lanham. 1982. *Renaissance and Renewal in the Twelfth Century*. Oxford: Clarendon Press.

Biblia Sacra iuxta vulgatam versionem. 1975. Ed. Robertus Weber et al. 2d rev. ed. Rome: Desclee.

Blair, Peter Hunter. 1976. *Northumbria in the Days of Bede*. London: Victor Gallancz, Ltd.

Blanch, Robert J. 1991. "Supplement to the *Gawain* Poet: An Annotated Bibliography, 1978–1985." *Chaucer Review* 25:4, 363–86.

Blanch, Robert J., Miriam Youngerman Miller, and Julian N. Wasserman, eds. 1991. *Text and Matter: New Critical Perspectives of the Pearl-Poet*. Troy, N.Y: Whitston Publishing Co.

Blanch, Robert J., and Julian N. Wasserman. 1995. *From Pearl to Gawain: Forme to Fynisment*. Gainesville: University Press of Florida.

Blenkner, Louis, O.S.B. 1968. "The Theological Structure of *Pearl*." *Traditio* 24:43–75. Reprinted in *The Middle English Pearl: Critical Essays*. Ed. John Conley. Notre Dame, Ind.: University of Notre Dame Press.

Boethius, *De Institutione Arithmetica*. See Masi, Michael.

Bower, Calvin M. 1967. *Boethius' The Principles of Music: An Introduction, Translation, and Commentary*. Ann Arbor, Mich.: University Microfilms. 67–15, 005.

Bowers, John M. 2001. *The Politics of Pearl: Court Poetry in the Age of Richard II*. Cambridge, England: Boydell and Brewer.

Boyer, Carl B. 1989. *A History of Mathematics*. 2d ed. Revised by Uta C. Merzbach. New York: John Wiley and Sons.

Breidert, Wolfgang. 1970. *Das aristotelische Kontinuum in der Scholastik.* Beiträge zur Geschichte der Philosophie und Theologie des Mittelalters, N.F. 1. Münster: Aschendorff.

Brewer, Derek, and Jonathan Gibson. 1997. *A Companion to the Gawain-Poet.* Cambridge, England: D. S. Brewer.

Brown, T. J. 1960. See Lindisfarne Gospels.

Burrow, John A. 1965. *A Reading of Sir Gawain and the Green Knight.* London: Routledge and Kegan Paul.

———. 1984. "*Sir Thopas:* An Agony in Three Fits." *Review of English Studies,* n.s., 22 (1971):54–58. Reprinted in *Essays on Medieval Literature.* Oxford: Clarendon Press.

Cahill, Thomas. 1995. *How the Irish Saved Civilization: The Untold Story of Ireland's Heroic Role From the Fall of Rome to the Rise of Medieval Europe.* New York: Doubleday.

Caldwell, John. 1981. "The *De Institutione Arithmetica* and the *De Institutione Musica.*" In *Boethius: His Life, Thought and Influence,* edited by Margaret Gibson. Oxford: Basil Blackwell.

Capella, Martianus. See Stahl, William Harris.

Catholic Encyclopedia, The. See Herbermann, Charles G.

Cawley, A. C., and J. J. Anderson, eds. 1976. *Pearl, Cleanness, Patience and Sir Gawain and the Green Knight.* London: Dent; New York: Dutton.

Chrétien de Troyes. 1992. *Le Chevalier de la charrette, ou Le roman de Lancelot.* Ed. Charles Méla. Paris: Librairie Générale Française.

Citrome, Jeremy J. 2001. "Medicine as Metaphor in the Middle English *Cleanness.*" *Chaucer Review* 35:260–80.

Cochrane, Louise. 1994. *Adelhard of Bath: The First English Scientist.* London: British Museum Press.

Conant, Kenneth John. 1963. "Mediaeval Excavations at Cluny." *Speculum* 38:1–45.

Condren, E. I. 1999. *Chaucer and the Energy of Creation: The Design and Organization of the Canterbury Tales.* Gainesville: University Press of Florida.

Conley, John. 1970. *The Middle English Pearl: Critical Essays.* Notre Dame, London: University of Notre Dame Press.

Connolly, Margaret, ed. 1993. *Contemplations of the Dread and Love of God.* EETS no. 303. Oxford: Oxford University Press.

Constable, Giles. See Benson, Robert L., and Giles Constable.

Cooper, R. A., and D. A. Pearsall. 1988. "The *Gawain* Poems: A Statistical Approach to the Question of Common Authorship." *Review of English Studies,* n.s., 39 (155):365–85.

Crawford, Donna. 1993. "The Architectonics of *Cleanness.*" *Studies in Philology,* 90:29–45.

Curtius, Ernst Robert. 1953. *European Literature and the Latin Middle Ages.* Trans. Willard R. Trask. New York: Pantheon Books.

Davenport, W. A. 1978. *The Art of the Gawain Poet.* London: Athlone.

Donaldson, E. Talbot. 1972. "Oysters, Forsooth: Two Readings in 'Pearl.'" *Neuphilologische Mitteilungen* 73:75–82.

Duckworth, George. 1962. *Structural Patterns in Virgil's "Aeneid": A Study in Mathematical Composition*. Ann Arbor: University of Michigan Press.

Duggan, H. N. 1997. "Meter, Stanza, Vocabulary, Dialect." In *A Companion to the Gawain-Poet*, edited by Derek Brewer and Jonathan Gibson. Cambridge, England: Boydell and Brewer.

Eckhardt, Caroline D., ed. 1980. *Essays in the Numerical Criticism of Literature*. Lewisberg, Pa.: Bucknell University Press.

Edwards, A.S.G. 1997. "The Manuscript: British Library MS Cotton Nero A.x." In *A Companion to the Gawain-Poet*, edited by Derek Brewer and Jonathan Gibson. Cambridge, England: Boydell and Brewer.

Edwards, Lewis. 1958. "Some English Examples of the Mediaeval Representations of Church and Synagogue." *Transactions of the Jewish Historical Society of England* 18:63–75.

Eldredge, Laurence. 1979. "Late Medieval Discussions of the Continuum and the Point of the Middle English *Patience*." *Vivarium* 17:90–115.

Euclid. 1987. *The Mediaeval Latin Translation of Euclid's Elements*. Ed. H.L.L. Busard. Stuttgart: Franz Steiner Verlag.

Everett, Dorothy. 1955. "The Alliterative Revival." In *Essays on Middle English Literature*, edited by Patricia Kean. Oxford: Oxford University Press.

Farley-Hills, David. 1971. See Nolan, Barbara, and David Farley-Hills.

Fisher, Barbara M. 1997. *Noble Numbers, Subtle Words*. Cranbury, N.J.: Associated University Presses and Fairleigh Dickenson University Press.

Foley, Michael. 1989. "The *Gawain*-Poet: An Annotated Bibliography, 1978–1985." *Chaucer Review* 23 (3): 251–82.

Fowler, Alastair, ed. 1970. *Silent Poetry: Essays in Numerological Analysis*. London: Routledge and Kegan Paul.

Fowler, D. H. 1987. *The Mathematics of Plato's Academy: A New Reconstruction*. Oxford: Clarendon Press.

Frischer, Bernard. 1991. *Shifting Paradigms: New Approaches to Horace's "Ars Poetica."* American Classical Studies, no. 27. Atlanta: Scholars Press.

Galway, Margaret. 1947. "Joan of Kent and the Order of the Garter." *University of Birmingham Historical Journal* 1:13–50.

Ghyka, Matila. 1977. *The Geometry of Art and Life*. New York: Dover Publications.

Gibson, Jonathan. See Brewer, Derek, and Jonathan Gibson.

Gilligan, Janet. 1986. "Neoplatonic Cosmology and the Middle English 'Patience.'" Ph.D. diss., Northern Illinois University. Abstract in *Dissertation Abstracts International* 8625551.

———. 1987. "Numerical Composition in the Middle English *Patience*." *Studia Neophilologica* 61:7–11.

Gollancz, I., ed. [1923] 1971. *Pearl, Cleanness, Patience and Sir Gawain*. Reproduced in facsimile from the unique MS. Cotton Nero A.x in the British Museum. With an introduction by I. Gollancz. Published for the Early English Text Society. Oxford: Oxford University Press.

Green, R. H. 1956. "Alan of Lille's *De planctu naturae.*" *Speculum* 31:649–74.

Greene, Brian. 1999. *The Elegant Universe: Superstrings, Hidden Dimensions, and the Quest for the Ultimate Theory.* New York: W. W. Norton and Co.

Greenwood, Ormerod, trans. 1956. *"Sir Gawain and the Green Knight": A Fourteenth Century Alliterative Poem now Attributed to Hugh Mascy.* London: Lion and Unicorn Press.

Guzzardo, John J. 1987. *Dante: Numerological Studies.* American University Studies, series 2, Romance Languages and Literature, vol. 59. New York: Peter Lang.

Hart, Thomas Elwood. 1980. "Tectonic Methodology and an Application to *Beowulf.*" In *Essays in the Numerical Criticism of Medieval Literature,* edited by Caroline D. Eckhardt. Lewisburg, Pa.: Bucknell University Press.

Haskins, C. H. 1960. *Studies in the History of Medieval Science.* New York: Ungar Publishing Co.

Hawkins, Sherman. 1964. "Chaucer's Prioress and the Sacrifice of Praise." *Journal of English and Germanic Philology* 63:599–624.

Heath, Sir Thomas. 1921. *A History of Greek Mathematics. Vol I From Thales to Euclid; vol.II From Aristarchus to Diophantus.* Oxford: Clarendon Press.

Heninger, S. K., Jr. See Peterson, R. G. 1977.

Herbermann, Charles G., et al. 1912. *The Catholic Encyclopedia.* New York: Encyclopedia Press.

Herbert, George. 1633. *The Bodleian Manuscript of George Herbert's Poems: A Facsimile of Tanner 307.* Introduction by Amy M. Charles and Mario A. Di Cesare. Vol. 3. Delmar, New York: Scholars' Facsimiles and Reprints.

Herz-Fischler, Roger. 1998. *A Mathematical History of the Golden Number.* New York: Dover Publications.

Hieatt, A. Kent. 1960. *Short Time's Endless Monument.* New York: Columbia University Press.

———. 1970. *"Sir Gawain:* Pentangle, *luf-lace,* Numerical Structure." In *Silent Poetry: Essays in Numerological Analysis,* edited by Alastair Fowler. London: Routledge and Kegan Paul. Originally appeared in *Papers on Language and Literature* 4 (1968):339–59.

Higgins, Dick. 1987. *Pattern Poetry: Guide to an Unknown Literature.* Albany: State University of New York Press.

Hiscock, Nigel. 1999. *The Wise Master Builder: Platonic Geometry in Plans of Medieval Abbeys and Cathedrals.* Aldershot, England: Ashgate Publishing.

Honnecourt, Villard de. 1962. *The Sketchbook of Villard de Honnecourt.* Ed. Theodore Bowie. Bloomington: Indiana University Press.

Hopper, Vincent Foster. 1938. *Medieval Number Symbolism: Its Sources, Meaning, and Influence on Thought and Expression.* Columbia University Studies in English and Comparative Literature, no. 132. New York: Cooper Square Publishers.

Horgan, A. D. 1981. "Justice in *The Pearl.*" *Review of English Studies* 32:173–80.

———. 1987. "Gawain's *Pure Pentaungel* and the Virtue of Faith." *Medium Ævum* 56:310–16.

Huntley, H. E. 1970. *The Divine Proportion: A Study in Mathematical Beauty.* New York: Dover Publications.

James, John. [1982] 1990. *The Master Masons of Chartres.* London: West Grinstead Publishing. Originally published as *Chartres: The Masons who Built a Legend.* London: Routledge and Keegan Paul.

Johnson, Lynn Staley. 1984. *The Voice of the Gawain-Poet.* Madison: University of Wisconsin Press.

Käsmann, Hans. 1974. "Numerical Structure in Fitt III of *Sir Gawain and the Green Knight.*" In *Chaucer and Middle English Studies in Honour of Rossell Hope Robbins,* edited by Beryl Rowland. London: Allen and Unwin; Kent, Ohio: Kent State University Press.

Keyes, Clinton Walker. 1970. *Cicero, De Re Publica,* with an English translation. Loeb Classical Library, vol. 16. Cambridge: Harvard University Press.

Klibansky, R. 1939. *The Continuity of the Platonic Tradition.* London: Warburg Institute.

Knowles, Dom David. 1955. *The Religious Orders in England.* Vol. 2. Cambridge: Cambridge University Press.

Koehler, Ludwig, and Walter Baumgartner, eds. 1953. *Lexicon in Veteris Testamenti Libros.* Leiden, Holland: E. J. Brill.

Laferrière, Daniel. See Peterson, R. G. 1977.

Le Grelle, G. 1949. "Le premier livre des Géorgiques, poème pythagoricien." *Études classiques* 17:139–235.

de Lettenhove, K. 1870. *Oeuvres de Froissart: Chroniques.* Vol. 1, pt. 1. Brussels, Belgium: V. Devaux et Cie.

Lewis, Charlton T., and Charles Short. [1879] 1962. *A Latin Dictionary.* Oxford: Clarendon Press.

Lindisfarne Gospels, The. 1960. *Evangeliorum Quattuor Codex Lindisfarnensis* [The Lindisfarne Gospels, a full facsimile in 2 vols.]. Ed. T. D. Kendrick et al. Lausanne, Switzerland: Urs Graf-Verlag.

Mann, Jill. 1986. "Price and Value in *Sir Gawain and the Green Knight.*" *Essays in Criticism* 36:294–318.

March, Lionel. 1996. "Renaissance Mathematics and Architectural Proportion in Alberti's *De re aedificatoria.*" *Architectural Quarterly* 2:54–65.

———. 1998. *Architectonics of Humanism: Essays on Number in Architecture.* Chichester, England: Academy Editions.

Marzac, Nicole. 1968. *Richard Rolle de Hampole: Vie et Oeuvres et Édition critique, traduite et commentée du Tractatus Super Apocalypsim.* Paris: Librairie Philosophique J. Vrin.

Masi, Michael. 1983. *Boethian Number Theory: A Translation of the De Institutione Arithmetica.* Studies in Classical Antiquity, vol. 6. Amsterdam: Rodopi.

McColly, W. B., and D. Weier. 1983. "Literary Attribution Likelihood Ratio Tests:

The Case of the Middle English *Pearl*-poems." *Computers and the Humanities* 17:65–75.

McIntosh, A. 1963. "A New Approach to Middle English Dialectology." *English Studies* 44:1–11.

Menninger, Karl. 1969. *Number Words and Number Symbols: A Cultural History of Numbers.* Trans. Paul Broneer. 1992. Reprint, New York: Dover Publications. Originally published 1957–58 as *Zahlwort und Ziffer: Eine Kulturgeschichte der Zahlen.* Göttingen, Germany: Vandenhoeck and Ruprecht Publishing Co.

Midmer, Roy. 1979. *English Mediaeval Monasteries (1066–1540).* Athens: University of Georgia Press.

Millar, E. G. 1923. *The Lindisfarne Gospels.* London: British Museum.

Miller, Miriam Youngerman. See Blanch, Robert J., Miriam Youngerman Miller, and Julian N. Wasserman.

Moorman, Charles. 1977. *The Works of the Gawain Poet.* Jackson: University Press of Mississippi.

Morse, Charlotte C. 1978. *The Pattern of Judgment in the Queste and Cleanness.* Columbia: University of Missouri Press.

Murdoch, John E. 1968. "The Medieval Euclid: Salient Aspects of the Translations of the *Elements* by Adelard of Bath and Campanus of Novara." *Revue de Synthèse* 89:67–94. *Colloques Textes des Rapports* of the XIIᵉ Congrès d'Histoire des Sciences. Paris: Éditions Albin Michel.

———. [1970] 1980. "Euclid." *Dictionary of Scientific Biography.* Ed. Charles Coulston Gillispie. New York: Charles Scribner's Sons.

Murdoch, John E., and Edward A. Synan. 1966. "Two Questions on the Continuum: Walter Chatton (?), O.F.M. and Adam Woodham, O.F.M." *Franciscan Studies* 26:212–88.

Murley, Clyde. 1937. "The Structure and Proportion of Catullus LXIV." *Transactions and Proceedings of the American Philological Association* 68:305–17.

Nelson, Cary. 1973. *The Incarnate Word.* Urbana: University of Illinois Press.

Nicomachus of Gerasa. [1926] 1972. *Introduction to Arithmetic.* Trans. M. L. D'Ooge, with Studies in Greek Arithmetic by F. D. Robbins and L. C. Karpinsky. New York: Johnson Reprint Corp.

Nolan, Barbara. 1977. *The Gothic Visionary Perspective.* Princeton, N.J.: Princeton University Press.

Nolan, Barbara, and David Farley-Hills. 1971. "The Authorship of *Pearl:* Two Notes." *Review of English Studies,* n.s., 22:295–302.

OED [The Compact Edition of the Oxford English Dictionary]. 1971. Ed. Sir James Augustus Henry Murray. Oxford: Oxford University Press.

Old Testament. 1987. *The NIV Interlinear Hebrew-English Old Testament.* Ed. John R. Kohlenberger III. Grand Rapids, Mich.: Zondervan Publishing House.

Otis, Brooks. 1970. *Ovid as an Epic Poet.* 2d ed. Cambridge: Cambridge University Press.

Oxford Latin Dictionary. 1983. Ed. P.G.W. Glare. Oxford: Clarendon Press.

Pacioli, Luca. 1956. *De divina proportione.* Fontes Ambrosiani, vol. 31. Milano: [Silvana Editrice?].

Pearsall, D. A. See Cooper, R. A., and D. A. Pearsall.

Peck, Russell A. 1980. "Number as Cosmic Language." In *Essays in the Numerical Criticism of Medieval Literature,* edited by Caroline D. Eckhardt. Lewisberg, Pa.: Bucknell University Press.

Peterson, C. J. 1974a. "*Pearl* and *St. Erkenwald:* Some Evidence for Authorship." *Review of English Studies* 25:49–53.

———. 1974b. "The *Pearl*-Poet and John Massey of Cotton, Cheshire." *Review of English Studies,* n.s., 25:257–66.

———. 1977. "Hoccleve, the Old Hall Manuscript, Cotton Nero A.x, and the *Pearl*-Poet." *Review of English Studies,* n.s., 28:49–55, with reply by Edward Wilson, 55–56.

Peterson, R. G. 1976. "Critical Calculations: Measure and Symmetry in Literature." *PMLA* 91:367–75.

———. 1977. "Forum." *PMLA* 92:126–29.

Plato. 1961. *The Collected Dialogues of Plato.* Ed. Edith Hamilton and Huntington Cairns. New York: Bollingen Foundation.

Platt, Colin. 1984. *The Abbeys and Priories of Medieval England.* London: Secker & Warburg, Ltd.

Prior, Sandra Pierson. 1996. *The Fayre Formez of the Pearl Poet.* Medieval Texts and Studies, no. 18. East Lansing: Michigan State University Press.

Rashdall, Hastings. [1895] 1936. *The Universities of Europe in the Middle Ages.* Ed. F. M. Powicke and A. B. Emden. Vol 1., 3d ed. Oxford: Clarendon Press.

Reuchlin, Johann. 1983. *Johann Reuchlin: De arte cabalistica, On the Art of the Kabbalah.* Trans. Martin and Sarah Goodman, with an introduction by G. Lloyd Jones. New York: Abaris Books.

Revised Medieval Latin Word-List From British and Irish Sources. 1965. Ed. R. E. Latham. London: Oxford, for the British Academy.

Ridley, Florence H. 1987. "The Prioress' Prologue and Tale." In *The Riverside Chaucer,* edited by Larry D. Benson, gen. ed. 3d ed. Boston: Houghton Mifflin.

Robertson, Michael. 1982. "Stanzaic Symmetry in *Sir Gawain and the Green Knight.*" *Speculum* 57:779–85.

Robson, C. A. 1961. "The Techniques of Symmetrical Composition in Medieval Narrative Poetry." *Studies in Medieval French presented to Alfred Ewert.* Oxford: Clarendon Press.

Rothschild, Victoria. 1984. "The *Parliament of Fowls:* Chaucer's Mirror up to Nature?" *Review of English Studies,* n.s., 35:164–84.

Russell, J. Stephen. 1998. *Chaucer and the Trivium: The Mindsong of the "Canterbury Tales."* Gainesville: University Press of Florida.

Scarry, Elaine. 1980. "The Well-Rounded Sphere: The Metaphysical Structure of the

Consolation of Philosophy." In *Essays in the Numerical Criticism of Literature,* edited by Caroline Eckhardt. Lewisberg, Pa.: Bucknell University Press.

Schlauch, Margaret. 1939. "The Allegory of Church and Synagogue." *Speculum* 14:448–64.

Schmidt, A.V.C. 1987. "'Latent Content' and 'The Testimony in the Text': Symbolic Meaning in *Sir Gawain and the Green Knight.*" *Review of English Studies,* n.s., 38 (150): 145–68.

Septuaginta. [1935] 1952. *Septuaginta; id est, Vetus Testamentum Graece iuxta lxx interpretes, edidit Alfred Rahlfs.* Editio quinta. Stuttgart, Germany: Privilegierte Wuerttembergische Bibelanstalt.

Shepherd, Geoffrey, ed. 1965. *Sir Philip Sidney: An Apology for Poetry or The Defence of Poesy.* London: Thomas Nelson and Sons.

Shoaf, R. A. 1984. *The Poem as Green Girdle: Commercialism in Sir Gawain and the Green Knight.* University of Florida Monographs, Humanities 55. Gainesville: University Press of Florida.

Simson, Otto von. [1956] 1989. *The Gothic Cathedral: Origins of Gothic Architecture and the Medieval Concept of Order.* 3d ed., expanded. Bollingen Series, no. XLVII. Princeton: Princeton University Press.

Singleton, Charles S. [1965] 1980. "The Poet's Number at the Center." In *Essays in the Numerical Criticism of Medieval Literature,* edited by Caroline D. Eckhardt. Lewisburg, Pa.: Bucknell University Press. Originally published in *Modern Language Notes* 80:1–10.

Souter, Alexander. 1949. *A Glossary of Later Latin to 600 A.D.* Oxford: Clarendon Press.

Southern, R. W. 1979. *Platonism, Scholastic Method and the School of Chartres.* Reading, England: Reading University Press.

———. 1982. "The Schools of Paris and the School of Chartres." In *Renaissance and Renewal in the Twelfth Century,* edited by Robert L. Benson and Giles Constable. Oxford: Clarendon Press.

Spearing, A. C. 1970. *The Gawain Poet: A Critical Study.* Cambridge: Cambridge University Press.

———. 1980. "*Purity* and Danger." *Essays in Criticism* 30:293–310.

Stahl, William Harris. 1971. *The Quadrivium of Martianus Capella.* Latin Traditions in the Mathematical Sciences, 50 B.C. to A.D. 1250. New York: Columbia University Press.

Stanbury, Sarah. 1991. *Seeing the Gawain-Poet: Description and the Art of Perception.* Philadelphia: University of Pennsylvania Press.

Stevick, Robert D. 1982. "A Formal Analogue of *Elene.*" *Studies in Medieval and Renaissance History* 5:47–104.

———. 1994. *The Earliest Irish and English Bookarts: Visual and Poetic Forms Before A.D. 1000.* Philadelphia: University of Pennsylvania Press.

Stock, Lorraine Kochanske. 1991. "The 'Poynt' of *Patience*." In *Text and Matter: New Critical Perspectives of the Pearl-Poet*, edited by Robert S. Blanch, Miriam Younger Miller, and Julian N. Wasserman. Troy, N.Y.: Whitston Publishing Co.

Synan, Edward A. See Murdoch, John E., and Edward A. Synan.

Tavernor, Robert. 1991. *Palladio and Palladianism*. New York: Thames and Hudson.

Taylor, A. E. [1928] 1962. *A Commentary on Plato's Timaeus*. Oxford: Clarendon Press.

Thorpe, Douglas. 1991. *A New Earth: The Labor of Language in Pearl, Herbert's Temple, and Blake's Jerusalem*. Washington, D.C.: Catholic University of America Press.

Tinkle, Theresa. 1988. "The Heart's Eye: Beatific Vision in *Purity*." *Studies in Philology* 88:451–70.

Tregelles, Samuel Prideaux. 1979. *Gesenius' Hebrew and Chaldee Lexicon to the Old Testament Scriptures*. Grand Rapids, Mich.: Wm. B. Eerdmans Publishing Co.

Trigg, Stephanie. 1991. "The Romance of Exchange: *Sir Gawain and the Green Knight*." *Viator* 22:251–66.

Underhill, Evelyn. [1955] 1970. *Mysticism: A Study in the Nature and Development of Man's Spiritual Consciousness*. New York: World Publishing Co.

Vergil, Polydore. 1950. *The Anglica Historia of Polydore Vergil*. Ed. and trans. Denys Hay. London: Royal Historical Society.

Virgil [Publius Vergilius Maro]. [1935] 1994. *Virgil I*. Ed. and trans. H. Rushton Fairclough. Loeb Classical Library, no. 63. New, rev. ed. Cambridge: Harvard University Press.

Vitruvius. [1931] 1955. *Vitruvius on Architecture*. Ed. Frank Granger. Loeb Classical Library. Cambridge: Harvard University Press.

Waldron, Ronald. See Andrew, Malcolm, and Ronald Waldron.

Wallace, David. 1991. "*Cleanness* and the Terms of Terror." In *Text and Matter: New Critical Perspectives of the Pearl-Poet*, edited by Robert J. Blanch, Miriam Youngerman Miller, and Julian N. Wasserman. Troy, N.Y.: Whitston Publishing Co.

Wanderer [Old English elegy]. 1936. *The Exeter Book*. Ed. George Phillip Krapp and Elliott Van Kirk Dobbie. Anglo Saxon Poetic Records, vol 3. New York: Columbia University Press.

Wasserman, Julian N. See Blanch, Robert J., and Julian N. Wasserman. See also Blanch, Robert, J., Miriam Youngerman Miller, and Julian N. Wasserman.

Weier, D. See McColly, W. B., and D. Weier.

Weiss, R. 1952. "England and the Decree of the Council of Vienne on the teaching of Greek, Arabic, Hebrew and Syriac." *Bibliothèque d'Humanisme et Renaissance* 14:1 ff.

Wenzel, Siegfried. 1967. *The Sin of Sloth: Acedia in Medieval Thought and Literature*. Chapel Hill: University of North Carolina Press.

White, Alison. 1981. "Boethius in the Medieval Quadrivium." In *Boethius: His Life, Thought and Influence,* edited by Margaret Gibson. Oxford: Basil Blackwell.

Whitman, Malcolm D. [1932] 1968. *Tennis: Origins and Mysteries.* With an historical bibliography by Robert W. Henderson. Detroit: Singing Tree Press.

Williams, Sister Margaret. 1970. *The Pearl Poet: His Complete Works.* New York: Vintage.

Wills, Garry. 1992. *Lincoln at Gettysburg: The Words That Remade America.* New York: Simon and Schuster [Touchstone Books].

Wilson, Edward. See Peterson, C. J. 1977.

Wycliffe, John. 1850. *The Holy Bible.* 4 vols. Trans. John Wycliffe and his followers. Ed. Rev. Josiah Forshall and Sir Frederic Madden. Oxford: Oxford University Press.

Zubov, V. P. 1961. "Jean Buridan et les concepts du point au quatorzième siècle." *Medieval and Renaissance Studies* 5:43–95.

Index

Ackerman, J. S., 173
Adelard of Bath, 5, 168
Adelricus me fecit, 166
Aers, David, 136, 182
Alberti, Leon Batista, 46, 90
Alcuin, 5
Alexander, Jonathan J. G., 178
Algebra: and al-Khwarizmi, 151
Allen, M.J.B., 26
Alliteration: in Cotton Nero A.x, 27–28, 44
Alliterative line. *See* Alliteration
Amiens, 23
Anderson, J. J. *See* Cawley, A. C., and J. J.
    Anderson
Andrew, Malcolm, 166; and Ronald Waldron,
    17, 19, 74, 136, 165, 172, 176, 184
Apocalypse, Book of the, 38, 72
Aquinas, Thomas, 175
Aristotle, 37, 175. *See also Pearl*
Arithmetic: and rhythm, 170
Arthur, Ross G., 114
Augustine, Saint, 4, 75; *The City of God*, 38;
    De civitate Dei, 177; *De libero arbitrio
    voluntatis*, 12–13; *Enchiridion*, 177

Babylonian quadratics, 159
Babylonian/Sumerian compromise, 24
Backhouse, Janet, 179
Baker, John, 169
Barbour, I. G., 166
Barrow, John D., 36
Batts, Michael S., 167
Baumgartner, Walter. *See* Koeler, Ludwig,
    and Walter Baumgartner

Bede, Venerable, 21, 86
Benjamin, Anna S., 12
Bennett, Michael J., 165
Benson, Larry, 2
Beowulf, 6
Bibla sacra, 169
Blanch, Robert J., 166; and Julian N.
    Wasserman, 166, 183
Blenkner, Louis, 174, 176–77
Boethius, 34, 62, 132; *Consolation of Phi-
    losophy*, 53, 87; *De musica*, 4
Bonacci, Filius. *See* Fibonacci, Leonardo of
    Pisa
Bonettus, Nicholas, 175
Bookart: early medieval insular, 87–91,
    178–79; and *Purity*, 90–98. *See also*
    Divine Proportion
Borges, Jorge Luis: and numerical construc-
    tion, 6–7, 169
Boyer, Carl B., and Uta C. Merzbach, 170,
    173, 176
Bradwardine, Thomas, 175
Brewer, Derek, and Jonathan Gibson, 166
Briedert, Wolfgang, 175
Burrow, John A., 118–19, 182

Caesura, 27–28
Cahill, Thomas, 178
Caldwell, John, 173
Campanus of Novara, 32, 173
Capella, Martianus, 4, 22, 34; *De nuptiis*,
    168; *The Marriage of Philology and Mer-
    cury*, 168
Catullus LXIV, 87

Cawley, A. C., and J. J. Anderson, 17, 136
Chartres, 23, 34–35, 168
Chartres, Thierry of, 34
Chaucer, Geoffrey, 17, 23, 87; *Canterbury Tales,* 75; *Ellesmere Manuscript,* 1; *Friar's Tale,* 183; *House of Fame,* 74; *Parliament of Fowls,* 6, 168; *Prioress's Tale,* 170, 181; *Summoner's Tale,* 183; *Tale of Sir Thopas,* 6; *Wife of Bath's Prologue and Tale,* 183
Chi-Rho symbol, 88, 105, 114
Chrétien de Troyes, 122
Cicero, 11, 169
Clannesse. *See Purity*
Clement V, Pope, 45
Cluny III: Great Church of, 21
Cochrane, Louise, 168
Collet, John, 46
Commensurable, 26
Condren, Edward I., 181, 183
Continuum, 43. *See also Pearl*
Convergent, 178, 185; rational, 29
Cooper, R. A., and D. A. Pearsall, 166
Cotton Nero A.x, 8, 13, 16–17, 19, 37, 41; EETS facsimile edition, 165; grouping of poems, 1–3, 76, 166; order of poems, 17, 28–31, 43–44, 48; size of poems, 76. *See also* Divine Proportion; Excess; Factors: in Cotton Nero A.x,; Infinity; Kabbalah; Mathematics; Number series and systems; Ratio
Cotton Nero A.x poet: identity of, 1–2, 8–89, 165–66, 179; influences on, 4, 37, 46, 89–90, 177. *See also* Northwest midlands
Counting system, medieval, 21
Crawford, Donna, 178
Curtius, Ernst, 5, 168
Cuthbert, St., 89

D'Alverny, 168
Dante Alighieri, 17; *Commedia,* 6, 22, 25; *Inferno,* 22, 25; *Paradiso,* 22; *Purgatorio,* 22, 74; *Vita Nuova,* 6
Da Vinci, Leonardo, 32, 173
Decimal system, 22, 24–25, 38, 178; historical context, 16, 178, 185–86; in *Patience,* 22, 108; in *Pearl,* 61; in *Sir Gawain,* 22

Defense of Poesy, The, 167
De Lettenhove, K., 182
Della Mirandola, Pico, 46
De Meun, Jean, 51, 80
Diagonal, 173
Divine Proportion, 7–10, 26, 31–37, 45, 48, 63, 154, 173; in bookart, early medieval insular, 88, 93–95; construction of, 149–51; and the dodecahedron, 64–65; as governing ratio of Cotton Nero A.x, 14–16, 45, 60, 90–91, 93, 107, 116, 139–40, 157; as a manifestation of Divinity, 33; in *Patience,* 112–13, 181; in *Pearl,* 58–59, 61–62, 180; and the pentangle, 40; in *Purity,* 84–87, 93, 95–96, 178; in *Sir Gawain,* 127–28, 138–39, 142–44, 185. *See also* Horace: and the Divine Proportion; Proportion; Ratio; Virgil: and the Divine Proportion
Divine Section. *See* Divine Proportion
Division into extreme and mean ratio. *See* Divine Proportion
Dodecadic time, 26
Dodecahedron, 36, 40, 76; divine rectangles within, 64–65, 108–10, 116, 139, 153–55; and the icosahedron, 153, 175–76; in *Patience,* 108–9; in *Pearl,* 60–65, 93, 147, 175–76; in *Purity,* 109; in *Sir Gawain,* 139; thematic and theological significance of, 63–64. *See also* Divine Proportion
Donaldson, Talbot, 58, 174–75
Dream of the Rood, 69
Duckworth, George, 7
Duggan, H. N., 165
Duodecimal system, 9, 21–22, 24–25, 38; in *Patience,* 108; in *Pearl,* 22, 60–61, 147; in *Purity,* 22, 83, 107–8

Ecclesiastes, 10–13
Edward III, 19, 89, 170
Edwards, A.S.G., 172, 173, 176
Eldredge, Laurence, 175
Elene, 88, 178
Erkenwald, St., 2
Eternity, 3, 16, 26, 45, 90; in *Pearl,* 55, 71; in *Purity,* 98; in *Sir Gawain,* 129

Euclid, 5, 31–32; *Elements*, 34, 168, 173, 175; theorems, 180
Euclidean geometry, 36, 88, 90, 97, 153
Euclidean-Pythagorean principles, 4
Everett, Dorothy, 75
Evodius, 12
Excess lines: in Cotton Nero A.x, 21, 27; in *Patience*, 21–22; in *Pearl*, 18–19; in *Purity*, 18–19; in *Sir Gawain*, 18–22
Expansion, 3, 16, 28, 40, 90; Kabbalist, 45–48, 105; from Old Law into New, 98, 104, 147; in *Patience*, 105, 107–8, 112–16; in *Pearl*, 49–51, 55, 64, 66, 128; possible error in, 157–58; in *Purity*, 86; in *Sir Gawain*, 128–29, 134, 142, 145, 185

Factors: in Cotton Nero A.x, 24, 147, 172
Farley-Hills, David. *See* Nolan, Barbara, and David Farley-Hills
Fibonacci, Leonardo of Pisa, 35, 186
Fibonacci series of numbers, 23, 35, 172
Ficino, Marsilio, 26
Fisher, Barbara M., 169
Foley, Michael, 166
Fractions: historical use of, 16, 176, 178, 185–86; problems with, 66, 172, 181
French, Old: narrative poetry, 87
Froissart, Jean, 119

Gall, Saint, 23
Garter, Order of the, 19, 170–71
Gawain-poet. *See* Cotton Nero A.x poet
Genesis, Book of, 38; in *Purity*, 78–79
Ghyka, Matila, 12, 167, 176
Gibson, Jonathan. *See* Brewer, Derek, and Jonathan Gibson
Golden, 26
Golden Mass, 183
Golden Section. *See* Divine Proportion; Kepler, Johannes
Golden time, 26
Gollancz, I., 19, 172
Goodman, Martin and Sarah, 105
Greek-Arabic science, 5
Greene, Brian, 166

Greenwood, Ormerod, 165
Grosseteste, Robert, 175

Hackstaff, L. H., 12
Hart, Thomas Elwood, 6, 167
Haskins, C. H., 168
Hawkins, Sherman, 181
Heath, Sir Thomas, 113, 173–74, 176
Heninger, S. K., 167
Herberman, Charles G., 183
Herbert, George, 167
Heron of Alexandria, 185–86
Herz-Fischler, Roger, 173
Hesiod, 8
Hieatt, A. Kent, 6, 131, 183–84
Higgins, Dick, 167
Hippasus of Metapontum, 35, 37
Hiscock, Nigel, 34
Hopper, Vincent Foster, 168
Horace: and the Divine Proportion, 7–9
Horgan, A. D., 183
Huntley, H. E., 172

Immaculate Conception, 177
Incommensurable, 10, 26, 37, 169, 175, 178
Infinity, 15, 36, 40–41, 178; in Cotton Nero A.x, 26, 41, 90, 116; in *Patience*, 43; in *Pearl*, 53–55, 58–59, 61; in *Purity*, 86; in *Sir Gawain*, 129, 134
Irrational number, 10, 30, 35, 37, 169

Jerome, Saint, 11
John, Gospel According to, 38, 72, 173
John the Canon, 175
John the Evangelist, 183
Jonas, Book of, 2, 89, 180; in *Patience*, 98–101, 107–8, 130
Judeo-Christian, 99, 180

Kabbalah: as a tool for reading Cotton Nero A.x, 45–48. *See also* Expansion
Käsmann, Hans, 183
Kepler, Johannes: on the Golden Section, 32–33, 35–37; in praise of five, 44–45, 47
Kings, Book of, 169
Knowles, Dom David, 179

Koehler, Ludwig, and Walter Baumgartner, 178

Laferrière, Daniel, 167
Langland, William, 1
Leonardo of Pisa. *See* Fibonacci, Leonardo of Pisa
Lewis, Charlton T., and Charles Short, 11, 169
Lindisfarne Gospels, 88–91, 94, 96, 116, 179
Luke, Gospel According to, 73

Mann, Jill, 182
March, Lionel, 46, 167, 169
Mark, Gospel According to, 116
Marlowe, Christopher: and numerical construction, 6
Martianus. *See* Capella, Martianus
Masi, Michael, 64
Mathematics: medieval, 4–5, 149, 151, 153–55, 172; as a device for understanding Cotton Nero A.x, 3–4, 7, 37–45, 147, 166; history of analytic reasoning, 10–13, 166–67; history of use in literature, 4–10, 167; and theology, 147; Timaean, 88
Matthew, Gospel According to, 54, 179
McColly, W. B., and D. Weier, 166
McIntosh, Angus, 165
Measure, 10, 12, 88
Menninger, Karl, 17, 170, 172
Merzbach, Uta C. *See* Boyer, Carl B., and Uta C. Merzbach
Michael's, Saint, at Hildesheim, 23
Midmer, Roy, 179
Mignot, Jean, 34
Milan cathedral, 34
Millar, E. G., 179
Milton, John, 174
Monasteries, 179
Moorman, Charles, 17
Morse, Charlotte, 75, 177, 180
Mount Auburn, 174
Murdoch, John E., 168; and Edward A. Synan, 175
Music, 4–5, 169, 171; harmony, 4, 31; key,

21–22, 27; in *Purity*, 82–83; in *Sir Gawain*, 132–38

Natural number system. *See* Number series and systems, integer
Neoplatonists, 177
Neopythagoreans, 36, 40
New Testament, 45, 69, 90, 107; in *Patience*, 103; in *Pearl*, 16, 47; in *Purity*, 79–80, 98; in *Sir Gawain*, 16, 47
Nicholas of Lyra, 45
Nichomachus of Gerasa, 169, 173; *Introductio arithmeticae*, 34
Nichomachus's tenth, 35
Nolan, Barbara, 49, 174; and David Farley-Hills, 165
Northwest midlands: dialect of, 1, 165; as home of Cotton Nero A.x poet, 89–90, 165
Number, 10, 12, 34, 36, 88, 172, 173; Arabic and Roman numerals, 171; and the Divine, 4–5; five, 45, 50, 128, 134, 183; in Gawain's first vesting scene, 39; twelve, 38, 170
Number series and systems, 16–26; in Cotton Nero A.x, 17–26; cube, 18; dozens, 22; square, 18; even, 18, 22; hexadic, 26; imperfection of whole-number systems, 26; integer, 18, 21–22, 25; odd, 18, 22; perfect, 18, 21, 26, 171; prime, 18, 170; sexagesimal, 22, 24–25, 176, 185–86; of twenties, 22; whole number, 24, 26–27, 36. *See also* Fibonacci series of numbers
Numeracy. *See* Numerical construction
Numerical construction: and literature, 3, 10, 24, 167; in *Purity*, 82–83, 178. *See also* Borges, Jorge Luis: and numerical construction; Horace: and the Divine Proportion; Marlowe, Christopher: and numerical construction; Shakespeare, William: and numerical construction; Virgil: and the Divine Proportion
Numerical design. *See* Numerical construction
Numerology, 3

Ockham, William of, 175
Old Law, 38, 170
Old Testament, 45–46, 69, 90, 107, 177; in
    Patience, 2, 16, 44, 47, 99, 103–4; in *Pu-
    rity*, 2, 16, 44, 47, 79–80, 98, 103
Ovid, 5

Pacioli, Luca, 32–33, 62–62, 173
Pappas, 173
Patience, 1–2, 15–19, 21–24, 27–28, 30, 38,
    41, 43–44, 75, 117, 171; cross of Christ
    in, 106–7, 114–16; dimensions of, 109–
    16, 139, 142, 181–82; divisions and deco-
    rated initials of, 108, 172, 176, 177, 181;
    God's justice and mercy in, 104, 139;
    Jonas in, 42, 99–104, 107, 130, 137–38;
    meter in, 99, 107; predestination and
    free will in, 99; Psalm 68 in, 102; shield
    design in, 110–14; thematic unity with
    Purity, *Pearl*, and *Sir Gawain*, 103–4,
    108–9. *See also* Decimal system; Divine
    Proportion; Dodecahedron; Duodecimal
    system; Expansion; Factors; Jonas, Book
    of; New Testament; Old Testament; Pen-
    tagon; Prime numbers; Ratio
Pearl, 1–3, 15–19, 23, 25, 27–28, 30, 41–44,
    48, 108, 117, 130, 147; continuum in, 50,
    59, 175; decorated initials in, 66–69, 71,
    177, 185; divisions of, 47, 61–62, 69–72,
    83–84, 143, 176, 180; Dreamer in, 3, 41,
    49–56, 58, 65, 69–73, 143, 146; Lamb in,
    41, 50, 56, 60, 70, 139; Maiden in, 41, 48,
    49–58, 60, 69–73; mathematical and theo-
    logical perfection in, 64; New Jerusalem
    in, 33, 38, 52, 71–73; "offys" in, 56–59,
    174–75; Old Jerusalem in, 71; parable of
    the vineyard in, 53–55, 64; Paradise in, 50,
    52; physicality in, 50–53, 55, 71, 174;
    Pygmalion and Aristotle in, 56–59, 63;
    rhyme scheme in, 23, 44, 49, 61–62, 174;
    spirit in, 50–53, 71. *See also* Decimal sys-
    tem; Divine Proportion; Dodecahedron;
    Duodecimal system; Eternity; Expansion;
    Factors; Infinity; New Testament; Penta-
    gon; Pentangle; Prime numbers; Salvation

Pearl-poet. *See* Cotton Nero A.x poet
Pearsall, D. A. *See* Cooper, R. A., and D. A.
    Pearsall
Pentaboron, 50
Pentagon, 36, 39–40, 116, 182; in *Patience*,
    108, 110–12; in *Pearl*, 60, 62, 65–66, 179;
    in *Purity*, 96–98, 180
Pentagrammaton, 46–47, 105
Pentangle, 36, 39–40, 62, 107, 116, 181–82;
    in *Patience*, 108, 168; in *Pearl*, 60, 180; in
    Purity, 96–98; in *Sir Gawain*, 39, 96, 98,
    114. *See also* Divine Proportion
Père Lachaise, 174
Peter of Spain, 40
Peterson, C. J., 165
Peterson, R. G., 167
Phi. *See* Divine Proportion; Proportion;
    Ratio
Phidias, 32
Piers Plowman, 69
Plato, 5, 40; *Epinomis*, 13; *Republic*, 36;
    Timaeus, 4, 168
Platonic solids, 40, 175–76. *See also* Dodeca-
    hedron
Platt, Colin, 179
Porphyry, 167
Prime numbers, 170; in *Patience*, 21–22, 24,
    107; in *Pearl*, 18, 22, 47, 67, 147; in *Pu-
    rity*, 83; in *Sir Gawain*, 18, 21–24, 47, 67,
    134, 147, 172
Prior, Sandra Pierson, 174
Proportion, 6, 12–13, 27–37, 168, 170; in
    the Book of Kells, 179; continuous, 31–
    32; defined, 31; Greek for "the indivis-
    ible," 9; harmonic, 32; *phi* as a propor-
    tion, 32; progressions, 31–32; in *Sir
    Gawain*, 132–35
Psalms, Book of, 11
Purity, 1–2, 15–19, 22–24, 27–28, 43–44, 99,
    103, 117, 139; Baltassar's Feast in, 41, 81–
    82, 178; as a blueprint for manuscript,
    90–98, 108–12, 137–38, 141–43, 154–55,
    157–58, 179, 181, 184; carpet page design
    in, 90–93, 179; cleanness in, 74, 82; criti-
    cal treatment of, 74–75; Daniel in, 81–82,

Purity—continued
178; divisions, sections, and decorated
initials of, 75–77, 80–81, 83–86, 142, 172,
176, 177; filth and uncleanness in, 74, 77–
78, 82; incarnation and Nativity in, 74,
80; Lot and his daughters in, 74, 78;
meter in, 107; Noe and the Flood in, 38,
74, 77, 79–80; parable of the wedding
feast in, 74, 77, 79, 177, 183; Sarah and
Abraham in, 74, 78–79; Sodoma and
Gomorra in, 74, 78–79. *See also* Bookart,
early medieval insular; Divine Proportion; Duodecimal system; Expansion; Factors; Genesis, Book of; Infinity; Music;
New Testament; Numerical construction;
Old Testament; Pentagon; Pentangle;
Prime numbers; Ratio; Wisdom, Book of
Pythagoreanism, 46, 105, 113, 149, 169, 175
Pythagorean theorem, 32, 35, 97, 109–10,
154, 172, 186
Pythagorean triangle, 24

Quadrivium, 4–5, 21, 34, 37, 40, 50, 88, 105,
147, 167–69, 171, 173

Raphael, 168
Rashdall, Hastings, 167
Ratio, 27–37; continuous, 26; in Cotton
Nero A.x, 27–31; as depicted in Villard
de Honnecourt's rotating squares, 28–
31; other definitions for, 10–13, 169; *phi*
as ratio, 32, 36; in the prime series, 23; in
Purity, 82–87; in *Sir Gawain*, 132–34
Reuchlin, Johann, 173; *De arte cabalistica*,
46–47, 105–6, 114, 181
Ridley, Florence, 170
Robertson, Michael, 183
Rolle, Richard, 69, 176–77
Roman de la Rose. See De Meun, Jean
Rothschild, Victoria, 6
Ruffus, Gerardus, 64
Russell, J. Stephen, 173

Salvation, 38, 45, 48, 90, 147; in *Pearl*, 49,
55, 64, 73; in *Purity*, 98
Santa Maria Novella, 46, 90

Saxony, Albert of, 175
Schlauch, Margaret, 181
Schmidt, A.V.C., 137, 183
Seafarer, 69
Septuagint, 12
Shakespeare, William: and numerical con-
struction, 6
Shepherd, Geoffrey, 167
Shoaf, R. A., 182
Short, Charles. *See* Lewis, Charlton T., and
Charles Short
Sidney, Philip, 4, 7
Singleton, Charles S., 3–4
Sir Gawain and the Green Knight, 1–3,
15–25, 27–28, 36, 38–39, 41–44, 48–49,
105, 116, 147, 165, 170; Bertilak's castle
in, 42, 123–24, 127, 130–35, 137–38,
143–45; bob-and-wheel in, 18, 23, 44,
47, 64, 147, 182; cross of Christ in, 107,
114–16, 137, 139–44, 182; cycle of nature in, 129; decorated initials in, 126,
128, 142, 177; design of, 126–28, 132–44;
Gawain's imperfection in, 136–37, 143–
46; Gawain's shield in, 39, 98, 114, 127;
Green Chapel in, 42, 127, 135, 137;
Green Knight in, 42, 117–27, 135–36;
gyng and *foin* in, 182; Henry James as a
window onto, 123–24; King Arthur in,
119–22; physical and spiritual in, 117,
124; *prayere* in, 184; Psalm 89:4 in, 129;
sections of, 84, 125–28, 130–43, 147,
183–85; Sir Gawain in, 3, 42, 114, 117–
20, 122–26, 128–38, 143–46, 169, 183;
verbal skills of Gawain in, 118, 120,
122–24, 135; worthiness of Arthurian
court in, 118–22. *See also* Divine Proportion; Dodecahedron; Eternity; Excess;
Expansion; Infinity; Music; New Testament; Number; Pentangle; Prime numbers; Proportion; Ratio
Snow, C. P., 37–38
Solomon, King, 10, 39, 98, 169
Souter, Alexander, 12
Southern, R. W., 168
Spearing, A. C., 17, 80, 123
Spenser, Edmund, 6

Stahl, William H., 168, 173
Stanbury, Sarah, 174
Stevick, Robert, 6, 88, 91–92, 178–79
Stock, Lorraine K., 180
Sufis, 177
Synan, Edward A. *See* Murdoch, John E.,
   and Edward A. Synan

Tanckius, 33, 36–37, 44
Tavernor, Robert, 90
Tennyson, Alfred, Lord, 119
Tetract, 171–72
Tetragrammaton, 46–47, 105
Theresa, Saint, 177
Thorpe, Douglas, 51, 174
Tinkle, Theresa, 173
Tregelles, Samuel Prideaux, 178
Trigg, Stephanie, 182
Trinity, 6, 22, 33–34, 41
Triple triangle, 181
Trivium, 34, 168
Troilus and Criseyde, 1

Underhill, Evelyn, 177

Villard de Honnecourt, 23, 28–31, 34
Virgil, and the Divine Proportion, 8–10, 32,
   169, 170
Vitruvius, 12, 170; *De architectura,* 89
Von Simson, Otto, 34, 173
Vulgate, Latin, 89, 177, 178

Waldron, Ronald. *See* Andrew, Malcolm,
   and Ronald Waldron
Wanderer, 27, 69
Wasserman, Julian N. *See* Blanch, Robert J.,
   and Julian N. Wasserman
Weier, D. *See* McColly, W. B., and D. Weier
Weight, 12, 88
Wenzel, Sigfried, 180
White, Alison, 173
William, Sister Margaret, 17
Wills, Garry, 174
Wisdom, Book of, 10, 12–13, 39, 82, 69
Wodeham, Adam, 175
Wycliffe, John, 169

Zero, 186
Zubov, V. P., 175

Edward I. Condren is professor of English at the University of California, Los Angeles, and author of *Chaucer and the Energy of Creation* (UPF, 1999).